O. Carl Simonton, M.D., D.A.B.R., is a radiation oncologist and medical director of the Cancer Counseling and Research Center in Fort Worth, Texas.

Stephanie Matthews-Simonton is a psychotherapist and director of the Center's intensive psychotherapy program.

James L. Creighton has worked with the Simontons and independently in cancer patient counseling and care.

THE TOTAL APPROACH THAT'S REVOLUTIONIZING CANCER TREATMENT

The Simontons are recognized worldwide as leaders in the holistic health movement. Their total approach to fighting cancer combines traditional medical management with psychological treatment—to create the most favorable environment, both internal and external, for recovery. And the results have been remarkable: the Simontons' patients have a survival rate twice the national norm and, in many cases, have experienced dramatic remissions or total cures.

Carl and Stephanie Simonton have worked with major hospitals and medical schools across the United States, helping them to establish cancer counseling programs like their own in Texas. Today they are considered the foremost practitioners in the field of psychological causes and treatment of cancer.

"A HUSBAND AND WIFE MEDICAL TEAM IS HELPING CANCER PATIENTS DIAGNOSED AS INCURABLY ILL THINK THEIR WAY TO SURVIVAL."   —*Associated Press*

GETTING WELL AGAIN

"Compared to U.S. national averages, the Simontons' 'terminally ill' patients have lived longer—in some cases experiencing dramatic remissions—and functioned more fully than typical cancer patients . . . In the burgeoning field of holistic health practice, [the Simontons] are bold and levelheaded pioneers."
        —*Association of Humanistic Psychology Newsletter*

"WE CAN ADD OUR OWN HEALING POWERS TO NORMAL MEDICAL TREATMENT AND INCREASE OUR CHANCES OF LONG-TERM, HIGH-QUALITY SURVIVAL . . . Underlying all the Simontons' work is the philosophy that we are all responsible for our own health and illnesses, and that we participate—whether consciously or unconsciously—in creating our physical, emotional, and spiritual health."   —*New Age*

"Carl and Stephanie Simonton are pioneering in the domain of mind-body communication and are getting remarkable results in cancer control."
                —Dr. Elmer Green,
                Menninger Foundation

"[The Simontons] have caught the very essence of the stress concept, especially as it concerns the goal of overcoming cancer."
                —Hans Selye, M.D., President
                International Institute of Stress

GETTING WELL AGAIN

*A Step-by-Step, Self-Help Guide
to Overcoming Cancer
for Patients and Their Families*

O. Carl Simonton, M.D.
Stephanie Matthews-Simonton
James L. Creighton

BANTAM BOOKS
Toronto / New York / London

This book is dedicated to the patients who have been willing to try to alter the course of their cancers through their mental and emotional processes and to the courage it takes to adopt that stance.

—CARL and STEPHANIE SIMONTON

I dedicate this book to my wife, Maggie Creighton, who first led me down these paths and supported me along the way.

—JAMES CREIGHTON

*This low-priced Bantam Book
has been completely reset in a type face
designed for easy reading, and was printed
from new plates. It contains the complete
text of the original hard-cover edition.*
NOT ONE WORD HAS BEEN OMITTED.

GETTING WELL AGAIN
A Bantam Book

PRINTING HISTORY
J.P. Tarcher edition published May 1978
2nd printing .... June 1978
13 printings through April 1980

Bantam edition | August 1980
2nd printing .... August 1980
3rd printing .... October 1980
4th printing .... June 1981

*Fictional names have been used for all the patients
mentioned in this book except for Bob Gilley.*

ISBN 0-553-20442-4

Published simultaneously in the United States and Canada

Bantam Books are published by Bantam Books, Inc. Its trademark, consisting of the words "Bantam Books" and the portrayal of a bantam, is Registered in U.S. Patent and Trademark Office and in other countries. Marca Registrada. Bantam Books, Inc., 666 Fifth Avenue, New York, New York 10103.

PRINTED IN THE UNITED STATES OF AMERICA

13 12 11 10 9 8 7 6 5 4

Contents

Acknowledgments

We are deeply grateful for the work of other researchers whose efforts have provided a foundation for our own work and for this book.

We want to express our appreciation for the support and encouragement of staff and friends at the University of Oregon Medical School, especially the Radiation Oncology Department, during the birth of this project; the Radiation Oncology Service and the Radiology Department at the medical center of Travis Air Force Base for the support in developing a formal program addressing the emotional needs of cancer patients; and a special appreciation for the support and wisdom of Oscar Morphis, senior oncologist of Oncology Associates in Fort Worth, Texas.

The interest and encouragement of our parents have been a great source of strength and we are deeply grateful to them.

The support of Robert F. White of Minnesota, Len and Anita Halpert of New York, and Dorothy Lyddon of California has been of much help and we thank them for it.

A grant from the Institute of Noetic Sciences, which accelerated our work and allowed us to broaden our research, has been quite helpful and is much appreciated.

In the actual writing of this book, we would like to thank Jeanne Achterberg-Lawlis, Anne Blocker, Bob Gilley, Frances Jaffer, Flint Sparks, and for her excellent help on many drafts, Sharon Lilly.

We would like to thank our editor, Victoria Pasternack, for her guidance and personal commitment to this book, and our publisher, Jeremy Tarcher, for his excellent help, advice, and friendship—without which this book would not be what it is today.

A special thanks to Reece and Doris Halsey in helping this book come into being.

We are especially thankful for the wisdom and guidance of John Gladfelter, whose counsel has dramatically improved the quality of our personal and professional lives.

Finally, we would like to thank our patients, who have shared so much of themselves with us and allowed us to share ourselves with them.

—CARL and STEPHANIE SIMONTON

I am grateful to my secretary, Marie Von Felton, who typed and retyped the manuscript through its many drafts.

—JAMES CREIGHTON

PART ONE

The Mind
and
Cancer

1

The Mind-Body Connection: A Psychological Approach to Cancer Treatment

Everyone participates in his or her health or illness at all times.

This book will show people with cancer or other serious illnesses how they can participate in getting well again. It will also show those who are not ill how they can participate in maintaining their health.

We use the word *participate* to indicate the vital role you play in creating your own level of health. Most of us assume that healing is something done *to* us, that if we have a medical problem our responsibility is simply to get to a physician who will then heal us. That's true to a degree, but it is only part of the story.

We all participate in our own health through our beliefs, our feelings, and our attitudes toward life, as well as in more direct ways, such as through exercise and diet. In addition, our response to medical treatment is influenced by our beliefs about the effectiveness of the treatment and by the confidence we have in the medical team.

This book in no way minimizes the role of the physician and other health professionals engaged in medical treatment.

Rather, *Getting Well Again* will describe what *you* can do in conjunction with medical treatment to gain the health you deserve.

Understanding how much you can participate in your health or illness is a significant first step for everyone in getting well. For many of our patients it is the critically important step. It may well be for you, too.

We are Carl and Stephanie Simonton, and we operate the Cancer Counseling and Research Center in Fort Worth, Texas. Carl, the medical director of the center, is a radiation oncologist, a physician specializing in the treatment of cancer. Stephanie is director of counseling and is trained in psychology.

Most of our patients, who come to us from all over the country, have received a "medically incurable" diagnosis from their doctors. According to national cancer statistics, they have an average life expectancy of one year. When these people believe that only medical treatment can help them—but their physicians have said that medicine is no longer of much avail and that they probably have only a few months to live— they feel doomed, trapped, helpless, and usually fulfill the doctors' expectations. But if patients mobilize their own resources and actively participate in their recovery, they may well exceed their life expectancy and significantly alter the quality of life.

The ideas and techniques described in this book are the approach we employ at our Cancer Counseling and Research Center to show cancer patients how they can participate in getting well again and live a rewarding and fulfilling life.

THE STARTING POINT:
THE "WILL TO LIVE"

Why do some patients recover their health and others die, when the diagnosis is the same for both? Carl became interested in this problem while he was completing his residency as a cancer specialist at the University of Oregon Medical School. There he noticed that patients who stated they wanted to live would often act as if they did not. There were lung cancer patients who refused to stop smoking, liver cancer patients who wouldn't cut down on alcohol, and others who wouldn't show up for treatment regularly.

In many cases, these were people whose medical prognosis indicated that, with treatment, they could look forward to many more years of life. Yet while they affirmed again and again that they had countless reasons to live, these patients showed a greater apathy, depression, and attitude of giving up than did a number of others diagnosed with terminal disease.

In the latter category was a small group of patients who had been sent home after minimal treatment, with little expectation that they would live to see their first follow-up appointment. Yet several years later, they were still arriving for their annual or semiannual examinations, remaining in quite good health, and inexplicably beating the statistics.

When Carl asked them to account for their good health they would frequently give such answers as, "I can't die until my son graduates from college," or "They need me too much at work," or "I won't die until I've solved the problem with my daughter." The common thread running through these replies was the belief that they *exerted some influence over the course of their disease.* The essential difference between these patients and those who would not cooperate was in their attitude toward their disease and their positive stance toward life. The patients who continued to do well, for one reason or another, had a stronger "will to live." This discovery fascinated us.

Stephanie, whose background was in motivational counseling, had an interest in unusual achievers—those people who in business seemed destined to go to the top. She had studied the behavior of exceptional performers and had taught the principles of that behavior to average achievers. It seemed reasonable to study cancer patients in the same way—to learn what those who were doing well had in common, and how they differed from those who were doing poorly.

If the difference between the patient who regains his health and the one who does not is in part a matter of attitude toward the disease and belief that he could somehow influence it, then, we wondered, how could we influence patients' beliefs in that positive direction? Might we be able to apply techniques from motivational psychology to induce and enhance a "will to live?" Beginning in 1969, we began looking at all the possibilities, exploring such diverse psychological techniques as encounter groups, group therapy, meditation, mental imagery, positive thinking, motivational techniques, "mind development" courses like Silva Mind Control and Mind Dynamics, and biofeedback.

From our study of biofeedback, we learned that certain

techniques were enabling people to influence their own internal body processes, such as heart rate and blood pressure. An important aspect of biofeedback, called visual imagery, was also a principal component of other techniques we had studied. The more we learned about the process, the more intrigued we became.

Essentially, the visual imagery process involved a period of relaxation, during which the patient would mentally picture a desired goal or result. With the cancer patient, this would mean his attempting to visualize the cancer, the treatment destroying it and, most importantly, his body's natural defenses helping him recover. After discussions with two leading biofeedback researchers, Drs. Joe Kamiya and Elmer Green, of the Menninger Clinic, we decided to use visual imagery techniques with cancer patients.

THE FIRST PATIENT:
A DRAMATIC EXAMPLE

The first patient with whom an attempt was made to apply our developing theories was a sixty-one-year-old man who came to the medical school in 1971 with a form of throat cancer that carried a grave prognosis. He was very weak, his weight had dropped from 130 to 98 pounds, he could barely swallow his own saliva, and was having difficulty breathing. There was less than a 5 percent chance that he would survive five years. Indeed, the medical school doctors had seriously debated whether to treat him at all, since it was distinctly possible that therapy would only make him more miserable without significantly diminishing his cancer.

Carl went into the examining room determined to help this man actively participate in his treatment. This was a case that justified using exceptional measures. Carl began treating the patient by explaining how the patient himself could influence the course of his own disease. Carl then outlined a program of relaxation and mental imagery based on the research we had been accumulating. The man was to set aside three, five- to fifteen-minute periods during the day—in the morning on arising, at noon after lunch, and at night before going to bed. During these periods he was first to compose himself by sitting quietly and concentrating on the muscles of his body, starting with his head and going all the way to his feet, telling each muscle group to relax. Then, in this more relaxed state, he was to picture himself in a pleasant, quiet place—sitting under a tree, by a creek, or anywhere that suited his fancy, so long as it was pleasurable. Following this he was to imagine his cancer vividly in whatever form it seemed to take.

Next, Carl asked him to picture his treatment, radiation therapy, as consisting of millions of tiny bullets of energy that would hit all the cells, both normal and cancerous, in their path. Because the cancer cells were weaker and more confused than the normal cells, they would not be able to repair the damage, Carl suggested, and so the normal cells would remain healthy while the cancer cells would die.

Carl then asked the patient to form a mental picture of the last and most important step—his body's white blood cells coming in, swarming over the cancer cells, picking up and carrying off the dead and dying ones, flushing them out of his body through his liver and kidneys. In his mind's eye he was to visualize his cancer decreasing in size and his health returning to normal. After he completed each such exercise, he was to go about whatever he had to do the rest of the day.

What happened was beyond any of Carl's previous experience in treating cancer patients with purely physical intervention. The radiation therapy worked exceptionally well, and the man showed almost no negative reaction to the radiation on his skin or in the mucous membranes of his mouth and throat. Halfway through treatment he was able to eat again. He gained strength and weight. The cancer progressively disappeared.

During the course of treatment—both the radiation therapy and the mental imagery—the patient reported missing only one mental imagery session on a day when he went for a drive with a friend and was caught in a traffic jam. He was most upset, both with himself and with his friend, for in missing just that one session he felt his control over his condition was slipping away.

Treating this patient in this way was very exciting, but it was also somewhat frightening. The possibilities for methods of healing that seemed to be opening up before us went beyond anything that Carl's formal medical education had prepared him for.

The patient continued to progress until finally, two months later, he showed no signs of cancer. The strength of his conviction that he could influence the course of his own illness was evident when, close to the end of his treatment, he said to Carl: "Doctor, in the beginning I needed you in order to get well. Now I think you could disappear and I could still make it on my own."

Following the remission of his cancer, the patient decided on his own to apply the mental imagery technique to alleviate his arthritis, which had troubled him for years. He mentally pictured his white blood cells smoothing over the joint surfaces of his arms and legs, carrying away any debris, until the surfaces became smooth and glistening. His arthritic symptoms progressively decreased, and although they returned from time to time, he was able to diminish them to the point where he could go stream fishing regularly, not an easy sport even without arthritis.

In addition, he decided to use the relaxation and imagery approach to influence his sex life. Although he had suffered from impotence for over twenty years, within a few weeks of practicing the imagery techniques he was able to resume full sexual activity, and his condition in all of these areas has remained healthy for over six years.

It is fortunate that the results of this first case were as dramatic as they were, for as we began to talk openly in medical circles about our experiences and to put forward the idea that patients had a much larger influence over the course of their disease than we gave them credit for, we received strong negative reactions. Indeed, there were many times when we, too, doubted our own conclusions. Like everyone else—and particularly anyone with medical training—we had been taught to see illness as "happening" to people, without any possibility of individual psychological control over its course, or little cause-and-effect relationship between the illness and what was going on in the rest of their lives.

However, we continued to use this new approach to cancer. Although it sometimes made no difference in the illness, in most cases it made significant changes in patients' responses to treatment. Today, in the more than seven years since Carl worked with that first patient, we have evolved a number of other processes in addition to mental imagery that we have used with patients, first at Travis Air Force Base, where Carl was chief of radiation therapy, and now at our center in Fort Worth. These techniques are the basis of "Pathways to Health," Part Two of *Getting Well Again*.

A WHOLE-PERSON APPROACH TO CANCER TREATMENT

Because cancer is such a dread disease, the minute people know someone has cancer, it often becomes the person's defining characteristic. The individual may play numerous other roles—parent, boss, lover—and have numerous valuable personal characteristics—intelligence, charm, a sense of humor—but from that moment on he or she is a "cancer patient." The person's full human identity is lost to his or her cancer identity. All anyone is aware of, often including the physician, is the physical fact of the cancer, and all treatment is aimed at the patient as a body, not as a person.

It is our central premise that an illness is not purely a physical problem but rather a problem of the whole person, that it includes not only body but mind and emotions. We believe that emotional and mental states play a significant role both in *susceptibility* to disease, including cancer, and in *recovery* from all disease. We believe that cancer is often an indication of problems elsewhere in an individual's life, problems aggravated or compounded by a series of stresses six to eighteen months prior to the onset of cancer. The cancer patient has typically responded to these problems and stresses with a deep sense of hopelessness, or "giving up." This emotional response, we believe, in turn triggers a set of physiological responses that suppress the body's natural defenses and make it susceptible to producing abnormal cells.

Assuming our beliefs are essentially accurate—and much of the next seven chapters will show you why we hold them as strongly as we do—then it becomes necessary for patient and physician in working toward recovery to consider not only what is happening on a physical level but, just as importantly, what is going on in the rest of the patient's life. If the total integrated system of mind, body and emotions, which constitutes the whole person, is not working in the direction of health, then purely physical interventions may not succeed. An effective treatment program, then, will deal with the total human being and not focus on the disease alone, for that would be like trying to treat a yellow fever epidemic with sulfa alone, without also draining the ditches in which the sickness-bearing mosquitoes breed.

THE RESULTS OF THIS APPROACH

After three years of teaching patients to use their minds and emotions to alter the course of their malignancies, we decided to conduct a study aimed at distinguishing the effects of emotional and medical treatments to demonstrate scientifically that the emotional treatment was indeed having an effect.

We began studying a group of patients with malignancies deemed medically incurable. Expected survival time for the average patient with such a malignancy is twelve months.

In the past four years, we have treated 159 patients with a diagonsis of medically incurable malignancy. Sixty-three of the patients are alive, with an average survival time of 24.4 months since the diagnosis. Life expectancy for this group, based on national norms, is 12 months. A matched control population is being developed and preliminary results indicate survival comparable with national norms and less than half the survival time of our patients. With the patients in our study who have died, their average survival time was 20.3 months. In other words, the patients in our study who are alive have lived, on the average, two times longer than patients who received medical treatment alone. Even those patients in the study who have died still lived one and one-half times longer than the control group.

As of January 1978, the status of the disease in the patients still living is as follows:

	Number of patients	Percent
No evidence of disease	14	22.2%
Tumor regressing	12	19.1%
Disease stable	17	27.1%
New tumor growth	20	31.8%

Keep in mind that 100 percent of these patients were considered medically incurable.

Of course, duration of life after diagnosis is only one aspect of the disease. Of equal (or perhaps greater) importance is the quality of life while the patient survives. There are few existing objective measures of quality of life; however, one measure we keep is the level of daily activity maintained during and after treatment compared to the level of activity prior to diagnosis. At present, 51 percent of our patients maintain the same level of activity they had prior to the diagnosis; 76 percent are at least 75 percent as active as they were prior to diagnosis. Based on our clinical experience, this level of activity for "medically incurable" patients is no less than extraordinary.

The results from our approach to cancer treatment make us confident that the conclusions we have drawn are correct—that an active and positive participation can influence the onset of the disease, the outcome of treatment, and quality of life.

Some people may be concerned that we are offering "false hope," that by suggesting people can influence the course of their disease we are raising unrealistic expectations. It is true that the course of cancer differs so dramatically from person to person that we would not presume to offer guarantees. There is always uncertainty, as there is with standard medical procedures, but hope, we feel, is an appropriate stance to take toward uncertainty.

As we shall see in detail in future chapters, expectancy, either positive or negative, can play a significant role in determining an outcome. A negative expectation will prevent the possibility of disappointment, but it may also contribute to a negative outcome that was not inevitable.

There are no guarantees at this time that a positive expectation of recovery will be realized. But without hope the person has only hopelessness (a feeling that, as we will see, is already too much a part of the cancer patient's life and personality). We do not deny the possibility of death; indeed, we work hard with our patients to help them confront it as a possible outcome. We also work to help them believe that they can influence their condition and that their mind, body, and emotions can work together to create health.

THEORY INTO PRACTICE

Getting Well Again is divided into two major parts. The first describes the theory on which our psychological approach to cancer treatment is based; the second presents a program for recovery for patients and their families. The chapters in Part One, "The Mind and Cancer," are not an effort to prove the validity of this approach to the scientific community. Rather, they are an effort to provide a simple, straightforward explanation so that you can evaluate for yourself whether our approach is reasonable and whether you wish to use it.

Part Two begins "Pathways to Health," the program we use with our patients at the Cancer Counseling and Research Center in Fort Worth. We urge you to try the specific techniques. Reading about them but not practicing them is no more effective than filling a prescription and not taking the pills. By participating in the program, you will participate in your health.

In the final chapter, we turn to the problems of living with a loved one who has a life-threatening disease. We describe some of the communication problems that occur, the kaleidoscope of feelings, and the possibility of increased closeness and love from the experience. If you have cancer, we not only encourage you to read this chapter but to give it to your spouse, your children, your family, and your close friends.

We invite all our readers to join us in the search for new methods for recovering from illness and maintaining health.

2

The Mysteries of Healing:
The Individual
and
His Beliefs

The awesome technology of modern medicine casts an image of such great potency and knowledge that it is hard to believe our individual resources can make much difference. Of course, no one would responsibly dismiss the advances of medicine in this age. Its accomplishments are among the greatest products of the human mind. In cancer treatment alone, great advances have been made in radiation therapy, in sophisticated procedures for chemotherapy, and in surgical techniques. As a result of this technology, from 30 to 40 percent of all cancer patients will be "cured" of their disease.

Some cancer patients receive their treatment from machines housed in special rooms posted with signs warning of the dangers of radiation. The patients are left alone to wonder why, if the treatment is supposed to do so much good, all the medical staff members avoid it so. Other machines emit such loud noises and whines that the patient must wear earmuffs. The latest diagnostic equipment is so vast that the patient is wheeled into the machine, where scans may be taken of cross sections of the body. Surgical teams use incredible sophisticated and expensive equipment in hours-long operations involving the most elaborate procedures. The technology is brilliant and powerful. Some cancer therapies are so potent, in fact, that patients fear the side effects of the treatment as much as the disease itself.

So much time, money, and knowledge have gone into our medical technology that it is easy to think of medical science as all-powerful. But when, in spite of everything, people still die, it is illness that seems all-powerful. The glittering machines, the giant laboratories, and the genuine medical accomplishments of our time can cause us to forget that many of the essential ingredients of healing are still mysterious. It is important that we remember the limits of our knowledge.

THE IMPORTANCE OF THE INDIVIDUAL

There is no cancer specialist who has not asked himself why one patient died whereas another, with virtually the same prognosis and the same treatment, recovered. Such a situation occurred with two patients who participated in our program. Each received the best available medical treatment. Each participated in the processes and techniques described in this book. But their responses were very different. Jerry Green and Bill Spinoza (fictitious names) had virtually indentical diagnoses of lung cancer, which had also spread to the brain.

The day he received his diagnosis, Jerry resigned from life. He quit his job and, after taking care of his financial affairs, he settled in front of the television set, staring blankly hour after hour. Within twenty-four hours he was experiencing severe pain and lack of energy.

No one was able to get him interested in much of anything. He did remember that he had always wanted to make some bar stools for the house, so for a week or two he worked in his shop, with some signs of increased energy and reduced pain. But as soon as the bar stools were completed, he returned to the TV. His wife reported that he did not really watch it as much as he watched the clock, for fear that he would miss the time for taking his pain medication. Jerry showed no signs of response to radiation therapy, and within three months he was dead. Jerry's wife later recalled that both his parents and many of his close relatives had died of cancer, and in fact, Jerry had warned her when they were first married that he would die of cancer, too.

Bill Spinoza was also diagnosed with cancer of the lung,

which had spread to his brain. The prognosis for his survival and the treatment were nearly identical to Jerry's. But Bill's response to the diagnosis was very different. For one thing, he took the illness as a time to review the priorities of his life. As a traveling sales manager he had been constantly on the go and, he said, had "never taken time to see the trees." Although he continued working, he rearranged his schedule so that he could take more time to do things that were enjoyable to him.

At our clinic, he participated actively in the therapy group and regularly used a mental imagery process he had learned there. He responded favorably to radiation therapy and became virtually symptom free. All the while he remained active. Approximately a year and a half after Bill left our program, he experienced several major emotional blows and, within a short time, he suffered a recurrence and died shortly thereafter.

Both patients had had the same diagnosis, both had received the same treatment. Yet Bill outlived Jerry by more than a year and considerably outlived the medical prognosis for that form of cancer. Furthermore, the *quality* of life that Bill lived was quite different; he was involved in life, active, enjoying his family and friends. Each patient responded to his treatment in ways that are not considered typical. Jerry's decline was more precipitous than would normally be expected. On the other hand, Bill outlived his prognosis by many months.

A MYSTERIOUS RECOVERY

While Bill's and Jerry's cases illustrate the differences that the individual's personality can make, the mysteries of recovery are even more dramatically illustrated in the case of Bob Gilley, a highly successful insurance executive from Charlotte, North Carolina. Bob had always had near-perfect health and, as a result, had never thought much about illness. For years he had been an avid racquetball player. However, in the months preceding his diagnosis Bob was aware that he was "down" emotionally, feeling discouraged and depressed about some relationships in his life. But when he went in for his annual physical examination in 1973 he was "feeling good" physically: in fact, he had played a rather strenuous hour of racquetball the morning of his exam.

By virtue of his business, Bob was very conscious of the

value of regular physical exams, although he usually approached them with boredom since they had rarely turned up any signs of illness. The EKG, the X-rays, the blood work were all normal, but after a thorough examination, a lump was discovered in his groin. A surgical biopsy was scheduled for the following week.

Bob described his experience recently in a presentation to cancer patients and health professionals interested in our approach:

> I was told that there would be a very small cut, perhaps an inch in length, much like the incision in an appendectomy. However, when I woke up several hours after the biopsy, I found that they had opened my whole abdomen, both vertically and horizontally.
>
> When the surgeon arrived, he told me it was very hard to diagnose the particular kind of tissue he had removed. It was some sort of a malignant mass, but I had a good chance of pulling through it. Early the next morning the chance was changed to 50 percent. When my own doctor arrived on the scene, the diagnosis was changed again. I was given a 30 percent chance of survival.
>
> After much debate, the pathologist, the oncologist, and the surgeon finally called it a "secondary undifferentiated carcinoma." The chances for my cure were dropped to less than 1 percent.

Bob was then sent to a very large cancer clinic for chemotherapy treatment:

> It was a bizarre experience. I arrived there very weak from surgery and for an entire day sat in a waiting room with hundreds of other cancer patients. Everyone seemed to be treated very impersonally, but I'm sure it was just because of the incredible case load. I became "Undifferentiated Carcinoma in Room 351-A."
>
> When I was strong enough, I got passes for everything: passes to go for a walk in the park, passes to go to breakfast, lunch, dinner—I even got passes to go to the bathroom at the service station across the street, because it was very important for me to

remain a member of the outside world and not become a patient entombed in a cancer hospital. I got more passes than anybody in the history of that clinic. I also ran my office from my hospital bed.

The chemotherapy types and dosages were finally decided upon, and I was introduced to another stressful aspect of cancer. Three-quarters of the time I remained deathly ill. I lost all my hair, my appetite, and a considerable amount of weight. I was constantly nauseated, had diarrhea, burned veins [veins irritated from chemotherapy], mouth blisters, and was pallid and weak. In a very short time I looked like a reject from a concentration camp.

I could tell that in the eyes of all but a few people—a very precious few who mattered—I was a dying man. During my months of intense chemotherapy, I was on a miracle chase, working with nutrition, vitamin therapy, faith healers, psychic readers, and so on. Many times I would scream, "Damn you, cancer! Get out of my body!"

Bob made several trips back to the cancer clinic, receiving intensive chemotherapy. At the end of a ten-month period he had reached the point where continued chemotherapy held little promise and high danger of causing deterioration of the heart muscles. And the mass in his groin had not diminished in size.

Bob heard about our program and attended one of our patient sessions in Fort Worth. Prior to the meeting he was sent some materials describing our work as well as a tape recording that taught him the mental imagery process. Although his initial stay was only for a few days, the first session gave him renewed hope. In Bob's words: "'When I got off the plane in Charlotte, my wife said, 'You look different.' And I *was* different. I had hope. I had returned home full of enthusiasm and new direction."

Bob's chemotherapy was discontinued and his local oncologist evaluated him monthly. Bob found the discipline of practicing mental imagery regularly to be difficult but he kept it up. He also began to exercise regularly and soon was able to play twenty minutes of light racquetball. He began to build up slowly, regaining some of his weight. But the spectre of cancer still hung on. As he reported:

No medical differences showed up for two, three, even four weeks. But I kept holding on to the belief that this system would work. After six weeks, I was examined by my doctor in Charlotte. As he began probing my body, I can't begin to describe the absolute terror that came over me. "Maybe it's spread!" I thought. "Maybe it's five times bigger than it was before." My doctor turned to me in amazement and said with a very tender expression, "It is considerably smaller. As a matter of fact, I would say that it's shrunk 75 percent in mass size." We rejoiced together, but cautiously.

Two weeks later—which was only two months after I had met the Simontons—I was given a gallium scan and various other tests and examinations. There was absolutely no disease present, only a residual scar nodule about the size of a small marble. Within two months of beginning relaxation and imagery, I was cancer-free! My doctors in Charlotte didn't believe it.

Over the next few months Bob's energy and vitality continued to increase, until he felt his energy and vitality were as great as or greater than they had been before his diagnosis.

Bob still had a good deal of work to do. In subsequent sessions with us, he began to resolve many of the personal problems that had caused him to be emotionally "down" before the onset of the cancer. He also worked hard on changing behaviors that were interfering with his relationships. At this writing, he continues to show no evidence of cancer. In fact, he reports that:

Today my vitality is greater than before the cancer. If I had no medical records, I could pass any insurance exam in America. I don't want to sound overly confident, because I have many down moments. Fears of the disease return when I have abdominal pain from indigestion, for instance. Sometimes I even doubt that all of this is a reality, and my logical mind says, "Maybe it was a delayed effect of the chemotherapy, or maybe it was the vitamins. Maybe there was no cancer there to begin with." But most of the time I feel very confident that this was the way for me, and it can be a way for many, many others.

Bob has done much to educate people in Charlotte about the role patients can play in overcoming cancer and has instituted a cancer counseling service known as Dayspring. He sums up his experience by saying: "I've learned a lot about my responsibility for my disease, my responsibility for healing, and about the techniques for unlocking powers that can be found within all of us."

"SPONTANEOUS" REMISSION AND THE PLACEBO EFFECT

Bob's case is dramatic because he did not appear to respond well to standard medical treatment, yet four years later he continues not to show any sign of cancer. His turnaround could have been a delayed response to the chemotherapy, although most physicians would not predict or expect such an occurrence. We believe that his recovery had to do with Bob himself. It cannot be attributed to a normal response to medical treatment. This is an apparent case of spontaneous remission; it "just happened."

When a disease does not proceed in ways that can be explained by physical intervention, the result is called "spontaneous." The word covers today's ignorance in much the same way as the term "spontaneous generation" covered medical ignorance during the late Middle Ages. In those times, no explanation was available as to why living organisms, such as maggots, could grow out of nonliving matter, such as spoiled foods, and so it was said they were "spontaneously" generated. (It was not until 1765 that Spallanzani showed that when food was placed in airtight jars the living organisms that normally appeared in spoiled food did not appear. In other words, something in the air carried the larvae. When no air reached the food, there was no "spontaneous generation.") "Spontaneous remission," too, results from processes or mechanisms that are not yet understood.

The number of spontaneous remissions from cancer appears to be small, though all estimates are guesses because we have no idea how many such remissions take place before patients are diagnosed as having the disease. Yet however many cases there are, none of them is "spontaneous." In each case there is some kind of cause-and-effect process. The process by which spontaneous remission takes place is simply beyond our present understanding. It may be that we are unable to recognize the processes because we are not paying sufficient attention to the effect on the body of the mental and emotional aspects of human beings, including their beliefs about their illness, their treatment, and their chances for recovery.

This exclusion of beliefs and feelings from medical practice is unwarranted and in a way, surprising, because it fails to take into account the significance of what many physicians regard as one of their most powerful drugs, the placebo. Every physician knows the effectiveness of treatments which use only a sugar pill or other medicineless preparation. This is known as the "placebo effect." A patient is told that a prescription will produce a certain beneficial side effect—and it does— even though there is no medication in the pill that could produce it.

A physician may give a placebo either because medicine is not required (for example, to a chronic complainer) or because an appropriate treatment is not available and the doctor does not want the patient to feel abandoned. (For obvious reasons, doctors do not frequently discuss placebos with their patients.) In many cases, the placebo proves to be exceedingly effective in reducing or eliminating physical symptoms, including ailments for which there are no known cures. The only active ingredient in the treatment appears to be the power of the *belief*—the *positive expectations*—patients have that they have received a helpful treatment. Since they believe the placebo is helpful, because the physician has created *positive expectations* about the results, the treatment does, in fact, help.

A striking illustration of the placebo effect occurred in a research study conducted with two groups of patients who had bleeding ulcers. One group was told by a physician that they were to receive a new drug that would undoubtedly produce relief. The second group was told by nurses that a new experimental drug would be administered, but that little was known about its effects. The same drug was then administered to both groups. Seventy percent of the patients in the first group showed significant improvement in their ulcers; in the second group 25 percent showed significant improvement. The only difference in treatment was the positive expectancy created in the first group by the physician.

Countless other studies have confirmed the results of positive expectancy on treatment.

• Dr. Henry K. Beecher and Dr. Louis Lasagna of Harvard University conducted a study of postoperative pain. Some patients were given morphine, others placebos. Fifty-two percent of the people who took the morphine reported relief from pain; 40 percent who took the placebos reported relief. In other words, the placebo was more than three-quarters as effective as morphine. In fact, Drs. Beecher and Lasagna discovered that the more severe the pain, the more effective the placebo.

• Eighty-three arthritic patients were given sugar pills instead of their usual medicine, aspirin or cortisone. A second group received their usual medication. The percentage of patients who reported relief was the same among those who received the sugar pills as among those who received conventional medication. In addition, when those patients who received sugar pills but reports no relief were given placebo injections of sterile water, 64 percent reported relief or improvement. (Apparently, injections inspired greater positive expectancy than did pills, regardless of the medical value of either.)

• Medical officials at the National Institute of Geriatrics in Bucharest, Romania, conducted a study of a new drug designed to enhance health and longevity by activating the endocrine system. One hundred fifty patients were divided into three equal groups. The first group received no medication, the second received a placebo, and the third was given the new drug. The three groups were then observed for several years.

Members of the group that received nothing had similar mortality rates and incidence of illness as people in the same age groups in the patients' geographical areas. The second group, which had re-received the placebo, showed a substantial improvement in health and a lower death rate than the first group. The third group, which had received the drug, showed about the same improvement over the placebo group that the placebo group showed over the first group. Thus, although the drug made an important difference in longevity and health, the placebo effect by itself was able to produce improvements in both the degree of illness and the length of life.

The placebo effect is not limited to the administration of sugar pills. Throughout medical history there have been countless paractices, such as "bleeding" the patient (which was common during the Middle Ages), that have no physiological basis for curing but still frequently worked, apparently because everyone—including the physician—believed in their efficacy. Indeed, some surgical procedures that were in vogue during the last fifty years seemed to produce remarkable results even though we now know that, in many cases, there are serious questions about their value. Thus, patients not infrequently reported feeling much better after unnecessary hysterectomies or tonsillectomies were performed. Once again, the results can be attributed to the patient's belief that the treatments would work and because of his confidence in the doctor.

The placebo effect may also account for a portion of the benefit received from real medication. The effect is created both by the doctor's manner in administering the drug and also by the process by which drugs are approved by the medical profession. Everyone knows that new drugs must undergo extensive testing by pharmaceutical companies and receive approval by agencies of the federal government. These same federal agencies are also actively involved in attempting to remove harmful foods and drugs from the market, further inspiring public confidence. So when research, testing, and approval by respected federal agencies are combined with a few publicly acclaimed successes, such as the polio vaccine, the ritual for establishing social belief in medical treatment is complete, and the public comes to believe that a medicine prescribed by a doctor *must* be effective.

A most dramatic case of the placebo effect has been reported by Dr. Bruno Klopfer, a researcher involved in the testing of the drug Krebiozen. In 1950, Krebiozen had received sensational national publicity as a "cure" for cancer and was being tested by the American Medical Association and the U.S. Food and Drug Administration.

One of Dr. Klopfer's patients had lymphosarcoma, a generalized, far-advanced malignancy involving the lymph nodes. The patient had huge tumor masses throughout his body and was in such desperate physical condition that he frequently had to take oxygen by mask, and fluid had to be removed from his chest every two days. When the patient discovered that Dr. Klopfer was involved in research on Krebiozen, he begged to be given Krebiozen treatments. Klopfer did so, and the patient's recovery was startling. Within a short time the tumors had shrunk dramatically, and the patient was able to resume a normal life, including flying his private plane.

Then as AMA and FDA reports of the negative results of Krebiozen started being publicized, the patient took a dramatic turn for the worse. Thinking the circumstances extreme enough to justify unusual measures, Klopfer told his patient that he had obtained a new, superrefined, double-strength Krebiozen that would produce better results. Actually, the injections Klopfer gave were simply sterile water. Yet the patient's recovery was even more remarkable. Once again the tumor masses melted, chest fluid vanished, and he became ambulatory and even went back to flying. The patient remained symptom-free for over two months. The patient's belief alone, independent of the value of the medication, produced his recovery.

Then further stories of the AMA and FDA's tests appeared in the press: "Nationwide tests show Krebiozen to be a worthless drug in the treatment of cancer." Within a few days the patient was dead.

PSYCHOSOMATIC HEALTH

How can the placebo effect be explained? Some will dismiss it by saying the patient's illness was "psychosomatic." It was "all in his head," a figment of his "imagination," and therefore not "real."

But this is a distortion of the meaning of the word *psychosomatic*, which simply means that an illness originated as a result of, or is aggravated by, an individual's psychological processes. It does not mean that the illness is any less real because it is not solely physical in origin—if any illness ever is. An ulcer may have originated as a result of, and be aggravated by, anxiety and tension. This does not make the ulcer any less real.

While almost everyone acknowledges that there are psychosomatic factors in high blood pressure, heart attacks, headaches, and certain skin disorders, the psychosomatic connection with cancer is not generally accepted even though the idea that such connections may exist is not a new or revolutionary one. As early as 1959, Dr. Eugene P. Pendergrass, president of the American Cancer Society, emphasized the necessity of treating the whole patient, not just the physical manifestations of cancer.

> Anyone who has had an extensive experience in the treatment of cancer is aware that there are great differences among patients. . . . I personally have observed cancer patients who have undergone successful treatment and were living and well for years. Then an emotional stress such as the death of a son in World War II, the infidelity of a daughter-in-law, or the burden of long unemployment seems to have been precipitating factors in the reactivation of their disease which resulted in death. . . . There is solid evidence that the course of the disease in general is affected by emotional distress. . . . Thus, we as doctors may begin to emphasize *treatment of the patient as a whole* as well as the disease from which the patient is suffering. We may learn how to influence general body systems and through them modify the neoplasm which resides within the body.
>
> As we go forward . . . searching for new means of controlling growth both within the cell and through systemic influences it is my sincere hope that we can widen the quest to include the distinct possibility that within one's mind is a power capable of exerting forces which can either enhance or inhibit the progress of this disease. [Emphasis added.]

The importance of Dr. Pendergrass's view is not just that it underscores the role that psychological factors play in aggravating a disease, it also emphasizes the possibility that psychological factors, including the patient's beliefs, may be mobilized to move toward health. Not only can mental and emotional conditions originate or aggravate physical conditions, they can also contribute to health. Just as one can become psychosomatically ill, so one who is ill can move in the other direction and become psychosomatically healthy.

Although at times we may say that someone "wanted" to make himself or herself sick, psychosomatic illness is generally attributed to unconscious processes. Basically our belief has been that the unconscious aspect of psychosomatic illness made it something that was beyond our control, and therefore something that simply "happened" to us. Although the mind might make the body sick, we did not think about the degree to which we might consciously influence the mind to make the body well again.

One of the greatest advances in modern medicine, however, is the new vision that doctors and others are gaining in regard to the amount of control a person may learn to exert over the mental processes that influence a wide variety of physical processes.

BIOFEEDBACK AND THE ABILITY TO INFLUENCE HEALTH

For years Westerners have heard reports about amazing feats of physical control performed most frequently by Indian yogis. They were, it was reported, able to stick large needles into parts of their bodies and not bleed or experience pain. Others were reported to have been buried in coffins in the ground for extended periods of time and, long after the normal consumption of air should have left them dead, emerged alive and healthy. Still other yogis were reported to be able to walk over burning coals and experience neither pain nor blistering. Most people doubted these reports or dismissed them as magician's tricks. But some researchers had learned from their own work that such reports might be true.

These exotic stories and common individual experiences are part of the impetus to the development of the new science of biofeedback. During the sixties biofeedback studies demonstrated how people could exercise substantial influence over bodily states that were formerly thought not to be subject to conscious control.

Researchers in biofeedback have discovered that it is possible for average people, not just yogis, to learn to control *voluntarily* heart rate, muscle tension, sweat-gland activity, skin temperature, and a wide range of internal physical states normally considered to be under *involuntary* control by the autonomic nervous system. The procedure by which the trainee learns to control these physical states is not very complex. Electrodes are attached to the skin of the person receiving the training so that a biofeedback machine can monitor some of his physiological functions, such as heart rate, brain waves, or muscle tension. The machine gives the trainee visual and/or sound signals that indicate what is happening to the physical function.

If, for example, you were learning how to alter your heart rate, a tone might sound at a higher frequency as the heart rate increased, and at a lower frequency as the heart rate declined. Initially, it might seem to you that the higher and lower frequency sounds were purely random, that there was no connection between what you were thinking and your heart rate. But soon you would become aware that you were experiencing certain thoughts or feelings when your heart rate declined, or that certain physical postures had an effect. Over time you would learn to exercise sufficient control over the physiological function to raise or lower the sound (and your heart rate) pretty much as you wished.

To date, every physiological function that can be accurately and predictably measured and "fed back" to trainees has been subject to learned control. Using biofeedback, people have been taught to reduce high blood pressure, eliminate migraine headaches, control irregular heartbeats, increase and decrease blood flow, cure insomnia, and control numerous other "involuntary" physiological functions.

Elmer and Alyce Green of the Menninger Clinic, pioneers in the field of biofeedback, have reported experiments in which trainees learned to control through their own volition a single nerve cell. They believe that biofeedback technique has clearly demonstrated the physiological principle that, "Every change in the physiological state is accompanied by an appropriate change in the mental emotional state, conscious or unconscious, and conversely, *every change in the mental emotional state, conscious or unconscious, is accompanied by an appropriate change in the physiological state.*" In other words, mind, body, and emotions are a unitary system—affect one and you affect the others. As Dr. Barbara Brown, another pioneer in biofeedback research, states:

> If some medical researchers are now teaching hearts, or the minds of hearts, to reverse a pathological condition, then medicine must be learning that relationships between mind and body are more pow-

erful than they once thought. The concept of "psychosomatic" is generally accepted as indicating the mental origin of physical pathology; research into biofeedback is the first medically testable indication that the *mind can relieve illnesses as well as create them*. [Emphasis added.]

A SYSTEM CONCEPT OF HEALTH

The results of countless placebo studies and the increasingly sophisticated use of biofeedback technology have caused the physical orientation of medicine to begin to undergo a change. It is no longer possible to see the body as an object waiting for replacement parts from the factory. Instead we now view the mind and body as an integrated *system*.

In this view, physical treatment remains an integral and essential part of the battle with a life-threatening disease such as cancer. Yet without beliefs—those of the patient and of the medical team—to support the treatment and create an expectancy of health, the physical treatment is incomplete. Recovery is more likely when we mobilize the whole person in the direction of health.

It is this concept, that the whole person be mobilized, that creates—even demands—a role for the patient in overcoming cancer and other diseases. The limits of the patient's responsibility extend far beyond getting himself to a physician who will "fix him up." Each person can assume responsibility for examining, even altering, beliefs and feelings that do not support the treatment, that do not move in the direction of affirming life and health.

Each of the next four chapters deals with one part of this changing conception of our role in illness and health. Each draws together a few more strands that tie the system together. The starting place is a definition of cancer that will be new to many, and an increased appreciation for our own resources to influence the disease.

3

The Search
for the
Causes of Cancer

Many of our patients come to us puzzling over what cancer is and what causes it. Most of them wonder, "Why me?" While we can offer a definition of the disease and describe the research into its causes, it is the third question—why a particular person contracts cancer—that is the real core of this book. However, we need to deal with the first two questions to set the stage for our evidence on "why you."

WHAT IS CANCER?

Because many people have lost a loved one to cancer or heard of the horrors of cancer, they assume it is a strong and powerful invader capable of ravaging the body. Actually, cellular biology tells us the opposite is true. A cancerous cell is, in fact, a weak and confused cell.

A cancer begins with a cell that contains incorrect genetic information so that it is unable to perform its intended function. This cell may receive the incorrect information because it has been exposed to harmful substances or chemicals or damaged by other external causes, or simply because in the process of constantly reproducing billions of cells the body will occasionally make an imperfect one. If this cell reproduces other cells with the same incorrect genetic makeup, then a tumor begins to form composed of a mass of these imperfect cells. Normally, the body's defenses, the immune system, would recognize these cells and destroy them. At a minimum, they would be walled off so they could not spread.

In the case of malignant cells, sufficient cellular changes take place so that they reproduce rapidly and begin to intrude on adjoining tissue. Whereas there is a form of "communication" between normal cells that prevents them from overreproducing, the malignant cells are sufficiently disorganized so that they do not respond to the communication of the cells around them, and they begin to reproduce recklessly. The body normally destroys them. But if it does not, the mass of faulty cells, the tumor, may begin to block proper functioning of body organs, either by expanding to the point that it puts physical pressure on other organs or by replacing enough healthy cells in an organ with malignant cells so that the organ is no longer able to function. In severe forms of cancer, malignant cells break loose from the original mass and are transported to other parts of the body, where they begin to reproduce and form new tumors. This breaking off and spreading is called "metastasis."

WHAT CAUSES CANCER?

Our patients have generally heard just enough about cancer research to believe that medical science is closing in on its causes. They tend to look for the culprit in external factors. By now everyone "knows" that cancer is caused by carcinogenic substances, or by genetic predisposition, or by radiation, or perhaps by diet. In reality, not one of these elements alone is a sufficient explanation for who gets cancer and who doesn't. Let's look at each separately.

Carcinogenic Substances

There is no question that there are harmful substances, including analine dyes, asbestos, coal tars, and other chemicals that apparently are able to affect the genetic information in cells and thus produce cancer. Research using laboratory animals has demonstrated that when they are exposed to large amounts of these harmful substances over a period of time, the substances have become known as "carcinogens," or cancer-producing agents.

One fact offered to support the argument that these substances are the cause of cancer is that the incidence of cancer has been found to climb markedly with increased levels of industrialization. Cancer is very prevalent in the United States, Western Europe, and other industrialized nations. Since a frequent by-product of industrialization is environmental pollution, which exposes people to an increasing amount of these carcinogens, it is argued that the increase in cancer is the result of the environmental pollution that accompanies industrialization. Indeed, the cancer incidence rates for the Soviet Union, which is not yet as industrialized as the United States, are virtually identical to those in the United States twenty years ago, and so it is suggested this time lag corresponds to the lag in industrialization.

Other researchers argue, on the other hand, that industrialized countries also have better medical care. Thus, people in less-developed countries die of other diseases or illnesses that are cured or prevented in industrialized countries, and so do not live long enough to contract cancer. While the fact that people live longer with better medical care may account for some of the increase in cancer deaths in industrialized societies, it doesn't satisfactorily explain the entire phenomenon.

If there were a direct, simple cause-and-effect relationship between harmful substances, chemicals, chronic irritants, and cancer, then increased exposure to these substances should cause an increase in cancer. On a broad statistical basis, there is an increased incidence of cancer with exposure to these substances, yet the vast majority of people exposed still do not get the disease and people who are apparently not exposed to exceptionally high levels of harmful substances still do get it.

In other words, exposure to carcinogens alone is not sufficient to cause cancer, nor does reduced exposure automatically eliminate cancer. On a person-by-person basis, additional explanations are needed.

Genetic Predisposition

The problem of explaining why one individual contracts cancer and another does not has led researchers to theorize that there could be a genetic predisposition that either causes some people to produce a greater number of abnormal cells or inclines them to have a weak immune response to abnormal cells. The observation that the incidence of cancer is substantially higher in some families than in others has been an impetus to a great deal of research in this area.

Indeed, special strains of experimental mice have been bred for use in cancer research precisely because of their increased susceptibility to cancer. Yet a major study conducted with these cancer-prone mice casts considerable doubt on any "it's genetics alone" theory. In the study, Dr. Vernon Riley, of the University of Washington, subjected a group of these mice to high levels of stress, while keeping a control group of the cancer-prone mice in a stress-free environment. At the time of the study, 80 percent of the mice would have been expected to develop cancer. As it turned out, however, 92 percent of the mice that had been placed under stress developed cancer, while only 7 percent of the stress-free mice did so. Thus, although all the mice had a genetic predisposition to cancer, the amount of stress in the environment had a very significant impact on the development of cancer.

Other efforts to explain cancer in terms of genetic predisposition have involved comparing cancer rates in different countries. For instance, the Japanese have one of the lowest rates of breast cancer in the world. Until a few years ago, it was thought this might be due to an inherited racial resistance, a genetic predisposition against breast cancer for all Japanese. But then the discovery was made that Japanese women living in the United States were four times more susceptible to breast cancer than were those living in Japan. Apparently, the differences in these cases are not racial, or genetic, but have something to do with living in Japan rather than in America.

Other cross-cultural studies have produced similarly inconclusive results. In addition, since genetic predisposition must be passed on from generation to generation, changes in predisposition in a whole society would occur very slowly. Therefore, the sharply increased incidence of cancer in industrialized society over the past twenty-five to fifty years is not readily explainable with the genetic argument.

Although genetic factors may play some role, we do not believe that by themselves they can explain the different patterns of cancer incidence throughout the world. It is important to consider the stressful changes that occur along with industrialization and integrate that information into our current thinking about cancer incidence.

Radiation

Still another suspect in the lineup of possible cancer causes is radiation, since it is well known that radiation can cause mutations in cells, which could in turn reproduce and lead to cancer. We are all subjected to many sources of radiation. First, the earth is constantly bombarded from outer space with what is called "cosmic radiation." It is possible that this radiation could cause occasional mutations resulting in cancer. But virtually no researchers seriously suggest that background radiation is a major cause of cancer. For one thing, all parts of the world are equally exposed to this form of radiation, which makes it difficult to explain major variations among different countries in incidence rates and kinds of cancer. If background radiation were a major cause of cancer, its effects should be relatively equal in all countries.

Another possibility being discussed lately is that fluorocarbons released from aerosol cans may be capable of destroying the protective layer of ozone in the atmosphere, leading to an increased exposure to ultraviolet radiation from the sun. Although this could certainly lead to potential health problems, high levels of ultraviolet rays are not normally associated with any cancer other than skin cancer. And since these changes in the atmosphere have not yet occurred, this source cannot account for present cases of cancer.

There has also been considerable discussion of the harmful effects of X-rays and other radiation used in medical diagnosis and treatment. The evidence is still unclear, and caution is certainly reasonable (for example, a correlation has been observed between using radiation to treat arthritis and subsequent development of leukemia). But citing this source of radiation as the cause of cancer suffers from the same problem as the harmful substance theory: many people who have been exposed to high levels of X-rays or other radiation do not get cancer, while people who have relatively low exposure still get the disease. Statistically it may be a factor, but for the patient who asks, "Why me?" it does not provide anything like a complete answer.

Diet

Including diet as a possible cause of cancer is relatively recent. Some researchers have suggested that the incidence of certain kinds of cancer may relate to the amount of fat in our

diets. Much animal experimentation has shown that when caloric intake is decreased, the incidence of cancer is lowered. It
appears that cancer, like other degenerative diseases, may
strike hardest the overfed.

For instance, Japan, where the diet is still predominately
based on fish and rice and contains substantially less fat than
does the American or European diet, has both a lower incidence of cancer and a substantially different profile in types of
cancers than the other industrialized countries. Since the incidence of cancer goes up sharply among Japanese living in
the United States, as discussed earlier, some researchers have
settled on differences in diet as a likely explanation.

There are factors other than diet that might explain the
low rate in Japan compared to other industrial nations. Cultural factors, for instance, may play a critical role since they,
more than diet, influence the way we live, our beliefs and feelings. Still, many nonfat-eating Japanese get cancer and many
fat-eating Westerners don't.

There are other population studies that cast doubt on the
theory of diet as a sole cause. One of the strangest findings of
cancer research comes from studies comparing disease incidence among institutionalized catatonic schizophrenics with institutionalized paranoid schizophrenics.

Catatonia is a form of mental illness in which individuals
wall themselves off from outside contact. Typically, catatonics
do not speak nor do they give any sign of recognition that
they have been spoken to. Frequently, they will not take the
initiative to eat or perform any other necessary physical function. They isolate and protect themselves from the outside
world. (They are also, it should be pointed out, protected
from the outside world.) Their susceptibility to cancer is very
low.

Unlike the catatonics who tune out the world, paranoids
are overly sensitive to the reactions of everyone around
them—they often suspect that everybody is plotting against
them. The incidence of cancer among paranoid schizophrenics
is higher than that of the normal population. It would appear
that the ability of the catatonic to close out the world provides
some form of protection against factors that may influence
cancer, whereas the paranoid has no such such protection.

The relationship between these two special populations
and the argument that diet has something to do with the incidence of cancer is as follows. In institutions, both kinds of pa-

tients, catatonics and paranoids, receive the same diet yet have sharply different incidences of cancer. In addition, they receive a diet very similar to the general diet in the United States, yet the incidence of cancer for both groups is different from that of the population at large. An explanation having to do with the psychology of people rather than the nature of diets is necessary to account for these differences.

Still, the fact that another population has a low incidence of cancer and eats a typical Western diet does not eliminate the possibility that Japan's incidence rates are related to diet. Instead, it suggests that we take a second look at what makes Japan distinctive. Although the Japanese diet is certainly unique among the industrialized nations, it is clear that Japanese culture is also unique. As feelings and beliefs are acknowledged to play a role in disease, then cultural factors may assume overwhelming importance in creating different rates of cancer incidence, since cultural patterns train people in their beliefs and feelings.

None of these theories by itself provides an adequate explanation of what causes cancer. Yet, part of any explanation must ultimately deal with one cause of illness—the suppression of the body's natural defenses against disease.

THE IMMUNE SYSTEM: OUR NATURAL DEFENSE AGAINST ILLNESS

A great deal of time, energy, and resources have been poured into the search for the causes of cancer, but one important fact is often overlooked: When exposed to known cancer-producing substances, most people still remain healthy. It is quite clear, for example, that the incidence of lung cancer goes up sharply with heavy smoking. But if all it took to get cancer was exposure to nicotine and tars, then all heavy smokers would contract the disease. Yet most heavy smokers do not get lung cancer. To understand the disease, then, we have to consider not only what causes some people to get cancer, we also have to consider what keeps most people from getting it—in other words, what maintains health?

One of the most important factors in sickness and health is the body's natural defenses. All of us are regularly exposed to disease, whether it is simply a cold, flu, or a more serious infectious disease. Yet the mere fact of exposure does not mean that we become ill. For the body's defense system—the *immune system*—is so powerful and effective that most people would not see a doctor for years unless reminded to take periodic checkups.

Greatly simplified, the immune system is composed of several kinds of cells designed to attack and destroy foreign substances. Anytime you see pus gathering in a cut, it is a reminder of the body's immune system at work. Pus is nothing more than a mass of white blood cells—a major part of the immune system—that have rushed to the site of the cut to isolate or destroy the infection. This self-healing process takes place constantly, on all levels within the body.

There are numerous cases on record in which chest X-rays revealed that individuals had at some time contracted mild cases of tuberculosis, for example, but that their bodies' defenses had fought back and destroyed the disease—all without the patients' being aware that they had even had any disease in the first place. In much the same way, the body does battle with cancerous cells on a routine basis, and routinely the cancerous cells are contained or destroyed so that they can do no harm.

In fact, the effectiveness of the body's natural defense system in rejecting anything foreign or abnormal is so great that it becomes a major problem in transplanting organs such as a heart or a kidney. Ordinarily this rejection phenomenon has great survival value, but in the case of a transplant, the foreign organ must be accepted by the body if the patient is to survive. For this reason, transplant patients are given a number of drugs designed to suppress the body's defenses. And here a problem arises, for the drugs that reduce the body's rejection of the transplanted organ also reduce the body's ability to defend itself against other dangers such as infectious disease or abnormal cells such as cancer. Hospitals therefore take great care to ensure that the transplant patient is not exposed to disease during this period, and the transplanted tissue is thoroughly checked to ensure that it is normal and healthy. But when something goes wrong with these painstaking procedures, the effect can be lethal.

Such a case was reported by Dr. Ronald Glasser in his book, *The Body Is the Hero*. In a rare incident, even though everything possible had been done to ensure that the kidney donor was healthy, a kidney with unobserved cancer nodules was placed in a person who had received drugs to suppress his immune system for the transplant. After the operation, the patient was given further medication to continue suppressing the immune system and thereby prevent the body from rejecting the kidney. Within days, the transplanted kidney began to enlarge. The reaction looked like some form of active rejection, but the kidney continued to function normally. A few days later, a routine X-ray revealed a tumor in the patient's chest. Since chest X-rays taken four days earlier had showed no such mass, clearly it was something that had developed since the operation.

A day later a similar tumor could be seen in the other lung. When an emergency operation was performed, the upper half of the transplanted kidney was found to be three times the size of its lower half. A biopsy of the abnormal portion showed it to be full of malignant cells. The physicians concluded that the masses in the lung were metastatic cancer (that is, malignant cells had broken away from the original cancerous mass and begun to reproduce in other parts of the body). The startling thing was the speed with which the masses had grown. Within days, cancerous masses had appeared that would normally have taken months or even years to develop. There was no choice but to stop administering the drugs that suppressed the body's defenses.

Glasser reports:

> Within days, as the patient's immune system came back to normal, the masses in his lung began to disappear and his transplanted kidney began to shrink in size. But with the stoppage of the drugs, it became obvious to the physicians that as the patient began to "reject" his cancerous cells, he also began to reject his transplanted kidney. They had no choice. They could not run the risk of the cancer returning, so they kept the patient off his immunosuppressive drugs; the cancer was destroyed but the kidney was also completely rejected. The rejected kidney was removed and the patient put back on chronic dialysis. He survived with no further evidence of cancer.

The physicians concluded that the donor's immune system had kept these cells in his own kidney in check, preventing them from spreading. Is is even possible that the donor's natural defenses were sufficiently strong that he might never have been aware of the presence of malignant cells, but when the organ was transplanted into a person whose defenses were suppressed by drugs, there was nothing to prevent them from running rampant. Despite the rapid spread of the cancer—and this is most important—when the body's normal defenses were allowed to function again, the cancer was quickly destroyed.

This story and a significant body of other research demonstrate that the development of a cancer does not require just the presence of abnormal cells, it also requires a *suppression of the body's normal defenses*. This research has led to broad medical acceptance of what is called the "surveillance theory" of cancer development.

The Surveillance Theory and Susceptibility to cancer

According to this theory, everyone produces abnormal cells in the body from time to time, either because of external factors or simply because of inaccurate cellular reproduction. Normally, the body's immune system keeps close watch out for any abnormal cells and destroys them (thus the term "surveillance"). For cancer to occur, then, the immune system must be inhibited in some way.

We will explore the possible causes of this suppression in later chapters, but the important point here is that something is happening in the person who contracts the cancer to create a susceptibility.

External agents, radiation, genetics, diet—all four factors may play a role in the causation of the disease, but none of them is a full explanation without considering why particular individuals, at particular points in their lives, contract cancer. They have certainly been exposed to harmful substances or radiation at other times. If there has been a genetic predisposition, it has been there all along. Their diet is likely to have been stable for a number of years. And, based on current medical theory, as we have said, abnormal cells are present in everybody's body occasionally throughout life. So, whether abnormal cells are created by external factors or simply occur naturally, the crucial questions become: What lapse in the body's defenses allows these cells to reproduce into a life-threatening tumor at this time? What inhibits the body's immune system from performing the function that it has performed successfully for many years?

The answers to these questions bring us back to emotional and mental factors in health and illness. The same factors that may determine why one patient lives and another with the identical diagnosis and treatment dies also influence why one person contracts a disease and another does not. As we shall see in the next two chapters, there are already several valuable clues to justify this line of assault on the causes.

First, there is a strong link between stress and illness. Second, the incidence of cancer in laboratory animals is greatly increased when they are placed under stress. Third, there are substantially different incidence rates for cancer among patients with different kinds of mental and emotional problems. These clues point to significant connections between emotional states and illness.

It is time to consider how the interrelationship of mind, body, and emotions may give us important new insights into the increased susceptibility to illness in general, cancer in particular, and into the question, "Why me?"

4

The Link
Between
Stress and Illness

There is a clear link between stress and illness, a link so strong that it is possible to predict illness based on the amount of stress in people's lives. Much of the early work demonstrating that the emotions can cause illness was undertaken by Hans Selye at the University of Prague in the 1920s. Recent studies involving both humans and laboratory animals have supported Selye's research and have also begun to reveal the physiological process by which emotional responses to stress can create susceptibility to disease. These findings are of critical importance to cancer patients, for they suggest that the effects of emotional stress can suppress the immune system, thus shackling the body's natural defenses against cancer and other disease.

MEASURING STRESS AND
PREDICTING ILLNESS

For years physicians have observed that illness is more likely to occur following highly stressful events in people's lives. Many doctors have noticed that when their patients suffered major emotional upsets there was an increase not only in diseases usually acknowledged to be susceptible to emotional

influence—ulcers, high blood pressure, heart disease, headaches—but also in infectious diseases, backaches, and even ac-
cidents.

The task of validating these observations scientifically
was undertaken by Dr. Thomas H. Holmes and his associates
at the University of Washington School of Medicine. They developed a means by which they could objectively measure the
amount of stress or emotional upset in a person's life. Dr.
Holmes and Dr. Rahe designed a scale that assigned numerical values to stressful events. Totaling the numerical values of
all the stressful events in a person's life could indicate the
amount of stress he or she was undergoing. The scale they
developed is shown in Table 1.

Table 1.
Social Readjustment Rating Scale

Event	Value
Death of spouse	100
Divorce	73
Marital separation	65
Jail term	63
Death of close family member	63
Personal injury or illness	53
Marriage	50
Fired from work	47
Marital reconciliation	45
Retirement	45
Change in family member's health	44
Pregnancy	40
Sex difficulties	39
Addition to family	39
Business readjustment	39
Change in financial status	38
Death of close friend	37
Change to different line of work	36
Change in number of marital arguments	36
Mortgage or loan over $10,000	31
Foreclosure of mortgage or loan	30
Change in work responsibilities	29
Son or daughter leaving home	29
Trouble with in-laws	29

Event	Value
Outstanding personal achievement	28
Spouse begins or stops work	26
Starting or finishing school	26
Change in living conditions	25
Revision of personal habits	24
Trouble with boss	23
Change in work hours, conditions	20
Change in residence	20
Change in schools	20
Change in recreational habits	19
Change in church activities	19
Change in social activities	18
Mortgage or loan under $10,000	17
Change in sleeping habits	16
Change in number of family gatherings	15
Change in eating habits	15
Vacation	13
Christmas season	12
Minor violation of the law	11

This scale includes events that we all recognize as stressful, such as death of a spouse, divorce, loss of a job, and other painful experiences. Interestingly, it also includes events such as marriage, pregnancy, or outstanding personal achievement, which are generally thought of as being happy experiences. Yet these are all experiences that may require us to change our habits, our ways of relating to people, or our self-images. They may be positive experiences, but they may also demand a great deal of introspection and may even cause unresolved emotional conflicts to surface. The key is the need to adapt to *change*, whether or not that change is in a positive or negative direction.

Using these objective measurements of the amount of observable change in people's lives, Holmes and his associates were able to predict illness with a high level of statistical accuracy. Forty-nine percent of the people who had accumulated scores of 300+ points within twelve months on the scale reported illness during the period of the study, while only 9 percent of those with scores below 200 reported illness during the same period. Another twelve-month study indicated that people with total point scores in the top third of those who participated in the study reported 90 percent more illness than did people in the bottom third.

Although using this scale makes it possible to predict the probability of illness based on the number of stressful events in a person's life, it is not possible to predict how an individual will react to stressful situations. Even in Holmes's study, 51 percent of the individuals with scores of 300 did not get sick during the period of the study. While stress may predispose to illness, the significant factor still seems to be how the individual copes with it.

Clearly the meaning of an event—even a stressful one—is construed differently from person to person. Loss of a job at age twenty will usually be less stressful than will loss of a job at fifty. When a person is enthusiastically looking forward to retirement, eager to spend time on a number of important projects, then retirement is much less stressful than it is when it is imposed by mandatory retirement rules. Some divorces are extremely bitter and shattering, while others are comparatively amiable. The same logic applies to all the other items on the stress list: since the events involve change, they will all produce some stress; but the amount of stress varies with the individual.

Stress may accumulate to the point that the individual simply can no longer cope and consequently becomes ill. But usually the relationship between stress and the individual's ability to cope is more complex. Holmes and Masuda acknowledge the significance of the individual's response in their analysis of why stress can lead to illness:

> The explanation, we suspect, is that the activity of coping can lower resistance to disease, *particularly when one's coping techniques are faulty:* when they lack relevance to the . . . problems to be solved. This approach to illness is a lesson in human finitude [reminding] us that we have only so much energy, no more. If it takes too much effort with the environment, we have less to spare for preventing disease. When life is too hectic, *and when coping attempts fail,* illness is the unhappy result. [Emphasis added.]

Research with animals corroborates the significance of these findings. Dr. Samudzhen demonstrated that the intensity of cancerous growth in experimental animals placed under stress was much higher than that in nonstressed animals. In 1955, Dr. Turkevich demonstrated that stressing of experimental animals has a stimulating effect on tumor development. And in a review of the studies in 1969, Dr. S. B. Friedman indicated that, "it now appears certain that environmental factors of a psychosocial nature can modify resistance to a number of infectious and neoplastic (cancerous) diseases." So many animal studies have demonstrated the link between stress and cancer that Dr. Friedman in a symposium of the New York Academy of Science suggested that no further animal research need be conducted in this area because the link had already been quite adequately proven.

While these studies clearly establish the fact that stress may often lead to illness, they stop short of describing *how* this happens on a physical level. Other researchers, however, have been able to describe the physiology of stress.

HOW STRESS INCREASES
SUSCEPTIBILITY TO ILLNESS

The medical community has been slow in acknowledging the role of stress in illness. In part this is due to the general physical orientation of the medical profession: physical ailments are produced by physical causes and should be treated with physical intervention. What has been missing from the studies to make them more acceptable to the medical community is the identification of a specific physiological mechanism by which emotional states contribute to the onset of illness. The delineation of just such a mechanism is emerging from recent research on the effects of chronic stress. To understand the findings, you may find it helpful to know a little more about the physiology of stress.

The human nervous system is the product of millions of years of evolution. For most of human existence the demands placed on the nervous system were very different from those placed on us by modern civilization. Survival in primitive societies required that humans be capable of immediately identifying a threat and making a quick decision whether to fight or flee. The nervous system is an external threat, our bodies are instantly primed (via a change in hormonal balances and nerve outputs) either to fight or flee.

But life in modern society requires that we frequently inhibit our fight-or-flee responses. When a policeman stops you to give you a speeding ticket or when your boss berates your performance, your body is instinctively mobilized by the threat. In these circumstances, however, either "fighting" or "fleeing" would be a socially inappropriate response, so you learn to override your reaction. Throughout the day, you constantly override your body's responses to stress—when a mistake is made, a taxi honks too loudly, you have to wait in lines, you miss a bus, and so on.

The body is designed so that moments of stress, followed by a physical reaction such as fighting or fleeing, do little harm. However, when the physiological response to stress is not discharged—because of the social consequences of "fighting" or "fleeing"—then there is a negative cumulative effect on the body. This is *chronic* stress, stress that is held in the body and not released. And chronic stress, it is increasingly recognized, plays a significant role in many illnesses.

Dr. Hans Selye, mentioned previously, an endocrinologist and director of the Institute on Experimental Medicine and Surgery at the University of Montreal, described the effects of chronic stress on the body. His description reads like a list of medical horrors.

To start with, chronic stress frequently produces hormonal imbalances. Since hormones play a critical role in regulating body functions, these imbalances can lead to high blood pressure and eventually damage to the kidneys. The damage to the kidneys can, in turn, lead to severe hypertension (high blood pressure), which will reinforce the chemical imbalance.

In addition, the hormonal changes resulting from stress can allow tears to develop in the walls of arteries. The body repairs these tears by a buildup of cholesterol plaques, a type of scar tissue. But too many plaques cause hardening of the arteries, arteriosclerosis. This, in turn, forces the heart to pump harder to circulate the blood, further increasing the blood pressure. When arteriosclerosis becomes far advanced, it diminishes the amount of blood and oxygen reaching the heart to the point that coronary failure may occur. The cholesterol plaques may also block the heart's major coronary arteries, causing part of the heart muscle to die, resulting in eventual heart failure. Normally, the body will make an effort to adjust to these problems, but under chronic stress the mechanisms responsible for reducing and adjusting hormonal imbalance are overriden. The imbalance just continues in an increasingly negative and life-threatening cycle.

This evidence clearly demonstrates the very real physical effects of stress. But it is still another effect that is of greatest importance to the cancer patient. Selye has discovered that chronic stress suppresses the immune system which is responsible for engulfing and destroying cancerous cells or alien microorganisms. The important point is this: The physical conditions Selye describes as being produced by stress are virtually identical to those under which an abnormal cell could reproduce and spread into a dangerous cancer. Not surprisingly, cancer patients frequently have weakened immune systems.

Selye's findings are confirmed by other researchers. Dr. R. W. Bathrop and his associates at the University of New South Wales, Australia, have conducted studies indicating that bereavement lowers the body's immune response. They tested twenty-six recently bereaved persons (ages twenty-five to sixty-five) at two weeks and six weeks after their spouses' death. A control group was established of twenty-six hospital employees who had not experienced any bereavement in the past two years. Lymphocyte function, a critical measure of the potency of the body's immune system, was significantly depressed in those who had lost a wife or husband. Since the immune system serves as a potent defense against the reproduction of cancerous cells, as we discussed in the last chapter, evidence that emotional loss can lead to a suppression of the immune system is an important clue to the causes of cancer.

Another study that points to mental factors leading to the suppression of the immune system was conducted by Dr. J. H. Humphrey and his associates at the British Medical Research Council. Their research demonstrates that the body's immunity to tuberculosis can be profoundly affected by hypnotic suggestion—clearly demonstrating the influence of mental and emotional stress on the body's defenses.

Finally, Dr. George Solomon of California State University has discovered that incisions in the hypothalamus—a portion of the brain that significantly affects endocrine production in the body—lead to a suppression of the immune system. The hypothalamus is also the portion of the brain considered most directly associated with emotions—another significant piece of evidence for those of us in cancer research seeking the causes of disease.

Dr. Solomon's work begins to specify the physiological mechanism by which stress could lead to a suppression of the immune system. When his work is combined with that of Selye and others, a picture begins to emerge of how emotional stress can create the conditions under which cancer can occur. What remains is the need for a sufficient understanding of the body to describe the precise links between cancer and stress.

A SUMMARY OF THE INDIVIDUAL FINDINGS: WE RETURN AGAIN TO THE INDIVIDUAL

Let us take a moment to summarize the major themes of the research:

- High levels of emotional stress increase susceptibility to illness.

- Chronic stress results in a suppression of the immune system, which in turn creates increased susceptibility to illness—and especially to cancer.

- Emotional stress, which suppresses the immune system, also leads to hormonal imbalances. These imbalances could increase the production of abnormal cells at precisely the time the body is least capable of destroying them.

It is significant that the amount of emotional stress caused by external events depends on how the individual interprets or copes with that event. Even though researchers are able to predict illness based on the number of stressful events in people's lives, a number of individuals in these studies did *not* get sick, even though they experienced high levels of stress. Once again, it is necessary to look at the individual's unique response to a stressful event.

Everyone has learned some ways of coping with stress that either reduce its emotional impact or decrease its effects on the body. Thus, the next step is to understand what kinds of coping reactions play a role in making people susceptible to cancer.

5

Personality, Stress, and Cancer

Most of the time, the ways in which we respond to the stresses of life are habitual, dictated by our unconscious beliefs about who we are, who we "should" be, and the way the world and other people are and should be. These patterns of behavior form a total orientation, or stance toward life. There is now a growing body of evidence that different stances toward life may be associated with particular diseases. For instance, in their popular book, *Type A Behavior and Your Heart,* Drs. Meyer Friedman and Ray Rosenman describe a set of behaviors—a stance toward life—that they believe substantially contributes to heart disease. They have called this perennially pressured, competitive stance the "Type A Personality."

There are numerous studies that show that in addition to heart disease personality types, there are many similar characteristics in people who get rheumatoid arthritis, stomach ulcers, asthma, and urinary tract irritation (among women). There is also an ancient body of observations, confirmed by many recent studies, that there are strong personality profile similarities among cancer patients.

A HISTORICAL LOOK AT THE CONNECTION BETWEEN CANCER AND EMOTIONS

The connection between cancer and emotional states has been observed for nearly 2000 years. In fact, it is the separation of cancer from emotional states that is the new and strange idea. Writing nearly 2000 years ago in the second century A.D., the physician Galen observed that cheerful women were less prone to cancer than were women of a depressed nature. Gendron, in a treatise written in 1701 inquiring into the nature and causes of cancer, cited the influence of the "disasters of life as occasion much trouble and grief." In an example still quoted in medical schools today, Gendron reported that:

> Mrs. Emerson, upon the death of their daughter, underwent great affliction and perceived her breast to swell, which soon after grew painful. At last it broke out in a most inveterate cancer, which consumed a great part of it in a short time. She had always enjoyed a perfect state of health.
>
> The wife of the Mate of a ship (who was taken some time ago by the French and put in prison) was thereby so much affected that her breast began to swell, and soon after broke out in a desperate cancer which had proceeded so far I could not undertake her case. She never before had any complaint in her breast.

In 1783, Burrows, in a comment that sounds remarkably like an early description of chronic stress, attributed the disease to "the uneasy passions of the mind with which the patient is strongly affected for a long time." By 1822, Nunn, in *Cancer of the Breast,* a widely recognized text, stated that emotional factors influenced the growth of tumors. As an illustration, he noted that a particular case coincided "with a shock to her nervous system caused by the death of her husband. Shortly thereafter the tumor again increased in size and the patient died."

In 1846, Dr. Walter Hyle Walshe published *The Nature and Treatment of Cancer,* an influential and definitive book covering nearly all that was known about cancer at that time. Walshe stated:

Much has been written on the influence of mental misery, sudden reverses of fortunes, and habitual gloominess of temper on the disposition of carcinomatous matter. If systematic writers can be credited, these constitute the most powerful cause of the disease. . . . Facts of a very convincing character in respect to the agency of the mind in the production of this disease are frequently observed. I have myself met with cases in which the connection appeared so clear that . . . questioning its reality would have seemed a struggle against reason.

In 1865, Dr. Claude Bernard wrote a classic text, *Experimental Medicine,* in which he reported observations similar to our own. Bernard cautioned that a living being must be considered as a harmonious whole. Although separate analysis of body parts was necessary for investigation, he said, the relations among the parts must also be considered. And, in another classic text, *Surgical Pathology,* published in 1870, Sir James Paget expressed his conviction that depression plays a vital role in the occurrence of cancer:

The cases are so frequent in which deep anxiety, deferred hope, and disappointment are quickly followed by the growth and increase of cancer that we can hardly doubt that mental depression is a weighty additive to the other influences favouring the development of the cancerous constitution.

The first statistical study of emotional states and cancer was undertaken in 1893 by Snow. In reporting this relatively sophisticated research in *Cancers and the Cancer-Process,* Snow stated:

Of 250 out- and in-patients with cancer of the mammary or uterus at the London Cancer Hospital, 43 gave histories permitting a suspicion of mechanical injury. Fifteen of these 43 also described themselves as having undergone much recent trouble. Thirty-two others spoke of hard work and privation. In 156 there had been much immediate antecedent trouble, often in very poignant form, [such] as the loss of a near relative. In 19, no causation-history could be proved.

Snow concluded that:

> Of all causes of the cancer-process in every shape, neurotic agencies are the most powerful. Of the most prevalent kinds, distress of mind is the one most commonly met with; exhausting toil and privation ranking next. These are direct exciting causes that exert a weighty predisposing influence towards the development of the rest. Idiots and lunatics are remarkably exempt from cancer in every shape.

Despite the apparent agreement among late nineteenth- and early twentieth-century experts that there was a connection between emotional states and cancer, interest waned in the face of general anesthesia, newly developing surgical procedures, and radiation therapy. The success of these physical therapies with many medical problems substantially strengthened the viewpoint that physical problems could be solved only with some form of physical treatment. In addition, physicians began to see stresses such as hard work and privation as inevitable; after all, even if they did play a role in the onset of cancer, what could a physician do about them? Finally, until the first third of the twentieth century the tools for dealing with emotional problems were still quite limited.

Yet it is one of the ironies of medical history that, as the emerging sciences of psychology and psychiatry developed the diagnostic tools to test the link between cancer and emotional states scientifically and the therapeutic tools to assist in dealing with emotional problems, medicine lost interest in the problem. The result has been two very distinct bodies of literature and research. The psychological literature is rich with descriptions of the emotional states related to cancer, but it often fails to suggest any physiological mechanisms that might explain this relationship. The medical literature is well grounded in physiology but, perhaps because it does not integrate psychological data into its research, it is unable to explain "spontaneous" remission or major differences in how individuals respond to treatment.

Coming from a medical background, Carl was startled to find substantial evidence of the links between emotional states and cancer in the psychological literature. We have since observed that few physicians are aware of this research. The price of this age of specialization is that persons in different disciplines working on the same problem often have little exchange of information. Each discipline develops its own specialized language, its own values, its own method of communicating information, and important information can be lost because the disciplines do not exchange findings effectively.

We have found that explaining the psychological literature to cancer patients is a particularly sensitive task. If we make a statement that, "Research indicates that cancer patints have certain traits . . . ," then many patients automatically assume the research says they personally have those traits. But statistical studies, by their very nature, are broad generalizations that apply to groups, not necessarily to a particular individual. In his book, *Mind as Healer, Mind as Slayer,* psychologist Kenneth R. Pelletier suggests that people should exercise caution in applying "personality profiles" to themselves:

> At present most of the research in personality and illness is centered around determining the characteristic patterns among people who have already contracted a particular disorder. Some of the personality characteristics typical of people with particular disorders may sound remarkably like your own. You should not be alarmed by this, since *it does not inevitably follow that you will incur the diseases associated with these characteristics.* These personality profiles are merely useful guidelines, to make people aware of what potentially hazardous behavior patterns might be. Self-assessment is seldom accurate, and analysis of behavior patterns should always rely on the interpretation of a skilled clinician. Personality profiles are only one element of diagnosis, and they are inconclusive in and of themselves. It is common among graduate students in any clinical area to imagine themselves stricken by each disorder that they are studying. With further training, they realize that diagnostic assessment is complex and indicative of a direction, rather than being definitive. Anyone approaching the subject area of personality

and disease requires a comparable note of caution. [Emphasis added.]

As we review the research on emotional states and cancer, then, we strongly suggest that if you are a cancer patient or someone with a fear of cancer, simply use the research as a starting point for your thinking and be aware of the fact that all of us have a tendency to see aspects of ourselves in these descriptions. People with similar personality traits don't all develop the same illness any more than all people subjected to the same carcinogenic agents develop cancer. Many other factors, as you now know, play a significant role.

THE PSYCHOLOGICAL EVIDENCE

One of the finest studies on emotional states and cancer was reported in *A Psychological Study of Cancer,* written in 1926 by Dr. Elida Evans, a Jungian psychoanalyst, with an introduction by Carl Jung. Jung wrote that he believed Evans had solved many of the mysteries of cancer—including why the course of the disease is not always predictable, why the disease can sometimes recur after many years with no sign of illness, and why it is a disease associated with industrialized society.

Based on her analysis of one hundred cancer patients, Evans concluded that many cancer patients had lost an important emotional relationship before the onset of the disease. She saw such patients as people who had invested their identity in one individual object or role (a person, a job, a home) rather than developing their own individuality. When the object or role was threatened or removed, such patients were thrown back on themselves, with few internal resources for coping. (We, too, have found the characteristic of putting others' needs before one's own in our patients, as you will see in the case histories that follow.) Evans also believed that cancer was a symptom of other unresolved problems in a patient's life, and her observations have since been confirmed and elaborated on by a number of other researchers.

Dr. Lawrence LeShan, an experimental psychologist by training and a clinical psychologist by experience, is the foremost theorist of the psychological life history of cancer patients. In his recently published book, *You Can Fight for Your Life: Emotional Factors in the Causation of Cancer,* he reports findings similar in many ways to those of Evans. Le-Shan identifies four typical components in the life histories of the more than 500 cancer patients with whom he worked:

• The patient's youth was marked by feelings of isolation, neglect, and despair, with intense interpersonal relationships appearing difficult and dangerous.

• In early adulthood, the patient was able to establish a strong, meaningful relationship with a person, or found great satisfaction in his or her vocation. A tremendous amount of energy was poured into this relationship or role. Indeed, it became the reason for living, the center of the patient's life.

• The relationship or role was then removed—through death, a move, a child leaving home, a retirement, or the like. The result was despair, as though the "bruise" left over from childhood had been painfully struck again.

• One of the fundamental characteristics of these patients was that the despair was "bottled up." These individuals were unable to let other people know when they felt hurt, angry, hostile. Others frequently viewed the cancer patients as unusually wonderful people, saying of them: "He's such a good, sweet man" or "She's a saint." LeShan concludes "The benign quality, the 'goodness' of these people was in fact a sign of their failure to believe in themselves sufficiently, and their lack of hope."

He describes the emotional state of his patients after they lost the crucial relationship or role as follows:

The growing despair that each of these people faced appear[s] to be strongly connected with the loss that each suffered in childhood. . . . they saw the end of the relationship as a disaster that they had always half expected. They had been waiting for it to end, waiting for rejection. And when it happened, they said to themselves, "Yes, I knew it was too good to be true." . . . From a superficial point of view, all managed to "adjust" to the blow. They continued to function. They went about their daily business. But the "color," the zest, the meaning went out of their lives. They no longer seemed attached to life.

To those around them, even people close to them, they seemed to be coping perfectly well . . . but in fact it was the false peace of despair that they felt. They were simply waiting to die. For that seemed the only way out. They were ready for death. In one very real sense they had already died. One patient said to me, "Last time I hoped, and look what happened. As soon as my defenses were down, of course I was left alone again. I'll never hope again. It's too much. It's better to stay in a shell."

And there they stayed, waiting without hope for death to release them. Within six months to eight years, among my patients, the terminal cancer appeared.

LeShan reports that 76 percent of all the cancer patients he interviewed shared this basic emotional life history. Of the cancer patients who entered into intensive psychotherapy with him, over 95 percent showed this pattern. Only 10 percent of a control group of noncancer patients revealed this pattern.

Although LeShan writes movingly and convincingly of his patients' emotional states, not all facets of his observations have yet been validated by other studies. But several key elements have been confirmed by a thirty-year study by Caroline B. Thomas, a psychologist at The Johns Hopkins University.

Dr. Thomas began interviewing medical students at Johns Hopkins in the 1940s and evaluating their psychological profiles. Since then, she has interviewed more than 1300 students and followed their history of illness. She reports that the most distinctive psychological profile belonged to students who subsequently developed cancer—more distinctive even than that of students who subsequently committed suicide. In particular, her data showed that students who subsequently developed cancer saw themselves as having experienced a lack of closeness with their parents, seldom demonstrated strong emotions, and were generally low gear.

Another element of LeShan's description, that cancer patients tend to be prone to feelings of hopelessness and helplessness even before the onset of their cancer, has been confirmed by two other studies.

• Drs. A. H. Schmale and H. Iker observed in their female cancer patients a particular kind of giving-up, a sense of hopeless frustration surrounding a conflict for which there was no resolution. Often this conflict occurred approximately six months prior to the cancer diagnosis. Schmale and Iker then studied a group of healthy women who were considered to be biologically predisposed to cancer of the cervix.

Using psychological measures that allowed them to identify a "helplessness-prone personality," in this group Schmale and Iker predicted which women would develop cancer—and were accurate 73.6 percent of the time. The researchers pointed out that this does not mean that feelings of helplessness *cause* cancer—these women appeared to have some predisposition to cervical cancer—but that the helplessness seemed to be an important element.

• Over a period of fifteen years, Dr. W. A. Greene studied the psychological and social experiences of patients who developed leukemia and lymphoma. He too observed that the loss of an important relationship was a significant element in the patient's life history. For both men and women, Green said, the greatest loss was the death or threat of death of a mother; or for men, a "mother figure," such as a wife. Other significant emotional events for women were menopause or a change of home; and for men, the loss or threat of loss of a job, and retirement or the threat of retirement.

Greene concluded that leukemia or lymphoma developed in an environmental setting in which the patient had dealt with a number of losses and separations that produced a psychological state of despair, hopelessness, and discontinuity.

Other studies have confirmed LeShan's description of the difficulty many cancer patients experience in expressing negative feelings and the need to constantly look good to others.

• Dr. D. M. Kissen has observed that the major difference between heavy smokers who get lung cancer and heavy smokers who do not is that the lung cancer patients have "poorly developed outlets for emotional discharge."

• E. M. Blumberg demonstrated that the rate of tumor growth can be predicted based on certain personality traits. The patients with fast-growing tumors attempted to give a good impression of themselves. They were also more defensive and less able to defend themselves against anxiety. In addition, they tended to reject affection, even though they wanted it. The slow-growing tumor group showed a greater ability to absorb emotional shocks and to reduce tension by physical activity. The difficulty for the patients with fast-growing tumors seemed to be that the emotional outlets were blocked by an extreme desire to make a good impression.

• Dr. B. Klopfer conducted a similar study in which tumor type (fast or slow growth) was predicted based on personality profiles. The variables that allowed the researchers to predict rapid growth were patients' ego defensiveness and loyalty to "their own version of reality." Klopfer believes that when too much energy is tied up defending the ego and the patient's way of seeing life, the body will not have the necessary vital energy to fight the cancer.

EXAMPLES FROM OUR PATIENTS' LIVES

In addition to the studies cited, experience with our patients leaves no reasonable doubt in our minds of a link between certain emotional states and cancer.

One of our earliest experiences occurred while Carl was still in residency and we had not yet begun to use the approach described in this book. Betty Johnson, a forty-year-old woman, came to the hospital with an advanced cancer of the kidney. She had been widowed during the preceding year but continued to live and work on the ranch left to her by her husband. An exploratory operation revealed that she had cancer that had spread outside the kidney, and that it would be impossible to remove the cancer surgically. She was treated with minimal doses of radiation but there was little expectation for improvement. Then she was sent home to her ranch, given only a few months to live.

Once home, she fell in love with one of the men who worked on her ranch and they were soon married. Despite the prognosis of imminent death, she showed no further signs of the illness for five years. Then her second husband left her after running through her money. Within a few weeks Betty had a major recurrence of the cancer and died shortly thereafter.

It would seem that her remarriage played a significant role in her apparent recovery, and that being deserted precipitated the recurrence of the disease and her death.

Day after day we find similar evidence of the link between emotional states and disease in the lives of the people we see, and one important result is that we have learned to listen to our patients more closely. When we considered cancer a purely physical problem, we viewed patients' descriptions of their emotional states as something to be responded to with sympathy and understanding but having little to do with the course of the disease. As we learned that the "whole person" participates in the course of disease, we began to pay very close attention to everything our patients said. One of the patients who taught us was Millie.

Millie Thomas was unique among our early patients in that she came to us already convinced that she had participated in her illness. She had been sent to see Carl by her physician, a thoracic surgeon, who had attended a lecture Carl had given. Millie was seventy years old, although she held herself so erect that she seemed younger. She had already been diagnosed as having cancer and had undergone surgery once to remove the diseased tissue.

Millie's opening statment to Carl was that she had brought the disease upon herself and she was afraid she would cause it to recur or to spread. She wanted help. She spoke so directly and with such force of intelligence that we had no immediate reply, except to ask her to explain.

Millie related that as she approached seventy and neared her mandatory retirement age as an elementary schoolteacher, her students seemed to annoy her more and her work became unpleasant. Unmarried, she shared her apartment with another older woman, whom she also found increasingly annoying. Her whole world seemed to be deteriorating.

She noticed that she had begun smoking more and that, as she inhaled the smoke, she was thinking it wouldn't be long until she would be dead. At night when she went to sleep, she was also aware of thinking that this was one less day she would have to live, that she had completed another day and there wouldn't be many more. For several months, she continued to smoke and to become more and more depressed. Then she developed an increasingly severe cough that eventually produced some blood.

When she saw her physician she was found to have lung cancer and underwent surgery. After the operation, her depression recurred and, as a result, she became apprehensive about the possibility of recreating the disease that she strongly believed she had participated in developing in the first place. When she voiced this fear to her surgeon, he remembered Carl's lecture and referred her for consultation.

Millie was the first patient to tell us that she had "made herself ill" and could relate the actual thought processes she had experienced. Having previously undergone some psychotherapy, she was more aware of her thoughts and feelings than many people. She required very little help in overcoming her fear and depression.

Although Millie was unusual in the degree of access she had to her inner self, we find that many of our patients—once they understand that their emotional states may have played a role in their disease—remember similar thoughts and feelings. Often they recall wishing they were dead or feeling hopeless and thinking that death was the only way out. Frequently these feelings occurred either because of a new demand that had been placed on them or because of an apparently unresolvable conflict.

For many of our patients, the conflict occurs when they discover their spouses have had affairs, particularly if they will not consider marriage counseling or if their religious beliefs prevent them from accepting the idea of divorce, but they nevertheless feel unwilling to stay in marriage. Edith Jones faced this problem in the extreme when she discovered that her husband, the father of their six children, was having extramarital affairs. She did not believe she could tolerate the situation but she also did not believe in divorce. There appeared to be no alternatives and so she felt trapped. She contracted cancer and soon died. For Edith, death represented a solution. Other women might have found a basis for continuing the relationship, and still others might have given themselves "permission" to obtain a divorce.

Several of our male patients have had conflicts centering on relatives in their businesses. This was the case with Rod Hansen, who singlehandedly had developed his small company into a successful enterprise. Because of close family ties, Rod took a relative into the business in a major supervisory role. The relative turned out to be incompetent to handle this level of responsibility, the business began to deteriorate, and the enterprise that Rod had poured himself into heart and soul ceased to be a pleasure—indeed, it because an intolerable problem to which he saw no solution.

Rod received his cancer diagnosis approximately one year after his business began deteriorating. After working with us at our clinic for some time, Rod learned how to confront his problems more directly. At one point he actually fired the relative, then subsequently brought him back in a lower position more appropriate to his abilities.

Another frequent life pattern found in the cancer patient is that of a woman who has invested all her emotional and much of her physical energy in her family. As chauffeur, cook, nursemaid, and counselor to her four offspring, June Larsen's days were a whirl of ballet classes, music lessons, football games, slumber parties, and P.T.A. meetings. Because her husband was a successful executive, with a major corporation and had to travel a great deal, responsibility for the children fell almost entirely on her. When she looked back on those years, she admits that she and her husband had come to have little in common other than the children.

As each child grew up and left home for college or marriage, June would go through a short bout of despondency, but soon she would snap back and throw herself with renewed energy into her remaining children's endeavors. When the last child went away to college, June felt "as if a part of my life had been cut out of me." She was deeply depressed and at a loss as to what to do with her time. She also made increasing demands on her husband, which he resented. Nothing seemed to lift her spirits, and within a year she was diagnosed as having breast cancer with bone metastases.

June's primary identity had been tied up in her children. When thrown back on her own resources she discovered that most of her skills were for nurturing others rather than for meeting her own needs. She felt forced to accept that there was little left of her marriage. While the actual external stress—the blow of her last child's leaving for college—may seem small, it totally undercut the role that had defined her for many years.

Because June's situation is so typical, we have seen many patients like her and have observed a number of different responses to this particular stress. Some women are able to establish a new identity apart from that of mother. In several cases, the marriage has been rebuilt so that it once again provides meaning. In our experience, the women patients who make the transition to a new role or who reestablish important relationships not only live longer—some now show no sign of illness—they also live much more active and rewarding lives.

For men and women who have had active careers, retirement often poses a number of problems. Sam Brown was an executive who did not really want to retire at age sixty-five, but it was such an established practice in his firm that he never questioned it. After the round of retirement parties wore off, however, Sam felt himself getting increasingly bored, and then depressed. As an executive in his firm, he had always felt important. Now he felt he had lost stature. When people asked what he did and he answered "retired," he didn't get the spark of interest and respect he was used to. In addition, he found he missed the excitement and stimulation of his work and of an occasional business trip. Although he had prepared financially for retirement, inflation had forced him to reduce his standard of living.

To complicate matters, Sam and his wife had not been close for a number of years. Conflicts that had been hidden while he spent many hours at the office now emerged, and he saw himself as a captive audience to her steadily increasing complaints. He came to realize how much of his self-esteem had been tied up in his work, and without it he felt useless and unproductive. He began to wonder whether he had really accomplished much in life after all. Finally, when several friends died a short time after their own retirements, Sam began to think more about death. Fourteen months after he retired he was diagnosed as having cancer of the bowel.

In addition to the sources of stress which we have seen in the preceding cases (loss of a spouse, financial difficulties, unwanted retirement, significant business setbacks, loss of life's purpose through children leaving home and deterioration of a marriage), another stress that we have seen frequently in our patients' lives prior to the onset of cancer is what has come to be called "the mid-life crisis." (In chapter 9, we will be examining one such case in detail.)

THE PSYCHOLOGICAL PROCESS OF ILLNESS

These cases typify the kinds of conflicts our patients have faced in the months preceding their illness. From our experience and from the research of others, we can identify five steps of a psychological process that frequently precedes the onset of cancer.

1. *Experiences in childhood result in decisions to be a certain kind of person.* Most of us remember a time in childhood when our parents did something we didn't like and we made an internal pledge: "When I grow up I'm never going to be like that." Or a time when some contemporary or adult did something that we regarded highly and we made an internal pledge to behave in a similar way whenever we could.

Many of these childhood decisions are positive and have an overall beneficial effect on our lives. Many of them, on the other hand, do not. In some cases, these decisions were made as the result of traumatic or painful experiences. If children see their parents engaged in terrible fights, for example, they may make the decision that expressing hostility is bad. Consequently, they set rules for themselves that they must always be good, pleasing, and cheerful, no matter what their real feelings are. The decision that the only way to be loved or receive approval in the family is to be a certain kind of all-loving person may last a lifetime, even when it makes life a terrible strain.

Or some children make an early decision that they are responsible for the feelings of other people, and whenever other people are unhappy or sad around them, it's their responsibility to help them feel better. Possibly such decisions are the best ones children can make at the time they are made, because the decisions enable them to get through difficult situations. However, in adult life these decisions of accommodation are probably no longer appropriate, since life circumstances are different from those that existed when the decisions were made.

Our main concern is that the decisions made in childhood limit a person's resources for coping with stresses. By adulthood, most of these childhood decisions are no longer conscious. The same ways of acting have been repeated so many times that awareness of our ever having made a choice is lost. But unless these choices are changed, they become the rules of the game of our life. Every need to be met, every problem to be solved must be handled within these limited choices made in early childhood.

Most of us tend to see ourselves as being the way we are just because "that's the way we are." But when the history of our choices is made conscious, new decisions can be made.

2. *The individual is rocked by a cluster of stressful life events.* Both the research and our own observations of patients indicate that major stresses are often a precursor to cancer. Frequently, clusters of stresses occur within a short period of time. The critical stresses we have identified are those that threaten personal identity. These may include the death of a spouse or loved one, retirement, the loss of a significant role.

3. *These stresses create a problem with which the individual does not know how to deal.* It is not just the stresses that create the problem, but the inability to cope with the stresses given the "rules" about the way he or she has to act and the role decided upon in early life. When the man who is unable to permit himself close relationships, and therefore finds meaning primarily in his work, is forced to retire, he cannot cope. The woman whose principal sense of identity is tied up in her husband cannot cope when she finds out he has been having an affair. The man who learned to rarely express his feelings finds he feels trapped when in a situation that can be improved only if he will express himself openly.

4. *The individual sees no way of changing the rules about how he or she must act and so feels trapped and helpless to resolve the problem.* Because the unconscious decisions of the "right way" to be form a significant part of their identity, these people may not see that change is possible or may even feel that to change significantly is to lose their identity. Most of our patients acknowledge that there was a time prior to the onset of their illness when they felt helpless, unable to solve or control problems in their lives, and found themselves "giving up."

They saw themselves as "victims"—months before the onset of cancer—because they no longer felt capable of altering their lives in ways that would resolve their problems or reduce their stresses. Life happened to them; they did not control it. They were acted upon rather than actors. The continued stresses were final proof to them that time and further developments would not improve their lot.

5. *The individual puts distance between himself or herself and the problem, becoming static, unchanging, rigid.* Once there is no hope, then the individual is just "running in place," never expecting to go anywhere. On the surface he or she may seem to be coping with life, but internally life seems to hold no further meaning, except in maintaining the conventions. Serious illness or death represents a solution, an exit, or a postponement of the problem.

Although many of our patients remember this thought sequence, others are not consciously aware of it. Most, however, will recall having had feelings of helplessness or hopelessness some months prior to the onset of the disease. This process does not *cause* cancer, rather it *permits* cancer to develop.

It is this giving up on life that plays a role in interfering with the immune system and may, through changes in hormonal balance, lead to an increase in the production of abnormal cells. Physically, it creates a climate that is right for the development of cancer.

The crucial point to remember is that all of us create the *meaning* of events in our lives. The individual who assumes the victim stance *participates* by assigning meanings to life events that prove there is no hope. Each of us *chooses*—although not always at a conscious level—how we are going to react. The intensity of the stress is determined by the meaning we assign to it and the rules we have established for how we will cope with stress.

In outlining this process it is not our intention to make anyone feel guilty or frightened—that would only make matters worse. Instead, we hope that if you can see yourself in this psychological process, you will recognize it as a call to action and make changes in your life. Since emotional states contribute to illness, they can also contribute to health. By acknowledging your own participation in the onset of the disease, you acknowledge your power to participate in regaining your health and you have also taken the first step toward getting well again.

GETTING WELL AGAIN

We have just described the psychological steps we have identified and observed in a patient's becoming ill. It's important to appreciate that many of these steps occur unconsciously, without the patient's awareness that he or she was even participating. The whole purpose of explaining the psychological steps in the spiral toward illness is to build a basis from which the patient can proceed to the steps in a spiral toward recovery.

By becoming aware of the spiral that occurred in the development of their own illness, many of our patients take the first step in altering its direction. Then, by changing attitudes and behavior, they can tip the scales in the direction of health.

We have observed four psychological steps that occur in the upward spiral of recovery:

1. *With the diagnosis of a life-threatening illness, the individual gains a new perspective on his or her problems.* Many of the rules by which an individual lives suddenly seem petty and insignificant in the face of death. In effect, the threat gives the individual permission to act in ways that did not seem permissible before. Held-in anger and hostility can now be expressed; assertive behavior is now allowed. Illness permits the person to say no.

2. *The individual makes a decision to alter behavior, to be a different kind of person.* Because the illness often suspends the rules, suddenly there are options. As behaviors change, apparently unresolvable conflicts may show signs of resolution. The individual begins to see that it is within his or her power to solve or cope with problems. He also discovers that life did not end when old rules were broken and that changes in behavior did not result in loss of identity. Thus, there is more freedom to act and more resources with which to live. Depression often lifts when repressed feelings have been released and increased psychological energy is available.

Based on these new experiences, the individual makes a decision to be a different kind of person; the disease serves as permission to change.

3. *Physical processes in the body respond to the feelings of hope and the renewed desire to live, creating a reinforcing cycle with the new mental state.* The renewed hope and desire to live initiate physical processes that result in improved

health. Since mind, body, and emotions act as a system, changes in the psychological state result in changes in the physical state. This is a continuing cycle, with an improved physical state bringing renewed hope in life and with renewed hope bringing additional physical improvement. (For a more detailed explanation of how this occurs, see Chapter 7, Figures 1 and 2.)

In most cases, this process has its ups and downs. Patients may do very well physically until their renewed physical health brings them face to face with one of their areas of psychological conflict. If one of the conflicts has had to do with a job, for example, the physical disability associated with the illness may have temporarily removed the conflict because the individual was unable to work. With physical health restored, however, the patient may be facing again the stressful life situation. And even with renewed hope and a different perception of self and the problem, these are usually difficult times. There may be temporary physical setbacks until the patient again feels confident enough to cope with the situation.

4. *The recovered patient is "weller than well."* Karl Menninger, founder of the Menninger Clinic, describes patients who have recovered from bouts with mental illness as frequently being "weller than well," meaning that the state of emotional health to which they have been restored is in fact superior to what they had considered "well" before their illness. Much the same observation applies to patients who have actively participated in recovery from cancer. They have a psychological strength, a positive self-concept, a sense of control over their lives that clearly represent an improved level of psychological development. Many patients who have been active in their recovery have a positively altered stance toward life. They expect that things will go well, and they are victims no longer.

6

Expectations about Cancer and Their Effects on Recovery

Most of us have either known or heard reports of an apparently healthy, vigorous person who died almost immediately after being diagnosed as having cancer. Such patients are often so intimidated by the cancer diagnosis and have such a negative expectancy of their ability to survive, that they may never even leave the hospital following the diagnosis. The course of the disease goes downhill far more rapidly than the physicians anticipated. To explain such cases, doctors sometimes speak of the patients' "giving up" or losing their "will to live."

Many doctors have also experienced cases in which, after a diagnosis of cancer, the patients maintained a positive expectancy and had an unusually good recovery. In these cases, the medical treatment is often given the major credit for the patients' return to good health.

In general, people are quicker to believe in the relationship between dying and a negative expectancy than in the relationship between getting well and a positive expectancy. We believe one of the reasons that positive expectancy has not been as fully recognized in medicine as negative expectancy is that it is often difficult to tell whether a patient is talking positively merely for the sake of the people around him or her or whether the words are a true reflection of feelings. When patients verbalize a positive expectancy, saying they are not going to die or they are going to "beat this thing," and yet crawl into bed and pull the covers over their heads, don't go to work, and exhibit other behavior incompatible with what they are saying, it is apparent to us that they do not really have a firm belief that they can get well.

It is entirely possible that patients are unaware of the negative expectancies they are expressing in their behavior, and that they are not conscious of their fear of cancer—which arises from having had friends or relatives who died of the disease and the generally pessimistic view our culture takes. We have learned to look at actions as well as words to read our patients' frames of mind, and the messages we get we take very seriously. We think that patients' beliefs about the effectiveness of treatment and about the potency of the body's natural defenses—that is, their positive or negative expectancy—are powerful determinants in the outcome of illness.

SELF-FULFILLING PROPHECY

We have all experienced what are called self-fulfilling prophecies—that is, because we expect something to happen, we act in ways that increase the likelihood that the expectation will be met. If, for instance, a patient expects that he will get well, he is likely to take his medicine and carry out the regimen prescribed by his physician, thereby increasing his chances for recovery. If he expects to die, it is likely that he won't feel that it is useful to do the things that his doctor indicates will be good for him. This simple example illustrates one of the basic characteristics of a self-fulfilling prophecy— the "reinforcing cycle": an expectation of success will often lead to success, which in turn provides evidence that the original expectation was correct. On the other hand, an expectation of failure will often result in an unsuccessful outcome, which in turn validates the negative expectation. In both cases, the outcome created by the expectation supports the validity of the original expectation. The expectancy, whether positive or negative, gets stronger the more the cycle is repeated.

The effect of self-fulfilling prophecies on the results of supposedly objective scientific experiments has been demonstrated by psychological research. In one study, Dr. R. Rosenthal told graduate students conducting animal experiments that certain rats were exceptionally bright and would complete a maze quite rapidly, while other rats were dull and would do poorly. Actually there were no differences in intelligence or prior performance time between the two groups, yet when the results of the maze runs were tabulated, the supposedly bright rats had performed substantially differently from the so-called dull rats. The apparent explanation is that the students handled the "bright" rats differently—perhaps giving them more attention at the end of each trip through the maze—which encouraged them to perform better than the rats that were expected to do poorly.

Rosenthal and his associates produced equally startling evidence on expectancy in a study conducted with children in a California public school district. A non-verbal intelligence test was administered to eighteen classrooms of elementary students at the beginning of the school year. The teachers were told that the test would predict which children were ready to bloom intellectually. Twenty percent of the students whom Rosenthal selected at random, and not on the basis of test scores, were then identified as being "intellectual bloomers," and their teachers were told that these students could be expected to show remarkable gains during the coming year. The only difference between these students and a control group was the expectancy created in the teachers' minds. Yet when both groups of students were retested eight months later, the randomly chosen "bloomers" had gained in I.Q. points over the control group.

This and subsequent studies have indicated that teachers unconsciously treat some students differently from others. They create a warmer social climate, are more responsive to the students' performances, teach them more sophisticated material, and give them more opportunity to question and to respond. These findings are significant because they show that altered expectancies resulting in unconscious changes in behavior can produce dramatic changes in outcome.

Carl confirmed the effects of positive expectancy in a study of 152 cancer patients at Travis Air Force Base, the major Air Force medical facility on the West Coast. Five staff members rated the patients on their attitude toward treatment and evaluated their responses to treatment over the next eighteen months. The results were clear: those patients with positive attitudes had better responses to treatment; those with negative attitudes had poorer responses. In fact, of the 152 patients only two who had shown a negative attitude had a good response to treatment.

The most significant finding of the study was that a *positive attitude toward treatment was a better predictor of response to treatment than was the severity of the disease*. That is, patients who had very serious prognoses but positive attitudes did better than patients who had relatively less serious prognoses but negative attitudes. In addition, patients who began to view their treatments positively often reported reduced side effects.

Expectancy can also work negatively. We became acutely aware of this through another experience Carl had at Travis, where he treated patients from all over the Pacific coast. Among them were several middle-aged Japanese. Although they were receiving standard radiation therapy of the kind and dosage given to other non-Japanese patients, they had extensive unpleasant side effects that could not be explained in terms of the treatment alone.

One Japanese was a retired major who had gone on after his military career to be a successful business executive. We were told that prior to his diagnosis, he was a very strong-willed, independent, responsible man who was not easily defeated. But since beginning radiation therapy he had become an invalid, refusing to do even the simplest tasks for himself. No amount of talking to him seemed to help, and he was going downhill very fast. We discussed his feelings with him, and after careful questioning it became clear that he had a deep fear of radiation, dating back to World War II. Suddenly we recognized that our Japanese patients' beliefs about radiation were created, probably on an unconscious level, by the effects of the atomic bomb. To a middle-aged Japanese, who recalled the destruction of Hiroshima and Nagasaki, radiation was forever associated with destruction and death.

We thoroughly discussed with him the difference between atom bomb irradiation and radiation therapy. It seemed nearly impossible to influence his beliefs about the effects of this treatment. Clearly his negative expectancy was contributing to his deteriorating condition.

It is frequently difficult to distinguish side effects that are inevitably associated with a treatment from those that are significantly affected by belief. Nausea, for example, is often reported as a side effect of certain forms of treatment, but many patients become nauseous *on the way* to their treatment. We might well ask: Is the nausea treatment-induced or belief-induced?

NEGATIVE SOCIAL BELIEFS ABOUT CANCER —AND THEIR EFFECTS

Our experiences dramatically confirm the power of negative expectations. That power is particularly frightening when we consider the general beliefs about cancer in our society and their probable effects on cancer patients. In somewhat oversimplified terms the beliefs about cancer in our society are:

1. Cancer is synonymous with death.
2. Cancer is something that strikes from without and there is no hope of controlling it.
3. The treatment—whether radiation, chemotherapy, or surgery—is drastic and negative and frequently has many undesirable side effects.

If expectancies contribute to outcomes, then these social beliefs are having a heavily negative effect. Newspapers and magazines carry stories of people who have died following a long battle with cancer. The overt inspirational message of these stories is usually how brave these people were. The hidden message is that they were brave in the face of their *inevitable* death. Often, when people speak of someone who has cancer, the tone of the conversation changes, there is an awkward silence, the listeners look away—all connoting the expectation of death.

Cancer patients, of course, become very sensitive to such negative messages. Many report that their friends, upon finding out about their illness, begin to avoid them, apparently not knowing how to relate to them any longer since they are already "as good as dead." Much of other people's avoidance of cancer patients is based on an avoidance of thinking about death, as well as the fear that somehow cancer is catching.

This tragic set of negative expectancies is communicated not only by friends and relatives but also at times by the medical profession. A physician who was previously an understanding expert with ready answers may, in the presence of a patient diagnosed with cancer, become a somewhat inept philosopher trying to comfort with platitudes in the face of what he regards as inevitable death. In many cases, the most profound communication from the physician is his evading the patient's questions. One patient described her physician when he came to her hospital room after a surgical biopsy to tell her she had cancer. He only came two feet inside the door and stood with his body against the wall. He quickly told her she had cancer, would need further treatment, and would be referred to another doctor. Then just as quickly he left the room. Naturally, the patient senses the physician's attitude through both verbal and nonverbal cues. The message is clear: The patient will not survive.

None of this is said in condemnation of other physicians—or of the patient's disconcerted friends and family. We are simply describing facts. We are all too aware of the times when our own negative expectancies have been communicated or when our own sense of inadequacy has contributed to the patient's feelings of helplessness. The lamentable outcome of all these communicated expectations of side effects, pain, and death is that they can work to create a self-fulfilling prophecy. With different beliefs and expectations, however, the outcome can be different.

BUILDING A POSITIVE SYSTEM OF BELIEFS

Asking people with cancer to change their beliefs, to understand that they can recover and live a full and rewarding life—despite their own fears about the disease and the negative expectations of the people around them—is asking for a great many acts of courage and personal strength. Yet all of our experience has shown us that many cancer patients have been capable of achieving this courage and strength. To help them in this effort we first attempt to counterbalance society's negative beliefs about cancer with positive counterparts. The two sets of beliefs are shown in Table 2.

Table 2.
Negative and Positive Beliefs

Negative Expectancy	Positive Expectancy
1. Cancer is synonymous with death.	1. Cancer is a disease that may or may not be fatal.
2. Cancer is something that strikes from without and	2. The body's own defenses are the mortal enemy of

there is no hope of controlling it.	cancer, however it is caused.
3. Medical treatment is drastic and ineffective and frequently has many negative side effects.	3. Medical treatment can be an important ally, "a friend in need," in support of the body's defenses.

The beliefs listed in the "positive expectancy" column are, as we have been showing, justified by modern scientific research—more justified that the "negative expectancy" beliefs. However, the difficulty in persuading people to change their beliefs from negative to positive is that they generally have had negative experiences that "prove" the validity of their beliefs. In effect, then, we seem to be asking that they deny their own experiences and take on beliefs inconsistent with what they "know." Our point is that the negative experiences these people have had were not necessarily inevitable; the experiences have been shaped in part by original negative expectancy.

The same power that allows us to create negative experiences can be used to create positive experiences. And while there may be limits to the role that expectancy plays, no one really knows what these limits are. Unquestionably, then, it is desirable to have expectancy working for, not against, the cancer patient.

Some readers may feel that since their own expectancy is negative, they are necessarily going to have a negative outcome. This is not the case. We have had many patients who started with a negative expectancy and learned a positive one. The essential first step in changing an expectancy is to become aware of what you believe and its potential effect. Just reading this chapter should do that for you. Later in the book (Chapter 14), we will describe step-by-step the methods that we use to help our patients work toward a positive expectancy.

The Question of "False Hope"

We are sometimes asked, "Aren't you giving your patients false hope?" Our answer is "No," we are giving our patients reasonable hope. Our approach does not guarantee recovery. But the question of "false hope" suggests that people should never have hope if there is a good chance they will be disappointed. Such a belief provides no basis for living a full life or for dealing with a threat to life.

We enter marriage with no guarantee that it will be a happy and fulfilling experience. If we approach marriage with the expectation that it is *bound* to fail, it certainly increases the probability that it will fail. A positive expectancy does not guarantee a successful marriage, but it increases the likelihood of a good marriage and improves the quality of the relationship.

Since the first pages of this book, we have discussed how significant we believe a patient's view of his or her own prospects for recovery to be in the process of getting well again. Patients who have worked hard using our approach have still died, although in many cases they have significantly outlived their prognoses—and lived a more rewarding life than they would have had they not actively participated in their treatment. Yet death appears inevitable for us all. And our program includes activities designed to help the patient confront the possibility of death openly—an attitude that frees energy for living.

People who are concerned about "false hope" often see themselves as realists, people who see life "as it really is." But a life view that does not include hope is not realism but pessimism. This stance may avoid disappointment, but it does so by actively shaping negative outcomes.

Hope is an important element in survival for the cancer patient. Indeed, hopelessness and helplessness are frequent precursors of cancer. The hope we try to impart is essentially a stance toward life. It is not just a matter of philosophy, but of survival. For each patient, the process of getting well includes redefining his or her own stance toward the experience of a life-threatening disease so that there is hope.

Another concern expressed by people who talk of false hope is that this approach to illness is some form of quackery. It is true there are a number of nontraditional approaches to cancer treatment that do not appear to have a scientific basis. Still, it is not always easy to make definitive judgments about their worth, for supporters of such approaches are occasionally able to point to recoveries reportedly occurring as a result of their treatments.

The case of Laetrile is probably the most notorious recent example of "miracle cures" for cancer. Although there are no studies in reputable medical journals documenting Laetrile's effectiveness, there are numerous cases of cancer patients who attribute their recovery to the use of the drug. The placebo effect may well be the explanation for these cures, although this, too, is still unproven. Yet, even if it is proven that Laetrile, or other nontraditional approaches to cancer treatment, work because of the placebo effect, this is still a significant finding, for it will further demonstrate the extraordinary degree to which *belief* can materially affect the outcome of treatment. Then, rather than focus solely on the form of medical treatment, medicine may begin to focus on the psychological power of belief itself.

By openly focusing on belief and using it to reinforce and support both the body's natural defenses and the best medical treatment available, we are in the process of developing a medical approach that is supported by scientific research. Continuing to ignore the role that the mind and emotions play in recovery—in spite of the medical evidence that now exists—may be considered a form of quackery because it disregards other proven techniques. The real issue is no longer *whether* the mind and emotions affect the course of treatment; the question is rather *how* to direct them most effectively in support of it.

Changing Your Beliefs

Some readers may still be having difficulties accepting the ideas we have proposed. This is not surprising. It has taken us years, not just a few hours of reading, to come to understand and accept these concepts. It could not be otherwise—and it should not be otherwise. Beliefs too quickly gained can be as quickly lost, while those arrived at over a period of time are more likely to be retained. Our experience has shown that patients who have slowly, sometimes even grudgingly, altered their beliefs have done particularly well in our program. The time taken in consideration and internal argument has allowed them to integrate their new beliefs into all aspects of their personality and behavior.

The starting point for changing negative beliefs, then, is simply to become aware of the manner in which beliefs affect outcomes in many areas of your daily life. Once you begin to see how the process of creating experiences through beliefs works for you, you may find it easier to apply that concept to illness and to use it to gain health.

It is also essential for you to understand that you can influence your own attitudes. When you are convinced it is desirable to do so, you are capable of changing them. All our patients, and we ourselves, continue to have doubts at times or become aware of vestiges of old beliefs. But it is the effort to acquire positive beliefs and the recognition that we can change that are the important elements.

Many of the techniques and processes we will describe are means of reinforcing beliefs or of assisting people to identify how a new belief applies to their lives. We welcome you to explore them with whatever degree of openness is comfortable for you. Simply by exposing yourself to these processes and ideas you will become sensitive to alternative ways of viewing life, and ultimately your beliefs may begin to change.

7

A Whole-Person Model
of
Cancer Recovery

Based on our work and that of our fellow researchers, we have developed a "mind/body model" to show how psychological and physical states work together in the onset of cancer. The purpose of this model is to try to integrate a number of research results that seem to be pointing in a similar direction. To understand what a model is, it is helpful to think of the research data as pieces of a puzzle. With only a few pieces, it is difficult to see a pattern. But as more pieces accumulate, patterns begin to emerge. A model is an effort to put the pieces into a pattern before all the pieces are present. But, just as with an incomplete puzzle, you can think you know how the pieces go together, only to find you need to make some changes to make the last pieces fit. In the same way, models often have to be adjusted and altered to incorporate new data.

A MIND/BODY MODEL OF
CANCER DEVELOPMENT

The mind/body model, shown in Figure 1, is the pattern we see emerging from the current research into the links between mind and body in the development of cancer. A step-by-step explanation of the process follows. We anticipate that

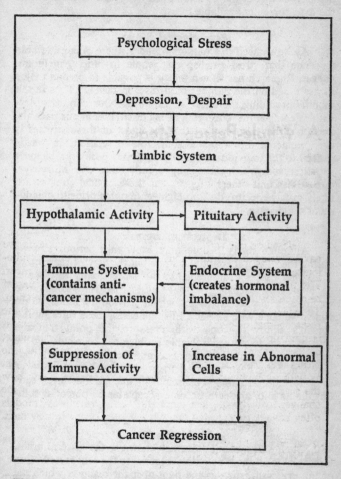

Figure 1. A Mind/Body Model of Cancer Development

further research will clarify and possibly alter some of its elements, but this is the clearest picture we can construct with the data currently available to us.

Psychological Stress

As we showed in Chapters 4 and 5, there is considerable evidence that stress predisposes people to illness, including cancer. Research has shown that it is possible to predict major illness based on the number of stresses in people's lives in the months preceding the onset of the illness. Our clinical observations confirm this clustering of major stresses in our patients' lives, but they also suggest that the effect of these stresses is even greater if they threaten some role or relationship that is central to the individual's identity or if they pose a problem or situation from which there is apparently no escape. Moreover, our studies and others suggest that these critical stresses are likely to have occurred six to eighteen months prior to diagnosis of the disease.

Depression, Despair

Although many people may experience serious stresses during their lives, it is not just stress but the way of reacting to stress that makes a difference in the susceptibility to disease. As previously discussed, we have all learned rules about who we are and how we are to act, which provide the limits within which we cope with stresses. In some cases, these rules limit a person's ability to cope with stress to the point that the stresses seem to pose unsolvable problems. The result can be depression, despair, hopelessness, and helplessness—all feelings that have been reported to precede cancer. Because of these feelings, at either a conscious or unconscious level, serious illness and/or death become acceptable as potential solutions.

Limbic System

The limbic system, otherwise known as the visceral brain, is integral to all those activities essential to the self-preservation of the organism, such as the fight-or-flight reaction which we discussed in Chapter 4. As a result, it is designed to record stress and its effects, in addition to all the other feelings and sensations of the body. The limbic system, then, records feelings of depression and despair being experienced by an individual.

Hypothalamic Activity

The major pathway by which the limbic system influences the body is through the hypothalamus, a small area in the brain. The messages that the hypothalamus receives from the limbic system are then translated in two important ways: First (as we described in Chapter 5), part of the hypothalamus—that part most responsive to human emotional stress—participates in controlling the immune system. Second, the hypothalamus plays a critical role in regulating the activity of the pituitary gland, which is turn regulates the remainder of the endocrine system with its vast range of hormonal control functions throughout the body.

Immune System

The immune system—the body's natural defense—is designed to contain or destroy any cancerous cells, which current medical thinking suggests we all have in our bodies from time to time. Suppression of the immune system, however, can result in cancerous growth. In this mind/body model, emotional stress, mediated by the limbic system via the hypothalamus, produces a suppression of the immune system, which leaves the body susceptible to the development of cancer.

Pituitary Activity/Endocrine System

To complicate matters, evidence suggests that the hypothalamus, responding to stress, triggers the pituitary gland in such a way that the hormonal balance of the body—mediated by the endocrine system—is changed. This is particularly significant since an imbalance in adrenal hormones has been shown to create a greater susceptibility to carcinogenic substances.

Increase in Abnormal Cells

The result of such an hormonal imbalance can be an increased production of abnormal cells in the body and a weakened ability of the immune system to combat these cells.

Cancerous Growth

With this sequence of physiological changes, optimal conditions are now created for cancer growth. That is, at the same time the body's defenses against intruders are lowest, the production of abnormal cells is increased. The result can be a life-threatening disease.

REVERSING THE CYCLE: A MIND/BODY MODEL OF RECOVERY

Our purpose in writing this book is to show that the cycle of cancer development can be reversed. The pathways by which feelings can be translated into physiological conditions conducive to cancer growth can also be used to restore health. Figure 2 summarizes how mind and body can interact to create health. The explanation starts again in the psychological realm.

Psychological Intervention

The first step toward recovery is to assist cancer patients in strengthening their beliefs in the effectiveness of treatment and the potency of their bodies' defenses. Then they can be taught to cope more effectively with the stresses in their lives. It is particularly important that there be a change either in patients' perceptions of themselves—so they believe they can solve whatever life problems faced them before the onset of the cancer—or in their perception of their problems—so they believe they can cope with them more effectively.

Hope, Anticipation

The results of patients' beliefs in their opportunities for recovery, coupled with their "redecision" about the problems they face, are an approach to life that includes hope and anticipation.

Limbic System

Altered feelings of hope and anticipation are recorded in the limbic system, just as were the previous feelings of hopelessness and despair.

Hypothalamic Activity

Once these feelings are recorded in the limbic system, messages are sent to the hypothalamus reflecting the altered emotional state—a state that includes an increased will to live. The hypothalamus then sends messages to the pituitary gland that reflect the altered emotional state.

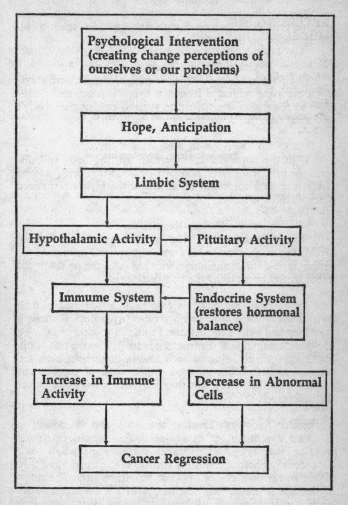

Figure 2. A Mind/Body Model of Recovery.

Immune System

The hypothalamus in turn reverses the suppression of the immune system, so that the body's defenses once again mobilize against abnormal cells.

Pituitary Activity/Endocrine System

The pituitary gland (which is part of the endocrine system), receiving messages from the hypothalamus, sends messages to the rest of the endocrine system, restoring the body's hormonal balance.

Decrease in Abnormal Cells

With the hormonal balance restored, the body will discontinue producing large numbers of abnormal cells, leaving fewer such cells for either treatment or the body's revitalized defenses to cope with.

Cancer Regression

Normal functioning of the immune system and reduced production of abnormal cells create the optimal conditions for cancer regression. Remaining abnormal cells can be destroyed either by treatment or by the body's defenses.

As we have said, patients who have participated in their own recovery often have much greater psychological strength than they had before the disease. From the process of facing a life-threatening illness, confronting basic life issues, and learning their power to influence their health, they emerge not just restored to health, but restored with a sense of potency and control over their lives that they may never have felt before the illness.

Cancer Recovery: Treating the Body and the Mind

Our description of cancer regression signals two pathways to recovery: either an increase in immune activity or a decrease in abnormal cells. Of course, the optimal conditions would be for both events to occur simultaneously. The thrust of medical treatment has been primarily the reduction of abnormal cells through irradiation or chemotherapy. Surgery is also a direct effort to remove all abnormal cells from the body.

Only immunotherapy, however, is aimed primarily at increasing immune activity. Immunotherapy focuses on stimulating the patient's existing immune system by introducing potentially stimulating substances, such as bacteria or altered cancer cells. As the immune system attacks these substances, it also attacks the cancer cells. Although immunotherapy is still in a relatively unrefined stage, in the future it may prove to be the superior method of treatment because it reinforces the body's natural functioning.

At present, however, if psychological intervention is capable of reversing the cycle of cancerous growth, then the body's natural functioning can contribute both to an increase in immune activity and to a decrease in abnormal cell production, while conventional medical treatment serves as an ally to destroy existing abnormal cells.

For the remainder of this book we will be describing the psychological processes we have developed for directing your mental and emotional states toward health.

PART TWO

Pathways
to
Health

8

The Program: Putting It to Work

The previous seven chapters were intended as a survey of the theoretical basis for our approach to cancer treatment. The rest of this book is devoted to the theory's practical application. We intend to introduce you to the processes we use with our patients at our Fort Worth Center. Whether you yourself have cancer, are the relative or friend of a cancer patient, or are an interested professional, by participating in the activities described in the next eleven chapters you will learn of a different way to think about illness and about how you may be able to influence the course of any disease.

Because we will be emphasizing the psychological processes used in our approach, we may appear to be neglecting or excluding physical treatment. This is by no means our intention. Although we believe medicine has developed too narrow a focus, concentrating primarily on physical symptoms, it has made monumental strides in developing and refining physical therapies. We encourage all cancer patients to obtain the best medical treatment they can find from a physician or health team they feel cares about them.

The second part of that statement—"from a physician or health team they feel cares about them"—is very important: We believe it interferes with therapy if patients feel they are being treated impersonally. Under such conditions, we encourage patients to attempt to alter the existing relationship and, if that does not work, to find a new physician or health team. It is important that patients see their treatment as an ally, a friend, and that they be aware of the effort and skill that have gone into developing the medical therapies that are currently available.

We are particularly concerned that the patient not decide to substitute psychological techniques for appropriate medical treatment. Rejecting medical treatment flies in the face of all our cultural beliefs about the physical nature of illness and the relative unimportance of mind and emotions in health. Few people can successfully turn their backs on decades of conditioning and substitute newly discovered ideas about their ability to influence the course of their disease.

For our patients, then, it is all too likely that if they were to discontinue physical therapies against their physicians' recommendations, they would never quite accept the idea that they had done the right thing. There is no reason to defy the accumulated wisdom of the medical community. Thus, we cannot emphasize too strongly the importance of pursuing both physical treatment *and* emotional interventions.

AN OVERVIEW OF PATHWAYS TO HEALTH

Below are brief summaries of the processes that can assist you in recovering and maintaining health. These techniques constitute a whole-person approach to cancer treatment, which deals with the individual's physical symptoms, his emotional orientation and problems, and his beliefs—both about his ability to recover and his capacity to solve his emotional problems. The interventions are designed to touch all parts of the system to restore the physical, mental, and emotional balance so that the whole person returns to health.

Chapter 9: "Participating in Your Health"

Since everyone participates in sickness or health, the first step is to assist patients in identifying how they participated in the onset of their disease. This process consists first of asking them to identify the major stresses occurring in their lives six to eighteen months prior to their diagnosis. The list of these stresses is used as a basis for discussing the patient's participation, which may have taken many forms. Some individuals may have participated by creating or allowing undue stresses in their lives or by refusing to recognize that they have emotional limits. Others may have subordinated their own needs to everybody else's until they had no strength left to devote to themselves. Still others may have participated by reacting to stresses with feelings of helplessness or hopelessness.

The object of such self-examination is not to invoke guilt but to identify behaviors to be changed if patients are to live full and healthy lives. By becoming aware of the stresses in their lives and finding more effective ways of coping with them, they can free energy to fight their disease and live richer lives.

Chapter 10: "The 'Benefits' of Illness"

We live in a culture that encourages hard work and bases self-esteem on productivity. It also generally discourages the expression of emotions, particularly sadness, grief, anger, and hostility. In such an accomplishment-oriented society, where people are discouraged from taking good care of themselves emotionally, illness can serve an important function.

After a patient has been diagnosed with a severe illness, emotion is expected and accepted. A patient, perhaps for the first time in his life, may give himself permission to do many things that he would not do it he were healthy, such as asking for help or for love and expressing unhappiness. Additionally, illness may give the patient an acceptable reason for not doing certain jobs that he had been reacting to with constant stress.

The focus of this chapter is on helping patients identify some of the benefits of their illness and also on helping them find ways to obtain and maintain those same emotional benefits as they recover.

Chapter 11: "Learning to Relax and Visualize Recovery"

Relaxation and mental imagery (visualization techniques) are excellent tools for creating and reinforcing patients' beliefs in their ability to recover from cancer. In the first part of this chapter, we provide a specific relaxation technique designed to break the cycle of tension and fear so common among cancer patients. In addition to unstressing their bodies, many patients discover that their psychological perspectives change when they are able to relax, permitting them to cope more effectively with their lives and their disease. Further, because the relaxation technique reduces tension and distraction, it prepares the patient for the mental imagery process, which we present in the second part of the chapter.

Since April 1971, when we first used visualization with a patient, it has been a central element in our approach. Not only does the mental imagery process create positive changes in expectancy, it is also a means for self-discovery in other areas of a patient's life. In this chapter we present detailed instructions for the relaxation/mental imagery process to help you learn how to visualize recovery from cancer and other illnesses.

Chapter 12: "The Value of Positive Mental Images"

Here we examine the symbols contained in your mental imagery as a key to identifying beliefs that may stand in the way of recovery. We also analyze examples drawn from our patients' experiences, and we teach you how to create more effective imagery for dealing with illness.

Chapter 13: "Overcoming Resentment"

In part, the stress and tension experienced by many patients may be due to a difficulty in expressing negative feelings, particularly anger and resentment. Holding in negative feelings has the effect of restressing the body and inhibiting recovery. But it is clearly not enough to moralize that people "should" or "ought" to release resentment. Instead, we teach our patients a specific process for releasing the past—for coming to terms with past relationships and overcoming resentment.

Chapter 14: "Creating the Future: Setting Goals"

On receiving a cancer diagnosis, there is a tendency to begin living life tentatively and conditionally. Frequently, people withdraw from relationships or refuse to make commitments. Not only does this establish the negative expectancy of death rather than recovery, this tentativeness can also significantly diminish the quality of life. Goals are important in maintaining a high quality of life. The will to live is certainly strengthened, even when life is threatened, if people ensure themselves of meaning and pleasure.

We assist our patients in setting three-month, six-month, and one-year goals as a statement that there are things they want to accomplish in life and an affirmation of their belief that they can live to accomplish these things. In setting goals we often identify other issues on which the patient needs to take action: Is there a tendency toward setting duty-oriented goals without counterbalancing them with goals that provide enjoyment? Does meeting these "duty" goals set in motion the same stresses that preceded the illness? In addition, we teach patients specific techniques for reinforcing their expectancy that they can meet their goals.

Chapter 15: "Finding Your Inner Guide to Health"

This process is a form of mental imagery. People sense and communicate with an "inner guide" while they are practicing mental imagery. Often the guide is a "wise man" or "wise woman" who serves as an image of the nurturing side of the personality. In some cases, patients have found that they can use their guide as a communication link to their unconscious, providing important information about their own psychological and physical workings.

Chapter 16: "Managing Pain"

While there is much about pain that we do not understand, there are several psychological processes for coping with it. Our approach to pain management is to use it as a biofeedback device. Pain, or the absence of pain, becomes a communication from the body about the various activities patients may be engaged in, or the thoughts and problems they may be working on mentally. We have also found that pain is intimately linked with fear, so that activities presented in other chapters for identifying and dealing with fear frequently lead to a reduction of pain.

Chapter 17: "Exercise"

We began paying more attention to exercise when we observed that many of our patients with the most dramatic recoveries from cancer were physically very active. Because physical activity appears to be a way of releasing stress and tension, it is also an effective way of changing one's state of mind. As a result, we have developed a program of physical exercise that we ask all our patients to try. We believe that regular exercise (and a sensible diet) provides a way for patients to participate in getting well.

Chapter 18: "Coping with the Fear of Recurrence and Death"

Death is an especially fearful subject in our culture because it is usually not discussed, examined, or understood. The recurrence of their disease is also a significant fear in the minds of cancer patients. Feelings constantly suppressed become bigger and more powerful, so that the fear of recurrence and death can become overwhelming. In addition, patients often feel cut off from their families because they are not able to discuss these real concerns openly.

In this chapter, we lead patients through a psychological process that helps them identify their feelings about these subjects and encourages them to examine their attitudes toward recurrence and their beliefs about what will happen to them physically as they come closer to death. The purpose of confronting the possibility of death openly is to remove it from the realm of forbidden topics and to clarify beliefs. Unconscious beliefs can influence how people live, so by examining their attitudes, cancer patients can improve the quality of their living.

Chapter 19: "The Family Support System"

This chapter concentrates on helping the family of the cancer patient understand their own feelings about coping with a potentially life-threatening disease, as well as being tolerant and accepting of their loved one. It suggests ways for establishing the honest, open communication and loving, supportive environment essential for improving the quality of living and creating the atmosphere for getting well again.

PUTTING THE PROGRAM TO WORK

The processes just described provide a variety of pathways to health. But since they are usually used under our direction, we have added a section outlining a simple six-week program of implementation, so that those of you who want to practice these techniques in your own life can get started as soon as you have finished reading Part Two of this book.

First, however, let us give you two crucial suggestions: do not delay receiving medical attention while you follow this program, which is designed to work *in support of your medical treatment,* not instead of it; and if you know people who can give you the psychological support you need, contact them right away—their counsel will help you put this program into practice.

Because any illness is a signal that there is something amiss in the unity of mind, body, and emotions, we have written these exercises so that they can be employed no matter what the ailment—from colds and headaches to cancer. Whether or not you have cancer, then, you will find value in walking these pathways with us.

The First Week

1. Reading. After you finish this book, we suggest you begin a reading program of books and articles that explain the interrelatedness of mind, body, and emotions. We provide each of our patients with a copy of Dr. Arnold Hutschnecker's *The Will to Live* because we believe it is particularly helpful. If you have some background in the sciences, you may also be interested in *Mind as Healer, Mind as Slayer,* by Dr. Kenneth Pelletier. We also recommend reading *Seeing With the Mind's Eye,* by Mike and Nancy Samuels. The librarian or the card catalogue in your public library can refer you to other good books and articles on the subject.

2. Relaxation/Mental Imagery. Start a regular program of the relaxation/mental imagery process (Chapters 11 and 12) three times a day. If you have made a tape of the mental imagery process, you may want to use it every time for the first week, then wean yourself from it by using it every other time the second week, only once a day the third week, and so on. During particularly stressful times, when you find the mental imagery process difficult, you may want to use the tape again to reinforce the process.

The Second Week

1. Relaxation/Mental Imagery. Continue your relaxation/ mental imagery exercises three times a day.

2. Stresses Prior to Your Illness. Complete the exercise in Chapter 9, in which you identify the stresses in your life six to eighteen months prior to the onset of your illness. Use this exercise as a starting point to explore how you may have participated in the onset of your disease.

3. The "Benefits" of Illness. Complete the exercise in Chapter 10, in which you identify the "benefits" you receive from your illness. This exercise is a starting point to explore your commitment to recovery.

The Third Week

1. Relaxation/Mental Imagery. Continue your relaxation/mental imagery exercises three times a day.

2. Physical Exercise. Begin a program of one hour of exercise (appropriate to your physical condition) three times a week.

3. Counseling. Find someone in your community—a minister, counselor, or psychotherapist—to whom you can talk about your experiences and feelings as you are doing this program. Naturally, it is important that the counselor understand the concepts in this book. It is also important that you select a counselor you believe really cares about whether or not you get well.

The Fourth Week

1. Relaxation/Mental Imagery. Continue your relaxation/mental imagery exercises three times a day.

2. Physical Exercise. Continue your physical exercise program of one hour of exercise three times a week.

3. Recurrence/Death Imagery. Have someone lead you through the recurrence/death mental imagery process described in Chapter 18. This will help you face your feelings about death and help reduce some of your fear.

4. Overcoming Resentment. Begin to use the mental imagery process for overcoming resentment, described in Chapter 13, whenever you find yourself harboring ill feelings. It is difficult to see good things happening to someone toward whom you feel hostility, but be aware of your responses to this activity from now on and you will find yourself gaining important insights.

The Fifth Week

1. Relaxation/Mental Imagery. Continue your relaxation/mental imagery exercises three times a day.

2. Physical Exercise. Continue your physical exercise program of one hour of exercise three times a week.

3. Recurrence/Death Imagery. Repeat the recurrence/death mental imagery process to see if there are remaining emotional issues that need to be resolved.

4. Goal Setting. Set three goals each for three months, six months, and one year away, as described in Chapter 14. Then begin to incorporate your goals into your mental imagery process, seeing yourself reaching your goals and exploring any problems you foresee in reaching them.

The Sixth Week

1. Relaxation/Mental Imagery. Continue your relaxation/mental imagery exercises three times a day.

2. Physical Exercise. Continue your physical exercise program of one hour of exercise three times a week.

3. Inner Guide. Have someone talk you through the Inner Guide mental imagery process described in Chapter 15. If you find that you make "contact" with an Inner Guide to health, then conversation with it can become a regular part of your mental imagery program.

After Six Weeks

Once you have reached this point, you will have intergrated many of these processes into everyday living. Continue using the relaxation/mental imagery process indefinitely. If you have reached the point where you show no signs of cancer, you may begin to change your imagery to "surveillance"—visualizing your white blood cells patrolling your body and destroying abnormal cells—and continue to see yourself as healthy and free from illness. As you regain your health, the amount of time you spend visualizing health can be shifted to working on goals, resentments, or conversations with your Inner Guide.

Setting goals and working to meet them is an ongoing process. Naturally, your goals may change as your health improves, so change them as you wish. The important thing is that you know what you want and are working to get it.

We also recommend that you continue the exercise program indefinitely. As you become healthier, you will want to increase the level of physical exertion until you are walking, jogging, or doing some other vigorous exercise for one hour three times a week.

The value of this program comes from actually, *doing* the activities, so we strongly encourage you to follow a schedule similar to the one described above. As you begin to see improvements in your frame of mind and your health, you will have the incentive you need to make the activities part of your life. Following this program is an affirmation that you believe you can influence your health.

9

Participating in Your Health

Dr. Elmer Green, a pioneer in the field of biofeedback, has said that when people are attempting to influence their health, it is equally important for them to learn what thoughts, attitudes, and behaviors they are engaged in when they become ill as it is when they are healthy. When people have feedback, or information, concerning both illness and health, they can then more consciously participate in their recovery.

Information about one's thoughts and feelings when health is deteriorating may be the most valuable information of all. The body is built with homeostatic mechanisms designed to keep it healthy and free of disease; it is when these mechanisms break down and illness results that we most need to concern ourselves with our thought processes and behaviors. When our body is moving in the direction of illness, it may be a sign that the coping mechanisms we are using to deal with stress are not effective.

If you think back, you will probably see how many small ailments in your life, such as colds or headaches, occurred when you were tired, overworked, under tension or emotional strain. You have probably said many times that you caught a cold because you were "run down," and you most likely meant not just physical fatigue but also emotional depletion, a lack of vigor and enthusiasm. At that moment, life seemed like a chore.

Serious ailments, too, such as heart attacks and ulcers, have been observed to follow periods of overwork, tension, pushing too hard. They tend to occur when the body has reached its upper limit and can carry no more, but the signals of this situation have been ignored. Anyone who has had an ulcer is aware of how it acts as a feedback device for emotional overload, an index of the "state of the organism," because pain from the ulcer is most likely to occur when one is tense or anxious. A physician friend says that in a way he regrets having had surgery for an ulcer because without the ulcer's reminder, he can't tell anymore when he is overly tense, and he worries about what other effects the tension might be having on his body.

All of us participate in becoming sick through a combination of mental, physical, and emotional factors. You may have neglected reasonable diet, exercise, or rest. You may have been very tense or anxious for a long period of time without doing enough to relax. You may have maintained unreasonable work loads or gotten so caught up in meeting everyone else's needs that you ignored your own. You may have maintained attitudes and beliefs that prevented you from having satisfying emotional experiences. In sum, you may have failed to recognize your physical and emotional limits.

To the extent that you ignored these legitimate needs, you participated in your own illness. When the body's and mind's requirements for relaxation, rest, exercise, emotional expression, even for meaning in life are neglected, then the body may communicate this failure to pay attention by getting sick.

JOHN BROWNING: A CASE HISTORY

The case of John Browning demonstrates how people participate both in the onset of—and recovery from—illness. This case is revealing because it suggests specific connections between emotional stresses and cancer.

John is a brilliant scientist who works for a world-renowned research firm. At the time of the onset of his cancer (of the pancreas), he was fifty years old. He was given a life expectancy of six to nine months. Professionally, he had always been an overachiever, but as he approached fifty, he be-

gan to face the fact that many of his childhood dreams would
not be reached. Although he had received considerable professional recognition, it had not been at the level he had hoped.
In effect, he was experiencing mid-life crisis.

In addition, in the months prior to the onset of his cancer, John's son went off to college. Almost every weekend for
many years, John had gone to athletic events with his son.
John took great pride in his son's aptitude for sports. After his
son's departure, however, John stopped attending sports
events entirely. Clearly, an era had ended.

The end of this period also raised new stresses between
John and his wife. His wife had not recently enjoyed sports
and had not participated in the family's many athletic pursuits. Instead, she had become involved with club work,
church work, and similar activities. Since John no longer
spent every weekend with his son, he and his wife were
thrown together as they had not been for a long time, and
they had to develop new ways of communicating and creating
interests in common.

Another of John's regrets was that some years earlier he
had left a university post to go to work for his present em-
ployer. His motivation had been the extra money he would
earn for his son's college education. But while his salary was
indeed substantially greater, he badly missed having people to
guide and instruct.

A great satisfaction in his present job was that he had
been able to produce a number of significant research break-
throughs by putting together a collection of scientists and
guiding them into an exceptionally creative team. His supervi-
sors had been so impressed with his performance that they put
him in charge of another major project as a reward. But to
John the new project felt more like a punishment than a reward, for it meant he had to leave his team. Like many of our
patients, however, John had extreme difficulty expressing his
feelings and never told his superiors how badly he felt about
the new assignment.

This inability to speak up for his needs became clear
after John entered into therapy with us. He told us he had
always prayed regularly, but he soon informed us that he had
never prayed for his own health. John believed it would be
wrong to ask for anything for himself in his prayers. These
attitudes traced back to his childhood. John's mother was, he
said, "a very pious and self-sacrificing person." John saw his

father, in contrast, as a "selfish person" who accumulated money and then spent most of it on himself. John took his mother's self-sacrificing attitude yet always believed he had inherited a selfish streak from his father.

But as John rejected his father's apparently immature and selfish behavior, he overcompensated because of his fear of being selfish. This showed up in his difficulties in communicating his needs and feelings to others, in investing his life with meaning by making himself responsible for others, and in abandoning pleasurable activities when they were not shared with his son. In short, John felt obliged to place everyone else's needs ahead of his own, and so when his son left for school, when John was removed from his work team, when his professional dreams were unfulfilled, his personal rules were such that he could see no way to meet his needs. He thus became extremely depressed.

Changing Beliefs

The first step for John, or for anyone else trying to get well, is to identify those attitudes and beliefs that lock him into a pattern of hopeless victim. The psychological reality is that if John were to hang onto his beliefs that everyone else's needs come first, he would indeed be powerless to meet his own emotional needs. Clearly, these beliefs need to change.

We worked with John to help him recognize the facets of himself he was ignoring, and also to help him change his perception in other areas in his life. As a result of those efforts, he reexamined his work situation and finally came to the understanding that his superiors had, in fact, been trying to reward him by giving him the new job assignment and had no way of knowing of his disappointment. We urged him—as we urge everyone—to take his emotional responses to life more seriously.

We also worked with John on his sense of failure because he had not realized his early dreams. Like many ambitious men, John had channeled his energy into developing primarily those parts of himself related to his work. Now, since the dreams were no longer attainable, we urged him to give himself permission to explore other interests or pursue other parts of himself that had been held in check. Finally, we worked with John on his sense of loss of his son, pointing out the degree to which he had vested so much of his personal happiness in someone else rather than himself, and helped him to see that he had an opportunity to renew his relationship with his wife.

None of this is meant as a criticism of John; many of us have experienced similar events and reacted similarly. The difficulty is that the beliefs John had adopted as a child in response to the conflict between his mother and father were blocking his finding alternative ways of responding to life's inevitable disappointments. The point is that there *are* alternatives. Whenever people feel boxed in and trapped, it is because they are limited by their own beliefs and habitual ways of responding.

BOB GILLEY: A CASE HISTORY

Sometimes life changes that precede an illness are what might normally be identified as positive changes. Bob Gilley, thirty-nine years old when he received his cancer diagnosis, is a good example of how individual the nature of a person's response to stress is. When Stephanie first began working with Bob to explore his own emotional participation in his illness, she concluded at the end of his first interview that perhaps our theories did not pertain to him.

On first examination, Bob's life seemed to be a model of the dynamic and successful young executive. He owned his own corporation and attained national recognition within his profession, receiving an award for maintaining the highest standards of production in his industry for over ten years. Even though in the past Bob had experienced many business difficulties with previous partners, he had formed a new partnership a few years before which seemed ideal.

Bob reported that early in their marriage he and his wife had had considerable difficulties, particularly when he was struggling to become a success. As his career became more and more successful, however, his marriage, on the surface, seemed to improve. Additionally, Bob and his wife had made the decision to adopt children some years before. Just prior to his diagnosis, they had completed the adoption of their second child. For all outward appearances, Bob seemed to have reached the top of the ladder and should have been enjoying the rewards of his years of struggle.

One of the first clues indicating that all was not as it seemed with Bob was a remark he made in his initial interview. He said that one of the few things he could remember in the year prior to his illness was a generalized feeling that was best characterized by the Peggy Lee song, "Is That All There Is?" To a man who had learned that the proof of his attainment and manhood rested in conquering difficulties, the attainment by age thirty-nine of most of his life's goals and ambitions left him adrift. For someone who had not learned to enjoy the peaceful times in life, the absence of turmoil and struggle was experienced as a loss.

Within a year, Bob was diagnosed as having an advanced cancer and was once again faced with a challenge and a battle to be won. In the months and years after Bob's diagnosis, much of his own emotional work and exploration has been in learning to enjoy the rewards of his struggles and to accept himself for who he is, rather than constantly needing to prove his worth by overcoming an obstacle or meeting a challenge head-on.

HOW YOU INTERPRET THE MEANING OF EVENTS

It's not hard to see how other people create the meaning of events in their lives (although it is not quite so easy to see how we ourselves do this). For example, the loss of a job can mean a number of things:

1. A defeat or a sign of failure.

2. A challenge.

3. A chance to start out fresh.

4. A sign that life is unfair.

Which of these meanings people attach to the experience is dependent on other beliefs they have:

1. Perceived opportunities to get other jobs.

2. The degree to which the job was a symbol of personal worth.

3. Beliefs about being in charge of one's life.

4. Their ability to create a positive new situation.

The principle that you create the meaning of events applies to all the stresses typically identified as occurring prior to the onset of cancer. As painful as some of these experiences can be—loss of a loved one or of an important role, for example—the amount of stress and particularly the degree to which these events make you feel hopeless and helpless are the result of the meaning you attach to the experience. You determine the significance of events.

By exploring the beliefs that limit your responses, by considering alternative interpretations of life's events and alternative ways of responding, it is possible for you to create positive meanings where negative ones existed before. When the crucial beliefs that have created the blockage in a healthy, forward flow to life are discovered and dislodged, the full energy of life can flow smoothly once again. And with that flow can come the vital force that will restore the body's natural defenses to normal potency.

Although the exact form this freeing up will take varies from person to person, it almost always involves giving oneself permission to experience life differently. Some people may participate in their health by saying no to others' expectations, others by saying yes to experiences and parts of themselves they have denied. When the energy begins to flow again, while there will still be problems and stresses to face, they will be faced with the belief that the problems can be solved or at the least coped with—with the belief that one has the power to make decisions that will contribute to getting well again.

IDENTIFYING YOUR PARTICIPATION IN ILLNESS

How do you start breaking up the logjam of beliefs and habitual ways of responding to stress? The best way we have found with our cancer patients is to ask them to identify the stresses going on in their lives in the six to eighteen months prior to the onset of the disease.

Because the link between emotional states and disease applies to susceptibility to *all* illness, not just cancer, the process of identifying the links between stress and illness is valuable for everyone, and so we ask all readers, cancer patients or not, to complete the activity below. (You may wish to refer back to the Holmes-Rahe stress chart in Chapter 4 for an idea of the variety of stresses that can lead to illness.) This exercise can help you translate the general concepts we have been describing into your personal experience.

1. Think of an illness you have now or have had in the past. If you have or have had cancer, use that for this exercise.

2. If you have cancer, take a piece of paper and list five major life changes or stresses that were going on six to eighteen months prior to the onset of your illness.

3. If your disease was something other than cancer, list the five major stresses that were going on in your life in the six months preceding the onset of the disease. (With diseases less severe than cancer, a shorter time span seems appropriate.)

4. If you experienced a recurrence of your disease at any time, make a list of five major stresses going on in your life in the six months prior to the recurrence.

If you do not take the time actually to do this exercise, if you just read through these questions without thinking deeply about the answers and then writing them down, you will not begin to get the benefit that is available to you from this book. This statement applies to all the exercises that will be presented in Part Two of this book.

Most people find when completing this exercise that the period before the onset of the disease held a number of major stresses. If you did not find any major external stresses—such as the death of a spouse, the loss of a job, or the like—be sure also to consider internal stresses. Were you wrestling internally with a psychological problem such as disappointment that youthful dreams were not being realized, major adjustments in a personal relationship, or an identity crisis? These may be every bit as significant in creating feelings of hopelessness or helplessness as very visible external stresses are.

If you did discover significant stresses in your life (whether external or internal) prior to the onset of the disease, examine how you participated in that stress, either by creating the stressful situation or by the manner in which you responded to it. Did you, for example, place yourself in a stressful situation by putting everybody else's needs first, by failing to say no, by ignoring your own mental, physical, and emotional limits? Or, if the event was something outside of our control, such as the death of a loved one, were there alternative ways of reacting? Did you permit yourself to grieve or did you determine not to show your emotions? Did you permit yourself to seek out and accept support from loving, nurturing friends during the stress?

The object of this kind of self-examination is to identify beliefs or behaviors that you want to change now. Because these beliefs have been threatening your health, they need to be consciously examined with an eye toward altering them.

The purpose of the next exercise—identifying the five major stresses in your life right now and determining alternative ways of responding—is *prevention*, which means acknowledging and then eliminating tensions that could predispose you to illness.

1. List the five greatest stresses in your life right now.

2. Examine ways you may be participating in maintaining the stresses.

3. Consider ways for removing the stresses from your life.

4. If there is no reasonable way to remove a stress, consider whether you are creating other supportive or nurturing elements in your life. Are you accepting the support of close friends? Are you making a point of giving yourself pleasurable experiences during stressful times? Are you permitting yourself to express your feelings about stressful situations?

5. Consider whether you could remove these stresses or balance them in your life if you put your own needs first more often. Do you permit yourself to consider what your own needs are? Have you attempted to find ways to meet them despite what you feel are the needs of others?

After you have completed this exercise, be sure to note any similarities between the ways you responded to stress prior to your illness and the ways you are responding now. If you find similarities, reexamine your behavior, since you may have habitual ways of responding that do not contribute to health.

ACCEPTING THE RESPONSIBILITY FOR YOUR HEALTH

When people begin to look at ways they may have participated in their development of cancer, it is a good idea to seek the aid and support of a trained counselor or therapist. Many times, just asking for help is the first step in breaking a "rule" one learned in early childhood and establishing a more healthy way of responding to stress. Unfortunately, many of us grew up with a culturally induced reluctance to seek help for emotional problems. Yet if we are diagnosed with a severe illness, we do not feel embarrassed or ashamed to seek the help of a physician who has spent many years learning about the body. Neither should we feel embarrassed about enlisting the help of a professional to learn the ways in which stress has played a role in our illness.

Most of our patients who go through this process of self-examination see important links between their emotional states and the onset of their disease, as well as the ways they participated in these emotional states. But, having seen how their beliefs and behaviors in response to stress may have contributed, some begin to feel guilty about their actions in the past. You may have similar feelings, so we would like to give you the same advice we give our patients.

First, it is not our intent, nor is it desirable, for you to feel guilty for having recognized that you've participated in your disease. There is a difference between being "to blame" for something and having "participated" in it. It makes no sense to blame persons living in this society for becoming ill in light of the rules they were taught for dealing with their emotions and feelings. (Few individuals in our culture have been taught how to deal with emotions and feelings appropriately.) Further, blame suggests a person consciously knew better and yet decided to respond or act in a self-damaging way. That is certainly not true of people who respond to stress by developing a physical illness. Like most people in our culture, you were probably not even aware of a link between emotional states and illness. Thus, the ways in which you did participate are almost certain to have been a result of unconscious beliefs and habitual behavior.

It is a particularly sad course of events, that many times those people who most steadfastly and responsibly attempt to live up to cultural rules develop the most serious illnesses. The literature describing the emotional aspects of cancer is replete with examples characterizing cancer patients in general as "too good to be true"—people who are kind, considerate, unselfish, and pleasant in the face of all adversity.

Individuals who begin to accept responsibility for influencing the state of their health deserve the greatest of congratulations. Not only are they willing to begin the process of exploring their own attitudes, emotions, and feelings—and the ways these contribute to their response to stressful situations—but they are also finding the courage to stand up to the cultural rules they were taught and to reject those that are not conducive to health.

The real point of a self-examination is to turn up clues on how you can participate in health through a process of recognizing and changing self-destructive beliefs. If you have participated in the onset of the disease, you also have the power to participate in your recovery.

10

The "Benefits" of Illness

In a culture where feelings are given little importance and emotional needs vital to a person's well-being are frequently ignored, disease can fulfill an important purpose: It can provide a way to meet the needs that a person has not found conscious ways of meeting.

Illness includes much pain and anguish, of course, but it also solves problems in people's lives. It serves as a "permission giver" by allowing people to engage in behavior they would not normally engage in if they were well. Think for a moment of some of the things that people get when they are sick: increased love and attention, time away from work, reduced responsibility, lessened demands, and so on. Because cancer patients are often people who have put everyone else's needs first, they have obviously had difficulty permitting themselves these freedoms without the illness. In this way, illness works to suspend many of the attitudes that block people from paying attention to their own emotional needs. In fact, when you are ill may be the only time it is acceptable to drop the responsibilities and pressures of your life and simply take care of yourself without guilt or the need to explain or justify.

Though illness can provide temporary respite, it can also be a trap. If you can experience attention, love, and relaxation only by getting sick, then part of you has a stake in staying sick. Obviously, we don't advocate using illness to gain a "breather." Cancer is a high price to pay to solve problems that could be solved instead by altering your rules so that you give yourself permission to pay attention to your needs.

SOLVING PROBLEMS THROUGH ILLNESS

Willie was a patient who fell into the trap of having a stake in staying ill. Before he joined the air force, Willie had lived at home with his parents and had gone to school. In his family, at school, and at his part-time job, he felt hounded by people who were continuously pushing him to do things he really did not want to do. To "show them all," he ran off and joined the military. Much to his dismay, he once again found himself surrounded by authority figures. Everyone outranked him and everywhere he turned, he was told what to do. Because he had enlisted and could not get out of the situation in less than four years, he felt trapped. What made it worse was that he felt he could not even complain about his fate to sympathetic listeners. During this time, Willie told us later, he fantasized about having a terminal disease, imagining how sorry everyone would be if they found out he was going to die.

After Willie developed a lump in his neck, he came in for surgery and was told that a biopsy showed he had a malignant lymphoma (Hodgkin's disease). When told of the diagnosis, he said he experienced a sense of excitement, almost happiness. Later, he became concerned about his unusual response to what most people would take as devastating news. It was this concern that led him to explore with us the psychological issues of his illness during the weeks he was receiving radiation therapy. During the course of this exploration he came to the realization that his sense of relief at the time of his diagnosis was because his illness "rescued" his from the trap he believed himself to be in and gave him a reason for allowing no further demands to be made on him. The dilemma, though, was that if he recovered he would again have to face the problem of his military obligation. This raised a considerable barrier to his commitment to getting well. Resolving this issue was a central focus of his psychological therapy—to which he responded well.

A similar problem was faced by another patient of ours, a young psychiatrist. Approximately six months before his diagnosis, a long-term patient of his tried to commit suicide and another person was killed as a result. To make matters worse, the psychiatrist had been developing new approaches to psychiatry, and several people who disagreed with his ideas used the tragedy as an opportunity to question his "unorthodox" methods, aggravating the guilt he was already feeling. He went into a deep depressive cycle in which he contemplated taking his own life on several occasions. Six months later, he was diagnosed as having advanced lymphosarcoma involving his lungs and liver.

The illness served several important psychological functions for the psychiatrist. One by-product was that it silenced his critics. After all, no one needed to or could decently criticize a "dying man." In addition, the disease appeased his guilt, atoning for the exaggerated sense of responsibility he felt for his patient's actions. Recovery, of course, would remove the source of his penance.

Fortunately, as a psychiatrist, he had developed a high level of insight into his own psychological processes and was able to resolve his feelings substantially. At the time of his original diagnosis, he was given less than a 10 percent chance of surviving five years. Today, after six years and despite two flare-ups of his disease, he has maintained an active psychiatric practice.

This patient was able to use the temporary "protection" offered by the disease to regroup his psychological forces so that he could cope more effectively once he got well. But some patients find no way to solve their problems except through illness. Another patient revealed that his disease was preceded by a great deal of stress in his professional life, a lack of time with his wife and children, and a pressure for financial success. His illness provided him with a generous disability allowance, ample time for family, and no pressure to produce. But his problems in going back to work have been insurmountable. Three times he reached the point where he was free of symptoms and could consider working again and each time, within weeks of his seriously contemplating returning to his profession, he had a serious flare-up.

In still another case, the patient was part-owner of a business and felt that her partners put an unreasonable amount of the burden of running the business on her. Yet she had great difficulty refusing their demands. Initially, her illness said no for her. Nobody would dare ask her to do anything while she was sick. But fortunately she realized that if she used the illness as a crutch, she might never get well. Instead, she is learning to say no without using illness as an excuse and has gone back to sharing the operation of the business, feeling good that she is able to assert her needs.

Several other patients have found that their disease temporarily removed them from an intolerable job. Again, because the disease only suspends the problem for them, it is important that they confront the personal attitudes and behaviors that permitted the situation to become intolerable in the first place—or they are likely to recreate the situation and the disease each time they return to work.

Illness gives patients temporary permission to act in more open ways emotionally. But if they cannot learn to give themselves that same permission when they are healthy, then the moment they get well the old rules again apply, and they find themselves in the psychologically and physically destructive situation that first contributed to their illness.

This concept also accounts for the depression some patients report when they are told they are in remission—or that their disease is much better. Rather than the elation they expected to experience as a result of their good news, many report being perplexed because they feel depressed. Even though consciously they are pleased that their disease is better, unconsciously they are experiencing a loss of the tool their illness provided. The feeling of depression at the prospect of better health is important feedback that there is still psychologically important work to do.

THE LEGITIMACY OF EMOTIONAL NEEDS

The recognition that changing behavior and attitudes may be a matter of life and death is a significant motivator for change. Many of our patients have reported that one of the benefits of their illness was that they could no longer ignore their true needs. The illness permitted them to override their social conditioning and begin to grow as human beings: to express their feelings and go about meeting their needs openly and directly. Without the incentive of the illness, they could have continued to live lives of quiet desperation.

It is essential to recognize that the needs being met through the illness are *fully legitimate* and *deserve* to be met. The body is demanding attention in the only way it knows how. Whether it is Willie's need to feel that he has some control over his life, the psychiatrist's need to resolve his guilt, the young professional's need to balance his work with other parts of his life, or the businesswoman's need to say no, all of these are needs that human beings must meet to maintain their physical and emotional health. From this viewpoint, the intent of the organism is constructive, even in illness. Illness is an opportunity for the individual to achieve emotional growth.

IDENTIFYING THE "BENEFITS" OF ILLNESS

The task that faces the patient includes: (1) identifying the needs being met through the illness, and (2) finding ways of meeting those needs directly without illness. How can you identify these needs? We invite you to participate in an exercise we use with our patients to help them begin to recognize the benefits of their illness.

Get a piece of paper and list the five most important benefits you received from a major illness in your life. (You may find that there are more than five.) If you have or have had cancer, use this as the basis for this exercise.

The following is an example of how the exercise can work. During the preparation of this book, we had a conference with a busisness associate in Vail, Colorado. We got through the conference ahead of schedule and our associate, a nonskier, decided he would take some skiing lessons. He returned from the lessons exhausted and flew home. By the next day, he had developed a case of the flu that kept him in bed for two full weeks. In an effort to get well again and to apply the concepts we had described to him in Vail, he discussed the situation proceding the onset of the flu and then listed six benefits he derived from his illness.

> At the time I became ill, I was having a lot of trouble finishing a job in which I had a great emotional and financial stake. It was very important to me that it be completed in a splendid fashion, but the work was going slowly and I had doubts about the product I was producing. By getting sick I was able to meet many needs at once:
>
> 1. I wanted my wife's help on the project but felt that, unless I literally couldn't do it myself, it would

be wrong for me to distract her from her own activities to help me.

2. I needed the excuse of "something beyond my control" for not finishing the project on time.

3. I may also have been preparing an excuse for any imperfections that might appear in it.

4. It gave me a reason to get seriously involved with my own health, which meant among other things resolving that when I got well I would find the time to play tennis, an activity that I enjoy but which I normally don't do because I'm "too busy."

5. It was a simple rest from my daily labors, which were giving me a lot of stress.

6. The work at Vail called up many memories of my father's own death from a brain tumor. The unresolved issues of that situation were very much on my mind.

Clearly his physical exhaustion, both from the unusual exertion of skiing and the stress of completing a major job, contributed to his susceptibility to disease. But, as his answers show, the disease also gave him permission to rest, to ask for help, to take care of himself, to recharge his energy, to release himself from the tension of meeting very high standards, to remake decisions regarding priorities and life-style—all of which he had been unable to do without the illness.

The final pressure, the feelings about his father's death, was stirred up by the discussion of our approach to cancer treatment. Getting comfortable with this approach required that he start to resolve his feelings about his father's death.

In going over the lists our patients write, we find five major areas in which they most frequently benefit from their illnesses:

1. Receiving permission to get out of dealing with a troublesome problem or situation.

2. Getting attention, care, nurturing from people around them.

3. Having an opportunity to regroup their psychological energy to deal with a problem or to gain a new perspective.

4. Gaining an incentive for personal growth or for modifying undesirable habits.

5. Not having to meet their own or others' high expectations.

Now review your own list. Consider what underlying needs were met by your illness: relief from stress, love and attention, an opportunity to renew your energy, and so forth. Next, try to identify the rules or beliefs that limit you from meeting each of these needs when you are well.

One of our patients discovered that she felt a lack of physical closeness from her husband, but it was unthinkable for her simply to ask for affection and caring when she was well. Now she has given herself permission to say to her husband at any time, "I want a hug." She also learned some important things about herself as she looked at why it was so difficult to ask for physical closeness from her husband.

Ask yourself if you have been unable to allow yourself periods of release from tension. What personal beliefs stop you from giving yourself this freedom without needing the illness as justification? You might believe, for example, that it is a "sign of weakness" to give in to pressure or tension, or that it is your duty to put others' needs ahead of your own. Because these rules are mostly unconscious, this self-examination will take effort. But taking preventive action to avoid future illness is worth your time and energy. Once you begin to become aware of your internal rules and are able to see alternative ways of viewing situations, you are on the road to a healthier life.

By using the lessons of illness as a starting point, we can educate ourselves to recognize our needs and take the opportunity to satisfy them. This is the creative use of illness.

11

Learning to Relax
and
Visualize Recovery

The first step in getting well is to understand how your beliefs and emotional responses have contributed to your illness. The next step is to find ways of influencing those responses in support of your treatment. In this chapter we will tell you about a relaxation process for reducing the effect on your body of stress and tension associated with the onset of cancer and with the fear of the disease, which itself becomes a major source of stress. We will also show you how to use mental imagery, once you are relaxed, to create positive beliefs that will activate your body's defenses against disease.

For many cancer patients, the body has become the enemy. It has betrayed them by getting sick and threatening their lives. They feel alienated from it and mistrust its ability to combat their disease. Learning to relax and influence the body, on the other hand, helps people accept their body once again and their ability to work with it toward health. The body again becomes a source of pleasure and comfort and an important source of feedback on how effectively people are living life.

Relaxation also helps reduce fear, which can become overwhelming at times with a life-threatening disease. Cancer patients are often terrified they will die a prolonged, painful death, impoverishing their families through medical expenses, and doing their children psychological harm by the absence of a parent. Such fears make it almost impossible for patients to develop a positive expectancy about the outcome of their illness. But learning to relax physically helps them break the cycle of tension and fear. For a few minutes at least, while they are relaxing their bodies, cancer is not the overriding reality of their lives. Many patients report that they have a different perspective and renewed energy after using relaxation techniques. It appears to be a way of recharging their batteries. With the fear reduced, it is easier to develop a more positive expectancy, resulting in a further decrease in fear.

It is important to note that, in clinical terms, relaxation does not mean spending an evening in front of the television, having a few drinks, or talking with friends. Although these certainly can be pleasurable activities, laboratory studies show that such forms of "relaxation" do *not* result in an adequate discharge of the physical effects of stress.

Regular physical exertion is one way of unstressing. Regular exercise acts out the equivalent of the "fight-or-flee" response, which we discussed in Chapter 4, permitting the body to discharge the buildup of tension. It is not accidental, in our opinion, that many patients who have done very well in our program engage in some form of regular physical exercise. Many joggers and runners say that running is their "therapy" and that during the running, they are able to get a perspective on their problems that they cannot get just by thinking about them. (Later in the book we have a chapter devoted to this subject.)

Still, it is not always possible for people to engage in physical activity whenever they feel stressed. Modern life often requires considerable effort to handle all the arrangements necessary for physical activity. Fortunately, researchers have developed a variety of simple relaxation techniques—certain forms of meditation and progressive relaxation, autogenic training, and self-hypnosis, to name a few. Most of these techniques involve some form of mental concentration. People may focus their attention on a symbol or a series of mental images designed to calm the mind, or they may go through a series of instructions in their mind to relax the body.

Dr. Herbert Benson of Harvard University has documented the positive physical benefits of several of these techniques for reducing stress in his book, *The Relaxation Response*. Although all of the body's physiological responses to these various mental relaxation techniques may not be understood, research has amply demonstrated that the techniques discharge the effects of stress to a much greater degree than do the activities conventionally considered relaxing.

THE RELAXATION TECHNIQUE

The relaxation technique we developed while working with our patients is taken largely from a program devised by Dr. Edmond Jacobson, who calls his technique "progressive relaxation." In practice, we combine this technique with the mental imagery process we describe later in this chapter. However, we have detailed the relaxation process separately here so that you will see its value for use anytime. We recommend to our patients that they complete the combined relaxation/mental imagery activity three times a day for ten to fifteen minutes each time. Most people feel relaxed the first time they use this technique. But since relaxation is something that can be learned and improved upon, you will find that you'll enter into increasingly relaxed states as the process is repeated.

To make the relaxation/mental imagery process easier to learn, we provide our patients with a cassette tape of instructions. You may also find it helpful to have a friend read the following instructions to you or to make a tape recording of them. Allow plenty of time for completing each step in a comfortable, relaxed manner.

1. Go to a quiet room with soft lighting. Shut the door and sit in a comfortable chair, feet flat on the floor, eyes closed.

2. Become aware of your breathing.

3. Take in a few deep breaths, and as you let out each breath, mentally say the word, "relax."

4. Concentrate on your face and feel any tension in your face and eyes. Make a mental picture of this tension—it might be a rope tied in a knot or a clenched fist—and then mentally picture it relaxing and becoming comfortable, like a limp rubber band.

5. Experience your face and eyes becoming relaxed. As they relax, feel a wave of relaxation spreading through your body.

6. Tense your eyes and face, squeezing tightly, then relax them and feel the relaxation spreading throughout your body.

7. Apply the previous instructions to other parts of your body. Move slowly down your body—jaw, neck, shoulders, back, upper and lower arms, hands, chest, abdomen, thighs, calves, ankles, feet, toes— until every part of your body is relaxed. For each part of the body, mentally picture the tension, then picture the tension melting away; tense the area, then relax it.

8. When you have relaxed each part of the body, rest quietly in this comfortable state for two to five minutes.

9. Then let the muscles in your eyelids lighten up, become ready to open your eyes, and become aware of the room.

10. Now let your eyes open, and you are ready to go on with your usual activities.

If you have not already done so, we encourage you to go through this process before reading on. You can find the relaxation it produces pleasurable and energizing.

People sometimes experience difficulty picturing the mental image or keeping their minds from wandering the first few times they try the process. There's no need to feel discouraged. It's very natural and criticizing yourself will only increase your tension. At the end of this chapter, when you are more familiar with relaxation and visualization techniques, we will deal with a few of the common problems patients have with these procedures and suggest how to overcome them.

The next section provides instructions for moving directly from the relaxation process into the mental imagery process. Although the relaxation technique is valuable by itself, as we said earlier, we use it primarily as a prelude to mental imagery, because the physical relaxation reduces tension that could distract from concentrating on the mental imagery. The relaxation technique is also a prelude to mental imagery in another sense: Learning to use mental guidance to produce physical relaxation should help strengthen your belief that you can use your mind in support of your body.

RELAXATION AND MENTAL IMAGERY

Relaxation and mental imagery are among the most valuable tools we have found to help patients learn to believe in their ability to recover from cancer. In fact, we mark as the conception of our present approach the first time Carl used mental imagery with a patient. Since then, we have discovered that mental imagery is not only an effective motivational tool for recovering health, but is also an important tool for self-discovery and for making creative change in other areas of life.

We owe our discovery of the relaxation and mental imagery process to Stephanie's background in motivational psychology. Because of her training, we were aware that this process for altering expectancies had been used by people in many different disciplines. The common thread running through these disciplines was that people created mental images of desired events. By forming an image, a person makes a clear mental statement of what he or she wants to happen. And, by repeating the statement, he or she soon comes to expect that the desired event will indeed occur. As a result of this positive expectation, the person begins to act in ways consistent with achieving the desired result and, in reality, helps to bring it about. (This is similar to the concept of self-fulfilling prophecy, which we discussed earlier in the book.)

For example, a golfer would visualize a beautiful golf swing with the golf ball going to the desired place. A business person would visualize a successful business meeting. A stage performer would visualize a smooth opening night. A person with a malignancy would picture the tumor shrinking and his body regaining health.

As we were learning of the effectiveness of the relaxation and mental imagery process, we were also learning of the evidence that biofeedback researchers were amassing (described more fully in Chapter 2), that people could learn how to control inner physiological states, such as heart rate, blood pressure, and skin temperature. When interviewed, these people frequently stated that they had not been able to command the body to alter the internal state but instead had learned a visual and symbolic language by which they communicated with the body.

One woman, who had a dangerously irregular heartbeat, created a picture in her mind's eye of a little girl on a swing. She would see the little girl rhythmically swinging back and forth whenever she needed to bring her heartbeat under control. Within a short time, she needed no heart medication and had no more difficulties. Her success and the experiences of thousands of others in using mental imagery to control body states suggested to us that mental imagery—used in conjunction with standard medical treatment—might be a way cancer patients could influence their immune systems to become more active in fighting their illness.

Carl first used the mental imagery technique in 1971 (as we described in Chapter 1) with a patient whose cancer was considered medically incurable. The patient practiced three times a day visualizing his cancer, his treatment coming in and destroying it, his white blood cells attacking the cancer cells and flushing them out of his body, and finally imagining himself regaining health. The results were spectacular: The "hopeless" patient overcame his disease and is still alive and healthy.

THE MENTAL IMAGERY PROCESS

In this section, we will lead you through the relaxation-mental imagery process, repeating the previous instructions for relaxation. In Chapter 12, we will identify beliefs inherent in mental imagery, provide a list of criteria for creating effective imagery, and analyze examples drawn from our patients' experiences.

You may want to tape-record instructions, as we do for our patients, or have a friend read them to you. If you are reading to someone else, be sure to read slowly. Allow the other person plenty of time to complete each step. Remember that we encourage our patients to take ten to fifteen minutes to complete the entire process and to practice it three times a day.

Even if you do not have cancer, we ask you to go through the cancer visualization once to give you an emotional understanding of this process and insight into how the cancer patient feels.

1. Go to a quiet room with soft lightning. Shut the door, sit in a comfortable chair, feet flat on the floor, eyes closed.

2. Become aware of your breathing.

3. Take in a few deep breaths, and as you let out each breath, mentally say the word, "relax."

4. Concentrate on your face and feel any tension in the muscles of your face and around your eyes. Make a mental picture of this tension—it might be a rope tied in a knot or a clenched fist—and then mentally picture it relaxing and becoming comfortable, like a limp rubber band.

5. Experience the muscles of your face and eyes becoming relaxed. As they relax, feel a wave of relaxation spreading through your body.

6. Tense the muscles of your face and around your eyes, squeezing tightly, then relax them and feel the relaxation spreading through your body.

7. Move slowly down your body—jaw, neck, shoulders, back, upper and lower arms, hands, chest, abdomen, thighs, calves, ankles, feet—until every part of your body is more relaxed. For each part of the body, mentally picture the tension, then picture the tension melting away, allowing relaxation.

8. Now picture yourself in pleasant, natural surroundings—wherever feels comfortable for you. Mentally fill in the details of color, sound, texture.

9. Continue to picture yourself in a very relaxed state in this natural place for two to three minutes.

10. Then mentally picture the cancer in either realistic or symbolic terms. Think of the cancer as consisting of very weak, confused cells. Remember that our bodies destroy cancerous cells thousands of times during a normal lifetime. As you picture your cancer, realize that your recovery requires that your body's own defenses return to a natural, healthy state.

11. If you are now receiving treatment, picture your treatment coming into your body in a way that you understand. If you are receiving radiation treatment, picture it as a beam of millions of bullets of energy hitting any cells in its path. The normal cells are able to repair any damage that is done, but the cancerous cells cannot because they are weak. (This is one of the basic facts upon which radiation therapy is built.) If you are receiving chemotherapy, picture that drug coming into your body and entering the bloodstream. Picture the drug acting like a poison. The normal cells are intelligent and strong and don't take up the poison so readily. But the cancer cell is a weak cell so it takes very little to kill it. It absorbs the poison, dies, and is flushed out of your body.

12. Picture your body's own white blood cells coming into the area where the cancer is, recognizing the abnormal cells, and destroying them. There is a vast army of white blood cells. They are very strong and aggressive. They are also very smart. There is no contest between them and the cancer cells; they will win the battle.

13. Picture the cancer shrinking. See the dead cells being carried away by the white blood cells and being flushed from your body through the liver and kidneys and eliminated in the urine and stool.

• This is your expectancy of what you want to happen.

• Continue to see the cancer shrinking, until it is all gone.

• See yourself having more energy and a better appetite and being able to feel comfortable and loved in your family as the cancer shrinks and finally disappears.

14. If you are experiencing pain anywhere in your body, picture the army of white blood cells flowing into that area and soothing the pain. Whatever the problem, give your body the command to heal itself. Visualize your body becoming well.

15. Imagine yourself well, free of disease, full of energy.

16. Picture yourself reaching your goals in life. See your purpose in life being fulfilled, the members of your family doing well, your relationships with people around you becoming more meaningful. Remember that having strong reasons for being well will help you get well, so use this time to focus clearly on your priorities in life.

17. Give yourself a mental pat on the back for participating in your recovery. See yourself doing this mental imagery exercise three times a day, staying awake and alert as you do it.

18. Then let the muscles in your eyelids lighten up, become ready to open your eyes, and become aware of the room.

19. Now let your eyes open, and you are ready to resume your usual activities.

If you have not done so already, please take the time now to go through this mental imagery process. When you have completed the entire exercise, draw a picture illustrating the images you created, so that you can analyze your imagery in more detail, according to the criteria and examples we will present in Chapter 12.

You needn't worry about not being able to "see" the imagery if you were able to "sense" or "imagine" or "think" it. The word describing what you were doing is much less important than the fact of your doing it. Also, if you found your mind drifting during the process, next time just bring it back gently to the imagery without being harsh on yourself. If you were aware, while going through the process, that you were unable to complete certain of the instructions because you could not believe or accept them, then you have begun to confront your attitudes about cancer and recovery. By now you know how important that recognition is.

MENTAL IMAGERY FOR OTHER ILLNESSES

Since many readers of this book do not have cancer but may want to use mental imagery to help deal with pain and other ailments, here is a short mental imagery process, which can be substituted for steps 10 through 19, the cancer portion of the previous activity.

1. Create a mental picture of any ailment or pain that you have now, visualizing it in a form that makes sense to you.

2. Picture any treatment you are receiving and see it either eliminating the source of the ailment or pain or strengthening your body's ability to heal itself.

3. Picture your body's natural defenses and natural processes eliminating the source of the ailment or pain.

4. Imagine yourself healthy and free of the ailment or pain.

5. See yourself proceeding successfully toward meeting your goals in life.

6. Give yourself a mental pat on the back for participating in your recovery. See yourself doing this relaxation/mental imagery exercise three times a day, staying awake and alert as you do it.

7. Let the muscles in your eyelids lighten up, become ready to open your eyes, and become aware of the room.

8. Now let your eyes open and you are ready to resume your usual activities.

As an example of how you can use mental imagery to deal with an illness other than cancer, if you have an ulcer, your mental picture of the ulcer might be a crater-type sore in the lining of the stomach or intestine, seeing it rough and raw. Picturing the treatment, visualize antacids coating the area, neutralizing the excess acid and having a soothing effect on the ulcer itself. Picture normal cells coming in and doubling, dividing, covering over the raw, ulcerated area. See your body's white blood cells picking up any debris and cleaning the area, making it a pink, healthy lining. The next step is to see yourself free from pain and healthy, able to deal with the stresses of life without producing ulcer symptoms.

If you have high blood pressure, you could use the imagery process to see the problem as little muscles in the walls of the blood vessels tightening down, so that it causes much higher pressure necessary for the blood to be driven through. Now, see the medication relaxing these little muscles in the blood vessels, your heart pumping evenly, with less resistance, and blood flowing smoothly through the vascular channels. See yourself as able to cope with the stresses of life without producing symptoms of tension.

If your illness is arthritis, first picture your joints very irritated and having little granules on the surfaces. Then see your white blood cells coming in, cleaning up the debris, picking up the little granules, and smoothing over the joint surfaces. Then see yourself active, doing what you like to do, free of joint pain.

When you complete one of these mental imagery processes for the first time, draw a picture of your imagery. It will help you identify your attitudes toward participating in your health.

THE VALUE OF RELAXATION AND MENTAL IMAGERY

To give you a better idea of what to expect from these exercises, the list below contains some of the benefits of the relaxation/mental imagery process.

1. The process can decrease fear. Most fear comes from feeling out of control—in the case of cancer, feeling your body is deteriorating and you are powerless. Relaxation and mental imagery help you see your role in regaining health so that you begin to sense your own control.

2. The process can bring about attitude changes and strengthen the "will to live."

3. It can effect physical changes, enhancing the immune system and altering the course of a malignancy. Since mental processes have a direct influence on the immune system and hormonal balances in the body, physical changes can be directly attributed to changes in thought patterns.

4. The process can serve as a method for evaluating current beliefs and altering those beliefs, if desired. Alterations in the symbols and pictures that you use can dynamically alter beliefs to those more compatible with health.

5. The process can be a tool for communicating with the unconscious—where many of our beliefs are at least partially buried.

6. It can be a general tool for decreasing tension and stress. The process of regular relaxation by itself can decrease tension and stress and have a significant effect on underlying body functions.

7. The process can be used to confront and alter the stance of hopelessness and helplessness. We have seen again and again how this underlying depression is a significant factor in the development of cancer. As people begin to picture their bodies regaining health, their ability to solve the problems that existed prior to the malignancy, they weaken their sense of helplessness and hopelessness. Indeed, as the patients proceed toward health, they gain a sense of confidence and optimism.

OVERCOMING POTENTIAL PROBLEMS WITH THE MENTAL IMAGERY PROCESS

Some people are more visual than others; they think in images. Some people tend to sense things. Others feel things. Some think in words. Because of these individual differences, we have found that when we use the word "see" in our instructions to the mental imagery process, some people might instead "feel" what it is like to be well. When we would say, "See yourself becoming well," they might have the "sensation" of energy and health. It has become increasingly clear to us that a person should stay with the process or way of thinking that he or she is most comfortable with, rather than trying to become primarily visual. In the long run, all types of thinking tend to intertwine. A person who is mostly visual will begin to become more feeling, and a person who is more feeling will begin to become more visual. Permit yourself to operate first in the sense that is most natural to you.

Another problem we have found to be very common during mental imagery is the tendency for a person's mind to wander. This often represents a lack of concentration, which can be aggravated by certain medications, by pain, or fear. From time to time it is a problem that affects everyone using the process regularly. One of the most effective ways for dealing with distraction is to stop the process and ask yourself what is going on: "Why is my mind wandering?" Pursue that line of thought for a short time, perhaps five minutes. Then focus back on the exercise and go through it with whatever degree of success you can attain.

A third difficulty is the feeling that saying the cancer is "shrinking" is actually lying to yourself. We've heard statements such as, "I've got a cancer growing on my shoulder, I can feel it, it's not possible for me to see it shrinking when I know it's growing bigger." The problem here is a confusion about the purpose of the mental imagery process. We are attempting to help the patient visualize the *desired outcome*, not what may be happening at the time. It is possible to picture the cancer shrinking even when in reality it may be growing; you are picturing in your mind what you want to come about. Understanding this distinction is very important. Mental imagery is not a method of self-deception; it is a method for self-direction.

Now that you know the basic relaxation/mental imagery process, the next chapter will help you interpret and develop specific mental images so that you can understand your underlying beliefs about cancer and create a more positive expectancy for recovery.

12

The Value
of
Positive Mental Images

We first began using mental imagery to motivate patients and provide them with a tool for influencing their immune systems, but we soon discovered that the activity revealed extremely important information about patients' beliefs. This discovery was somewhat accidental. When we first began assigning the mental imagery process, we would ask our patients whether they were practicing it regularly, but we did not try to ascertain *what* their imagery was. However, when one patient's condition went steadily downhill, even though he steadfastly maintained he was using the process three times a day, we asked him specifically to describe the content of his imagery.

His answer confirmed our fears. When asked what his cancer looked like, he said, "It looks like a big black rat." When asked how he envisioned his treatment, which consisted of chemotherapy in the form of small yellow pills, he replied, "I see the little yellow pills going into my bloodstream, and once in a while the rat eats one of these pills." Asked what happened when the rat ate the pills, he said, "Well, he's sick for a while, but he always gets better, and then he bites me all the harder." When we asked about his white blood cell imagery, he replied, "They look like eggs in an incubator. You

know how eggs sit under the warm light? Well, they're incu-
bating in there, and one day they're going to hatch."

The imagery paralleled his deteriorating condition. First
of all, the cancer was strong and powerful—a "big black rat."
The treatment was weak and impotent, "tiny pills" that the rat
ate only occasionally and that had only a temporary effect on
him. Finally, the white blood cells, the representatives of the
body's natural defenses, were completely immobile. Our patient had created an almost perfect image of total suppression
of the immune system and had been faithfully repeating this
imagery three times a day.

We soon discovered that other patients also showed
strongly negative expectancies in their imagery. One patient
reported that, "I visualize my cancer as a big rock. Every
once in a while, these little scrub brushes come to clean up
around the edges of the rock, but they can't do much good."
Again, the cancer appeared strong and impregnable while the
body's defenses were puny and impotent, unable to "do much
good."

Another patient reported that he saw his white blood
cells "as a snowstorm that sweeps over my whole body and
obliterates most of the cancer cells in a single pass, but a few
pop back." Here the body's defenses appeared to be more potent, but they did not really destroy the cancer cells, they only
glossed over them. Moreover, since snowflakes have no direc-
tionality or intelligence, this imagery revealed that the patient
did not see his body's defenses as actually recognizing and
destroying the cells: their impact was by sheer numbers.

These experiences made us realize how important it was
to examine the contents of our patients' imagery closely to see
what expectancies were being communicated. Since then, we
have used the significance of the imagery to determine
whether patients show a general pattern of glossing over, or
trying to hide, negative feelings or otherwise impede their
treatments.

We have also discovered that the content of the imagery
varies with the patient's psychological state at a particular
time. For instance, the scientist John Browning, whose case
was reported in Chapter 10, had developed a strong mental
image for his white blood cells (see Figure 3), visualizing
them as a vast army of white knights on white horses who
would line up, their lances gleaming in the sunlight, and

charge through the landscape killing the cancer cells, which were small, slow-moving creatures.

But just prior to his two recurrences, John found his imagery changing. Sometimes he visualized black knights in the ranks of his army, which he took to mean enemy knights. At other times he imagined his knights' lances bent and limp, as if made of rubber, so that clearly they could do no damage. Or the knights' horses would be the size of dogs, so that they were ungainly and ineffective. We were soon able to observe a correlation between the imagery and events in John's life, and we realized that the imagery could be used as general feedback on his psychological progress.

THE CRITERIA FOR EFFECTIVE IMAGERY

With the assistance of Dr. Jean Achterberg-Lawlis, a research psychologist, we have developed a list of tentative cri-

Figure 3. John Browning's Mental Imagery: White Knights, on White Horses.

teria that can be used to evaluate the content of one's mental imagery. In our treatment center, patients use the criteria to analyze each other's imagery and to suggest alternatives that contain more positive expectancies. Representing cancer cells as ants, for instance, we have found is generally a negative symbol. Have you ever been able to get rid of the ants at a picnic? Crabs, the traditional symbol for cancer, and other crustaceans are also negative symbols. These beasts are tenacious, they hang on. They also have hard shells, making them relatively impregnable, and most people are afraid of them— the crab symbolizes the potency and the fear of the disease.

Interpreting mental imagery is similar to interpreting dreams: It involves a highly personal, symbolic language. To translate the beliefs inherent in an image, then, you must "try on" the image internally, identifying the meaning of its characteristics for you. The emotional meaning of a particular symbol may vary greatly for different individuals, so that a symbol that means strength and power to you may mean anger and hostility to someone else. Thus, you should not automatically accept anyone else's interpretation of your symbols. And, of course, your imagery need not be literally correct: there are no ants, crabs, white knights, or black rats crawling around in your body. Whatever the image, its importance lies in the meaning it holds for you, a meaning which, in this circumstance, it is up to you to recognize. Our experience has been that patients have a good feel for this kind of interpretation.

Despite all the potential for individual variations, our research indicates that effective images generally contain the features listed below. But because imagery is highly individual, what we are pointing out are the significant *qualities* of the symbols, not the symbols themselves. We will deal with problems related to effective mental imagery in the next section.

1. The cancer cells are weak and confused. It is important to depict your cancer cells as anything soft that can be broken down, like hamburger meat or fish eggs.

2. The treatment is strong and powerful. Your imagery should communicate the belief that the treatment is clearly capable of destroying the cancer. The imagery is strengthened if there is ample interaction between the treatment and the cancer, so that the impact of the treatment on the cancer is visible and understandable.

For example, if the cancer is pictured as a gray glob of cells, the treatment might be a yellowish or greenish fluid that flows over the cancer, breaking it down and making it shrink so that the white blood cells can easily destroy it.

3. The healthy cells have no difficulty repairing any slight damage the treatment might do. Since the treatment usually touches all cells, not just the cancerous cells, you should visualize your normal, healthy cells as being strong enough so that the treatment does little damage to them, and they are capable of repairing any minimal damage. The cancerous cells are destroyed by the treatment because they are weak and confused.

4. The army of white blood cells is vast and overwhelms the cancer cells. The white blood cells are a symbol of your body's natural healing process, so your imagery should reflect vast numbers of these cells and great strength. The victory of the white cells over the cancer should be seen as inevitable.

5. The white blood cells are aggressive, eager for battle, quick to seek out the cancer cells and destroy them. Again, the white blood cells are a symbol of your own defenses—that part of you that will help you recover—so make them intelligent, capable, strong. Visualize your white blood cells overwhelming the cancer cells, leaving no doubt about which cells are stronger.

6. The dead cancer cells are flushed from the body normally and naturally. Flushing dead cells from the body is a wholly natural process, requiring no special effort or magic. By imagining this process, you are communicating your confidence in your body's normal functioning.

7. By the end of the imagery, you are healthy and free of cancer. This image represents your desire for the final outcome: it is important that you see your body clearly as healthy, vital, and energetic.

8. You see yourself reaching your goals in life, fulfilling your life's purpose. This imagery communicates the fact that you have powerful reasons for living. You are confirming your confidence that you can recover and your commitment to living.

Our experience indicates that people who do very well in our program have developed imagery that matches these criteria. Yet none of our patients have started out with imagery containing all these elements. You may need to experiment before you find strong enough images to capture your new positive expectancy. Use the criteria to help you identify images that need strengthening or changing. Although it is not possible to provide a medically correct "prescription" of images, it is essential that you see your body's natural defenses triumphing over the disease. Strong images represent a strong belief in recovery.

It is important that in your imagery the most potent factor in overcoming your malignancy be your white blood cells, rather than, for example, chemotherapy. Patients often have reported seeing the white blood cells coming in and attacking but leaving behind some cancerous cells for the chemotherapy to eliminate. This indicates a basic belief that the medicine will get them well. While we in cancer therapy appreciate that medicine can do a great deal, we believe that the body's basic defenses eliminating the cancerous cells is the essential aspect in regaining health.

OVERCOMING PROBLEMS IN YOUR MENTAL IMAGERY

Now that you are familiar with the criteria for creating effective mental imagery, let's take a closer look at the mental imagery activity you just completed, the possible beliefs inherent in those images, some of the common problems patients face in creating such images, and some of the ways they have gone about overcoming the problems.

Imagery of the Cancer Cells

If you had difficulty visualizing the cancer, this may represent a strong fear of the disease and is often accompanied by a lack of confidence that your body can naturally and normally defend against the cancer. If you had difficulty seeing the cancerous cells as weak and confused, and instead saw them as strong—like stones or a predatory animal—or if you saw the cancer more vividly than other symbols in your imagery, you may have a much stronger belief in the potency of the disease than in the potency of treatment or of your body's defenses.

It is common to have difficulty picturing the cancer. If you are having trouble with this, picture a mass of gray cells wherever you know (or believe) the cancer to be in your body. Black and red are two very common colors that people use to describe their cancer, but these colors tend to have strong emotional connotations. Gray is a much more neutral color, and part of our approach is an attempt to neutralize the feelings about cancer.

Thus, we would suggest using gray rather than a stronger color. Or, you might picture the cancer as broken up hamburger meat and your white blood cells as large numbers of white dogs coming in to devour the hamburger, licking the surrounding areas clean and going on to patrol the other parts of your body. The basic image of the cancer cells should be that they are neutral, weak, and disorganized.

Imagery of the Treatment

It is important to visualize your treatment as a friend and ally. Our patients frequently report reduced side effects to treatment as a result of changing their attitudes in positive, supportive directions. For instance, one patient who had feared his treatment began calling the machine giving him radiation "George," and holding mental conversations with "George" about all the good things the treatment was going to do for him. In addition, the patient made efforts to engage the doctor and nurses in friendly conversations, which included thanking them for their efforts. Shortly after this change in attitude, he began to experience fewer and fewer side effects from the radiation. Personalize your treatment, make it a helpful friend who is working with you to overcome the disease.

Imagery of the White Blood Cells

This, we believe, is the most crucial symbol of the imagery process because it represents your beliefs about the body's natural defenses. The essential relationship between the white blood cells and the cancer is the strength and number of the white blood cells relative to the cancerous cells. The healthiest images are those in which the cancer is significantly outnumbered and overpowered by the white blood cells.

One way to strengthen the imagery of your white blood cells is to do the following: Assume your images of your white blood cells are fish swimming in and eating up the grayish cancer cells. Project this image as if it were on a screen that you're viewing in your mind's eye. When you have that image very clear, then *become* one of the fish and lead the rest of the pack into the attack. Feel yourself as the fish eating the cancer cells, destroying them, cleaning up any remaining debris. Hear the sounds and feel the emotions that are appropriate to the situation.

Again, the vividness of the imagery is important. Do you see the imagery of your white blood cells with the same or greater clarity than you see the cancer? Or do you see the cancer with greater vividness and clarity? If the cancer is more vivid, then, as previously mentioned, you probably have a greater belief in the power of the cancer than you do in the potency of your body's defenses, and so you will need to consciously strengthen the imagery representing your white blood cells.

In addition, the traits you attribute to the white blood cells often describe significant psychological issues you are facing. For example, patients who do not see the white blood cells attacking or destroying the cancer cells usually have difficulty expressing anger and hostility and have a strong need to impress others. These problems may have contributed to the onset of the disease and are standing in the way of recovery.

With this is mind, think of the white cell as having those characteristics that you consider most admirable and strong in yourself.

Imagery of Flushing Out Dead Cells

As we have said, how you see the dead and dying cells flushed from the body by natural and normal processes indicates your confidence in your body's natural functioning.

Some of our patients include in their imagery some form of magic or divine intervention to get the cancer cells out of the body. This is another representation of their belief in the power of cancer—that is, even when the cancer cells are dead, they are still so powerful that it takes a special intervention to rid the body of them.

Imagery of a Healthy Self

Since this is the desired outcome, how you visualize yourself regaining health, vitality, and energy is important. If you can see the battle, the cancer, the treatment, and the white blood cells but have great difficulty seeing yourself regaining health, you are quite possibly having difficulties believing you can recover. Try visualizing yourself engaging in activities you would pursue if you were healthy or having the overall feelings you would have if you were well. Picture yourself at the healthiest time in your life and create images of the present, feeling just that way.

Imagery of Your Goals

Goal setting (discussed in detail in Chapter 14) is a highly significant phase of the visualization process. If you have difficulty seeing yourself as healthy and well and engaged in happy pursuits, this may suggest you doubt your ability to recover. Try to see yourself reaching your goals and enjoying the satisfaction of having done so.

DRAWINGS AND INTERPRETATIONS OF OUR PATIENTS' MENTAL IMAGERY

We asked you to draw a sketch of your mental imagery for a simple reason. The drawing documents your beliefs at a particular time so you can later compare how your beliefs have evolved. In our program, we ask our patients to draw such pictures every three months and then to describe them aloud to us. By comparing their drawings from the initial session with the drawings from follow-up sessions, we are able to see how the patients are dealing with the cancer and how their beliefs are changing. Here are four case histories showing how imagery and beliefs changed over time.

Betty

Betty, thirty-five, was first diagnosed with breast cancer in 1973 and had one breast removed surgically. Later she had

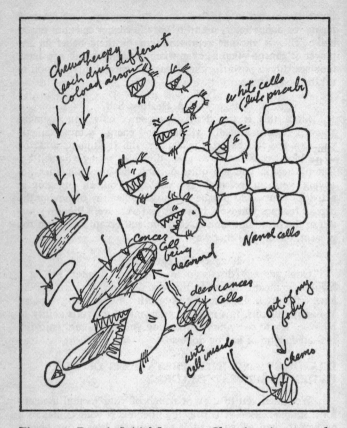

Figure 4. Betty's Initial Imagery, Showing Anger and, Hostility.

a second cancer requiring that her other breast be removed. When she began working with us in Fort Worth, she was receiving chemotherapy.

Betty's initial imagery (Figure 4) left little doubt that the white blood cells were going to win. Her first drawing showed ferocious-looking white blood cells with sharp, aggressive teeth. She noted that they were "like piranha," the voracious fish of South American rivers. Our experience tells us that such sharp teeth often indicate strong anger and hostility, and during her first session with us Betty did express much anger and hostility. Over the short term this works for her in her imagery; because of the potency of the symbol, there is little doubt that the white blood cells will win.

There are two other elements in the drawings we see as less positive. First, the cancer cells are either quite large or the cancer is drawn as a cluster of cells. It is good if patients are able to see the individual cancer cells. Those who do not visualize the individual cells often have difficulty looking at the component parts of a problem and instead are overwhelmed by the whole.

The second problem in Betty's imagery is that the chemotherapy is represented by sharp, pointed arrows. This is a very common symbol, but it often represents a fear of the treatment and a belief that the chemotherapy will have a detrimental effect on normal cells as well as cancerous ones. While such a belief has a basis in the experience of many patients, it is possible that the side effects will be reduced if another sym-

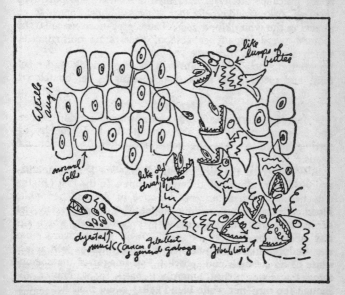

Figure 5. Betty's Imagery Six Months Later.

bol for the treatment, such as an individual rubbing "chemotherapy ointment" on cancerous cells, is pictured.

In Betty's second drawing six months later (Figure 5), the piranhas (white blood cells) were still there, but the teeth were less pronounced—though still quite effective—and now there were prominent eyes in the fish, indicating alertness and purposeful direction. At this meeting, Betty seemed considerably less angry and told the group that she had spent a great deal of time working on that aspect of her life.

Now, the cancerous cells were depicted as small and grapelike, and entwined with the normal cells. She associated this image with a great deal of fear which she had been experiencing recently. (We have often observed that vinelike, entangling symbols and fingerlike projections generally represent fear.) In working with Betty, it became clear to us that in addition to being more aware of her fear of dying, and particularly of dying alone, she was also afraid of getting well and facing the problems that she had suspended during her illness.

Betty had also picked up some erroneous information about precancerous cells, and in this drawing she portrayed them as corkscrewlike cells that at times almost appear to be attacking the white blood cells. These precancerous cells, she thought, were actually capable of penetrating normal cells, which is medically incorrect.

Betty is now doing quite well, both physically and mentally, and receives her primary counseling in her hometown.

Jennifer

Jennifer, thirty years old, had advanced ovarian cancer, and presented herself as a shy woman who had difficulty asserting herself so that she could meet her own emotional needs.

When given the assignment of drawing her mental imagery, Jennifer drew two different pictures. In the first (Figure 6), she showed her cancer as a cube of ice and her white blood cells as the sun, melting the ice. Her chemotherapy was depicted as white dust sprinkled over her cancer, which she had labeled the "cancer monster." Obviously, the word *monster* captured her dread and fear of the cancer, as well as her sense of its strength and ferocity. Her image for the chemotherapy was weak: dust is hardly a match for a monster. Although the sun (her white blood cells) could melt her cancer

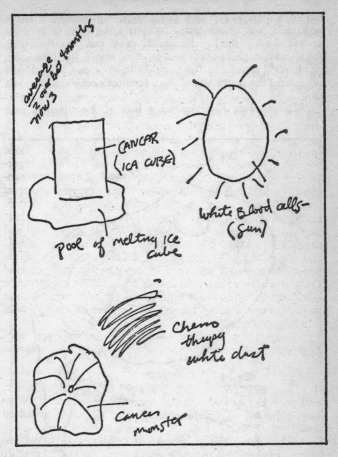

Figure 6. Jennifer's Mental Imagery; First Visit.

ice cube, it is a rather passive symbol with little direction or intentionality; that is, while the sun is shining, it incidentally melts the cancer.

Her second drawing (Figure 7) presented her as being in an even more hopeless position. Her cancer was portrayed as logs in a logjam, and one single man, representing a white blood cell, was shown trying to unjam the logs. Only if he succeeded could the logs be floated away, and even then they would remain unchanged; that is, they would still be cancer logs floating around in the body. With only one white blood cell against the entire jam of logs, Jennifer's odds did not look good.

The drawing also showed a lack of assertiveness and

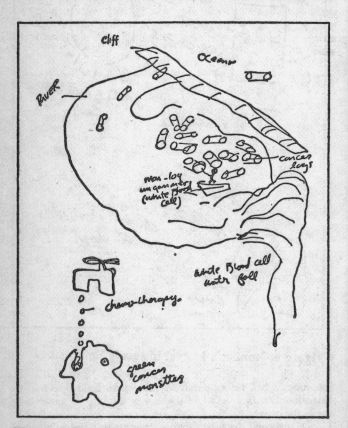

Figure 7. Jennifer's Mental Imagery; First Visit.

power—the kind of energy that might be able to break up the logjam in her life. (People who draw only one image of the white blood cells tend to have a feeling that if anything gets done in their lives, they have to do it all by themselves with no outside help. This feeling intensifies their sense of helplessness and hopelessness.)

The image of her chemotherapy was still weak. It appeared to be dripping some kind of poison into the cancer, again labeled "cancer monster," but did not seem to affect it greatly. In fact, the monster seemed to have a humanoid face, an eye and mouth, indicating intelligence and alertness with which it could defend itself.

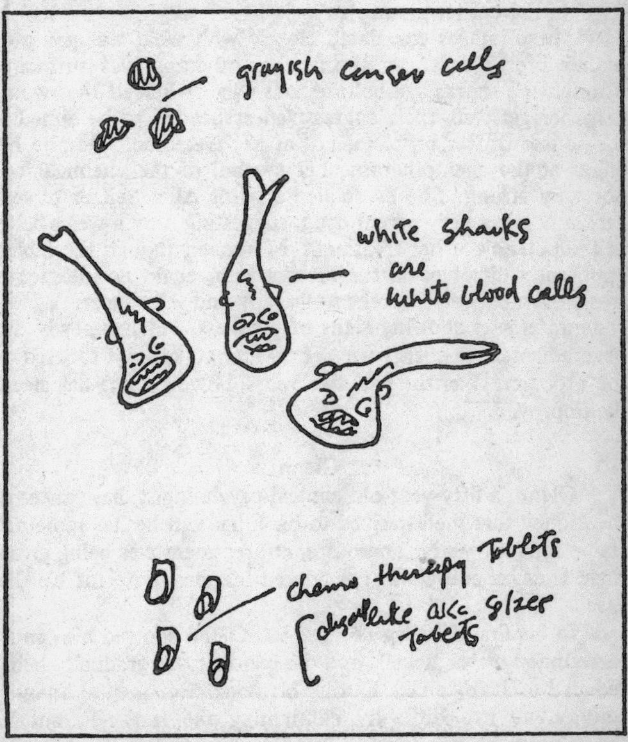

Figure 8. Jennifer's Mental Imagery, Six Months Later.

Taken together, Jennifer's first drawings indicate a confusion, an inability to stay with one image, and little belief that either her chemotherapy or her body's defenses could significantly influence the cancer.

Six months later, Jennifer's drawing (Figure 8) showed definite improvement. Her white blood cells were now depicted as white sharks with angry, pointed teeth. For Jennifer to show signs of anger or aggression, and sharks are certainly aggressive, was a major step forward. The cancer cells were also far smaller and less malevolent. Unfortunately, there was no interaction between the sharks and the cancer cells; in fact, the sharks seemed to be aiming their aggressiveness toward the chemotherapy (which looked remarkably like the "cancer logs" in her earlier picture).

These images correlated closely with what was going on in her life: Her anger at the chemotherapy was surfacing. Though the sharks symbolized that part of herself that would help her get well, their aggressiveness needed to be aimed at the source of her problem, not at her treatment. Despite her anger at the chemotherapy, her symbol of the chemical was not very strong: She associated it with Alka Seltzer tablets, certainly not a very potent drug, suggesting only a weak belief in the potency of her treatment. Moreover, though the tablets apparently dissolved in the bloodstream, again no interaction was shown between the chemotherapy and the cancer.

Jennifer was showing signs of progress, but her newly discovered assertive energy was, at that point, still not focused on the problem. Over the past two years, however, she has steadily improved.

Glenn

Glenn, a fifty-year-old clinical psychologist, has cancer of the kidney that metastasized to his lung, and he has remained stable for four years. Therefore, no treatment was being given, since chemotherapy was considered inappropriate for his disease.

In his first drawing (Figure 9), Glenn showed his cancer surrounded by white cells and the cancer mass gradually being reduced to a single cell. During his relaxation/mental imagery activity, he had difficulty eliminating the last cell, but he found when he was jogging that he could see the final cancer cell being absorbed by a giant white cell and disappearing.

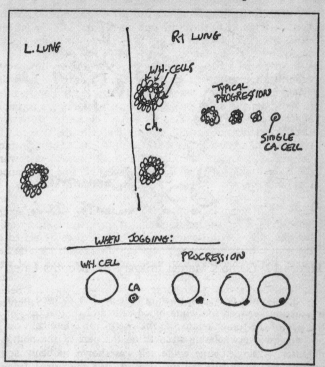

Figure 9. Glenn's Initial Mental Imagery.

Although in the drawing he does finally succeed in eliminating the cancer, there were some weaknesses in the imagery. The white blood cells seemed to work around the periphery of the cancer; there was little interaction, and they met the cancer only on the surface. (This desire to stay on the surface of the problem sometimes indicates an unwillingness to investigate the details of why one has developed cancer.) Also, destroying the last cancer cell required a tremendous effort on Glenn's part: He had to be jogging before it could occur. There appeared to be something almost magical about that last cell, almost a hanging on to the disease and an indication that it would take a very large white cell and an extraordinary event finally to get rid of the cancer.

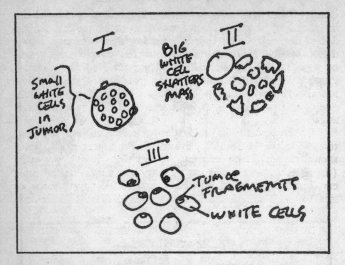

Figure 10. Glenn's Mental Imagery Six Months Later.

Six months later, his drawing (Figure 10) showed more interaction between the white blood cells and the cancer, yet the size of the tumor relative to the size of the white cells did not suggest overwhelming strength on the part of the body's defenses. A single, large white cell was shown suddenly appearing and shattering the tumor mass, and the tumor fragments were then absorbed by the ordinary white cells. Again, the drawing showed that an extraordinary event was required, and that until this magical event occurred, the cancer would remain intact. To us, Glenn's picture illustrated an unwillingness to deal with small component problems and a tendency to wait for the one event that would explain and remedy everything.

Similar to his imagery, Glenn's cancer has not regressed, though his general health is superb and he continues as professor and long-distance runner.

Charles

Charles was a successful businessman who, shortly after his retirement at sixty-two developed multiple myeloma, a cancer of the bone marrow. Although the disease showed up in laboratory studies, Charles was free of symptoms, so his doctor decided to wait before beginning chemotherapy. Now, three years later, his lab reports show less disease than when he was diagnosed, and he has still not received any chemotherapy. In addition to participating in our program, Charles has also had several years of private psychotherapy in which one of the problems dealt with was his difficulty expressing anger.

There were strong similarities between Charles's two pictures (Figures 11 and 12), drawn almost a year apart. Both showed a positive expectancy, in that the white blood cells (the sharks or large fish) were clearly overwhelming the cancer. The most dramatic difference between the two drawings was in their size: the first drawing filled almost the entire

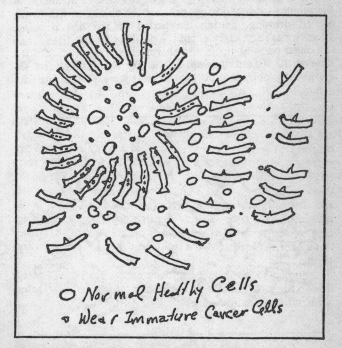

Figure 11. Charles' Initial Mental Imagery.

page, the second occupied a much smaller space. The second indicated how much smaller a part of the cancer occupies in Charles's life, for at that point his blood chemistry showed the cancer decreasing, he had no physical symptoms, and his physical condition had remained excellent—regularly beating the authors at tennis at the age of sixty-five.

Another sign of progress was that in the first picture, the cancer was shown as being largely surrounded in a highly organized manner by white blood cells; in effect, the cancer was walled-off, much as Charles had walled off problems in his life. By the second drawing, there was much less organization. We correlated these images with less need on Charles's part to protect himself emotionally and a greater willingness to interact openly with the problems in his life.

One difficulty was suggested by the lack of definition of the mouths—the major weapon—of the sharks or fish in the second drawing. During the period of the first drawing, Charles was very angry about the death of a close friend, and the anger showed up in the sharp, aggressive teeth. By the time of the second drawing, he was expressing much less anger about problems in his life, an issue we explored with him again.

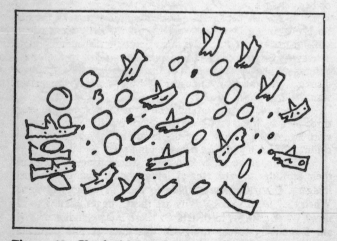

Figure 12. Charles' Mental Imagery One Year Later.

IMAGERY AS A DESCRIPTION OF SELF

These interpretations of our patients' drawings take into account as much as possible all the significant problems and psychological issues they are facing. We come to understand the drawing within the context of what we know of the patient's personality and life situation. Thus, it represented progress for Betty to tone down the anger and hostility expressed in her piranhalike fish, while it represented progress for Jennifer to portray her defenses as sharks. In one case, Betty's anger and hostility were causing her to reject the acceptance, approval, and recognition she desperately wanted and now had some hope of getting; in the other, Jennifer, a passive person, desperately needed the energizing that anger often accomplishes, even though she still had to learn how to use the anger effectively.

We are often able to use the imagery not just as an indicator of patients' beliefs about cancer but also as a description of their situations in life. In making this interpretation, we see the symbols of the cancer as the part of the person that wants to die or that is killing him or her, and the white blood cells as the part of the person that wants to live or that will help him or her get well.

The disease becomes a physical manifestation of the battle being waged between two parts of the self: the toxic or self-destructive parts and the nurturing or life-sustaining parts. The symbolic potency of the cancer in relation to the body's defenses is not just a measure of the patient's beliefs about the disease but is also an indicator of how strongly the patient wants to live or die.

Our patients go through the drawing procedure every three months when they return to Fort Worth for a follow-up visit. Even though they are fully aware of the use of this procedure, they still generate revealing imagery.

We encourage them to use the whole process, including their attitudes toward mental imagery and changes in their imagery, as an important guide to their psychological states. When they learn to ask, "Why are these images coming to me now? What changes in beliefs do these images indicate? Why am I choosing to see things in this light at this particular time?" they are participating in the process of expectancy and taking a measure of control over it.

Use relaxation/mental imagery time as an opportunity to work on other issues in your life. During the first weeks and months, the necessary emphasis is on getting well. Obviously, without health your ability to concentrate on other problems is limited. But as you begin to regain health, we urge you to seek ways to apply the process to a wide variety of life's problems. As we have stated, the imagery of positive expectancies, which is also the principle of the self-fulfilling prophecy, can help you succeed in a limitless number of ways.

13

Overcoming
Resentment

Processes that help people release resentment, express negative feelings, and forgive past wrongs (whether real or imagined) may well be a major part of the preventive medicine of the future. And because cancer patients often have unresolved resentments, and other emotional ties to the past (as we have seen, perceived abandonment or rejection by one or both parents may be an antecedent to the development of cancer), helping our patients learn to release the past is often essential in helping them get well.

We experience stress not only when we go through the experience that created the resentment but we reexperience it each time we recall the event. This locked-in or long-term stress and the tension that results can produce serious inhibitions of the body's natural defenses, as we and other researchers have shown.

Resentment is not the same as anger: Anger is generally a single, relatively short-lived emotion (one with which we are all familiar), whereas resentment is a long-term restressing process.

Suppose, for example, you are driving down the street and a carload of teenagers coming from the opposite direction almost hits your car. You experience a stress reaction: Your heart beats faster, your breathing speeds up, the adrenaline flows, and so on. Generally, two emotions are experienced with this event. The first is fear, then anger over the driver's carelessness. These reactions are normal.

When the event has passed, however, our actions and reactions become increasingly significant. One response to this event would be to catch up with the teenagers and talk to them about their way of driving. If they apologized or explained why they were driving in a careless manner—perhaps because they were in an emergency situation or late to work—the anger probably would be dissipated. However, this kind of follow-through is almost always impractical.

When we have no outward action available to diffuse the emotions that are connected to the past event, like that of the careless teenagers, the anger may well generalize to other teenagers in other cars (or even other drivers in general), causing us to retain the anger we felt at the time of the initial occurrence. If these feelings are not released, they often result in resentment and stress.

Some people allow resentments from countless sources to mount for years. Many adults carry such feelings from childhood experiences, which they remember in great detail. These may be over what they felt was a lack of parental love, over rejection by other children or by a teacher, over specific acts of parental cruelty, and endless other painful experiences. People who carry such resentments continually recreate the painful event or events in their heads. This may even go on long after the offending person has died.

No matter how justified those feelings may have been when the experience first occurred, continuing to carry them has tremendous physical and emotional costs. If you are harboring such feelings, the first thing you must acknowledge is that you—not the other person—are the ultimate source of your own stress.

TECHNIQUES FOR FORGIVING OLD HURTS— OUR OWN EXPERIENCE

It is one thing to know that you need to learn to release resentments and forgive; it is quite another to find an effective way to do so. Religious leaders of all persuasions and philosophers of every school plead the case for forgiveness. They wouldn't need to do so if forgiving were easy. But they also wouldn't suggest it if it were impossible.

A book by Emmett Fox, entitled *Sermon on the Mount*, gave us a specific, practical process to use for forgiving (we will describe it in a moment). At first glance, the process seems quite simple. The essence of it is to become aware of the person toward whom you feel resentment and to picture good things happening to him or her. We wondered whether it was an effective tool, for it seemed to deny the validity of one's feelings, and recognizing that validity is an essential element in fulfilling one's own needs. However, we decided to try it.

Initially, we discovered that it was difficult to see good things happening to a person toward whom we felt anger and hostility. But then as we continued to use the process, we began to get a different perspective on our relationship to the person resented and on his behavior. For instance, we still might not approve of the way a person had handled a particular situation, but after using the process we could generally understand the situation better and begin to see how we may have contributed to the situation.

Over time, as we repeated the imagery process—especially when one of us found ourselves recreating the distressing event—we began to succeed in picturing good things happening to the other person and we felt better for it. In addition, any face-to-face dealings with the other person became more relaxed and pleasant. The resentment imagery process had helped relieve stress that we might have carried around for much longer. We discovered that we had not denied our original response of anger and hurt, but rather had derived a new understanding and attitude that relieved our own discomfort. The benefits were clear.

MENTAL IMAGERY FOR OVERCOMING RESENTMENT

The imagery process we used is presented below. Before you apply it, however, you may need to identify appropriate targets for the process. They are not hard to detect. If you find yourself nursing an old hurt, reliving a distressing episode, thinking over and over about what you should have done or said, recalling the other person's reprehensible behavior, then you have unresolved feelings about an experience which could be dealt with using Emmett Fox's technique. Here is how it works:

1. Sit in a comfortable chair, feet flat on the floor, eyes closed.

2. If you feel tense or distracted, use the relaxation process described in Chapter 11 to get ready.

3. Create a clear picture in your mind of the person toward whom you feel resentment.

4. Picture good things happening to that person. See him or her receive love or attention or money, whatever you believe that person would see as a good thing.

5. Be aware of your own reactions. If you have difficulty seeing good things happening to the person, it is a natural reaction. It will become easier with practice.

6. Think about the role you may have played in the stressful scene and how you might reinterpret the event and the other person's behavior. Imagine how the situation might look from the other person's point of view.

7. Be aware of how much more relaxed, less resentful you feel. Tell yourself you will carry this new understanding with you.

8. You are now ready to open your eyes and resume your usual activities.

The imagery process generally takes less than five minutes to complete. Use it whenever you become aware of rerunning an unpleasant, painful, or angering episode from the past. There may be months when it is unnecessary for you to use it at all, and there may be days when you use it half a dozen times.

You can even use it at the time an unpleasant situation is occurring. For instance, in an episode such as the one with teenagers cutting in front of you, you could picture them getting to where they are going, having a good time, being successful in school and sports. You might begin to consider your own youth and the times you did foolish things and even gain an understanding of some of the teenagers' stresses.

OUR PATIENTS' EXPERIENCES WITH THE RESENTMENT IMAGERY PROCESS

We have frequently observed over the last several years that after our patients have forgiven others, the final person to forgive is themselves—for their own participation in the event and their contributions to the discomfort and stress that followed it. This can be an especially important process for people with malignancy, because they often find themselves victims of a guilt-resentment cycle for having the disease and having given their families pain and stress. Three examples may clarify how this process has actually worked.

Edith

Edith, fifty-three, had breast cancer that had spread to her bones and intestines. An only child, she had been extremely fond of her father, a charming, successful man, but she felt that her mother consumed so much of her father's attention that there was none left for her. She felt angry toward her mother and competed with her for her father's love.

While Edith was in her forties, her father died of cancer. She suffered a great sense of loss from his death and now found herself responsible for caring for her mother, who was quite elderly and living in a nursing home. Her mother complained bitterly if Edith did not visit her every day, and even when she did visit regularly, her mother invariably evoked feelings of guilt and inadequacy. Edith not only had the present inconvenience and emotional turmoil of caring for her mother, but she also felt forced to cope with earlier unresolved feelings of resentment. Shortly after her father's death, Edith developed breast cancer.

After she became aware of her resentment, we suggested that she visualize good things happening to her mother. While practicing this exercise for several weeks, Edith gained new insights into her mother's loneliness, particularly since her widowhood, and began to see that her mother's demands and complaints were not aimed at her personally but came out of her fears and frustration. She also became aware of her own feelings of insecurity and inadequacy generated by her father's death.

As a result of these recognitions, Edith was able to make decisions about whether or not to visit her mother without feeling guilty when she did not visit her. She also discovered that when she reacted less defensively to her mother's comments, her mother's behavior became gentler. An unexpected payoff from resolving her feelings about her mother was that Edith found she was able to communicate more satisfactorily with her own children.

Edith had a dramatic remission of her widespread metastases and has been able to remain very active for the past three years.

Betty

Betty, thirty-five, whom we spoke of in Chapter 12, was experiencing much anger and hostility. She was quick to challenge almost everything—the temperature of the room, the quality of the food, anyone who asked her why she smoked, and so on. After a very upsetting conflict with a member of our staff, Betty tried the resentment imagery process and discovered she had a seemingly endless list of things about which she could feel resentful. Indeed, she even found that she would seek out other people's difficulties and start resenting for them. For instance, at our residential treatment center, she discovered that the staff cook and the cook's husband were unhappy with the center's manager and planned to quit, and she brought their resentment up at our group meetings.

As she became aware of the role these feelings played in her approach to life, she also recognized that she had learned this approach from her mother, whose attitude had been that "the world was picking on her." (Betty's mother, incidentally, had died of breast cancer.)

We worked with Betty again after she had been using the resentment imagery process for six months, and it was quickly apparent that she had changed significantly. Gradually, she had learned to catch herself when she started to collect resentments and recognize that, even if injustices did exist, she was damaging her own health by going out of her way to look for them. Her facial expression had softened, she was much more direct in expressing her feelings, and she felt less depressed and anxious. Psychological tests that we gave her also indicated that she spent less time repressing and denying her feelings, showed increased resiliency and, in general, felt better about herself.

Ellen

At thirty-two, Ellen had breast cancer with bone metastases. During her initial work with us, she began to realize that she had spent much of her life blaming her parents, particularly her mother, for having damaged her psychologically in her early childhood. She blamed much of the pain in her life on that perceived hurt.

When we asked her to use the resentment imagery process and report on it, she said that at first she had great difficulty creating a picture of her mother. Then, after forcing herself to picture her mother and see good things happening to her, Ellen discovered that she was really angry with herself for having messed up her own life. She realized that she had used the resentment toward her mother as an excuse to avoid facing her anger at herself, and she saw that the person she really needed to forgive was herself.

Ellen began visualizing hugging herself, patting herself on the back, seeing good things come about in her life. She changed noticeably. Whereas she had formerly shown very little emotion and often felt extremely depressed, now she began to show signs of vitality and energy.

Importantly, Ellen learned to use her feelings toward her mother as feedback. Whenever she found herself raking over old resentments toward her mother, she knew she was covering up anger at herself. At such times, she would visualize herself with greater self-acceptance and more responsibility for solving her own problems. One year later, psychological tests indicate that considerable psychological improvement has taken place. Her physical health has also improved greatly. She is very active and has no evidence of disease at this time.

GAINING INSIGHT INTO YOUR RESENTMENT

The resentment imagery process is not a way to avoid expressing true feelings by turning them into unnaturally positive images. Rather, it is a way to gain insight into your old hurts and relieve the damaging side effects. After using the process repeatedly, our patients have shown—both through subjective reports and objective psychological tests—*less* tendency to repress and deny their feelings. They become able to deal with their feelings more effectively, and as a result, experience less stress and tension.

Since one does not simply turn negative feelings into positive feelings, it takes a great deal of effort to begin to visualize good things happening to a person toward whom you feel resentment. In the attempt, however, you begin to confront your own role in reacting to the hurtful situation as you did. You may find, as have a number of our patients, that some of your resentment toward the other person may be because you yourself reacted in a way you didn't approve of, and you wish you had reacted differently.

You may find in practicing the resentment imagery process, that no matter how hard you try, you just won't let the other person off the hook. Usually, this means you have a stake in continuing the resentment; you are getting something out of it. It might be that your resentment allows you to continue playing the victim, a role that permits you to feel sorry for yourself without having to take responsibility for changing your life. Or you may find that you have carried resentment over a long period of time because you have difficulty accepting the fact that you felt angry or hurt in the first place, and you continue to resent the other person for "making" you feel that way.

To make peace with another person's behavior, then, requires that you take a close look at your own. If you can forgive yourself, you can forgive others. If you cannot forgive others, it is usually because you are not extending forgiveness to yourself.

While releasing resentment frees your body from stress, you will also gain a sense of accomplishment as your feelings surrounding old events begin to change, and you will recognize a new sense of freedom and control as you discover that you are no longer victimized by your feelings. By allowing the energy tied up in resentment to be redirected toward constructive decisions, you will be much closer to leading the kind of life you want to live. These gains will enhance your body's ability to eliminate cancer and dramatically improve the quality of your life.

14

Creating the Future: Setting Goals

While in specialty training at the medical school, Carl developed an interest in why some cancer patients responded especially well to treatment. To see if he could find some answers, he decided to interview those patients in the cancer clinic who showed exceptionally good responses, and he discovered a strikingly similar theme in their answers: All had very strong reasons for wanting to live, could elaborate their reasons in great detail, and felt that this intense attachment to a goal in life was an explanation for their unusually positive progress.

These reasons, or goals, ranged from a strong desire to complete an important business arrangement or to oversee and complete the harvest of that season's crops to a fervent need to communicate certain messages to their children, which would help them to function as independent adults. Whatever the goals, they had special meaning to the patients—strong enough, apparently, to significantly enhance their will to live. From these experiences and essentially similar observations by others, it became clear to Carl that building a strong attachment to significant goals could be a major source of the inner strength a cancer patient needs to regain health.

Unquestionably, it takes courage to live in a way that

makes life worthwhile after being diagnosed with cancer. It takes courage because, if life is worth living, then there is much to lose. Most people think if they were told they had a life-threatening disease, they would do all the things they had postponed doing, be all the things they had put off being, live their remaining months to the hilt. In fact, most do just the opposite: They stop living. Life becomes neutral, conditional. This may be, in part, an unconscious preparation for death, for if life is lived in low gear, then its loss does not seem so great.

Once cancer patients fear they will die soon, their tendency is to feel that the family resources involved in improving the quality of life should be used for someone "who's going to be around longer." As Carl found with his patients at the medical school, those who *are* "around longer" are precisely the ones who make life worth living by investing themselves in something significant to live for.

THE BENEFITS OF SETTING GOALS

Throughout this book, we have pointed out that people who continually ignore their emotional needs pay the price physically. Good health, in contrast, is the result of paying attention to your needs—mental, physical, and emotional—and then translating this awareness into action. The most effective tool we have found for getting our patients to take specific, positive action is to ask them to set new life goals. For some of them, this is the first time they have consciously formulated their reasons for living.

By asking our patients to set goals, we help them conceptualize and focus their reasons for living, reestablishing their connection with life. It is a way of saying that there are things you want out of life and will make an effort to achieve. It is a way to transform emotional, mental, and physical needs into life-affirming behavior, to reinvest yourself in life. The will to live is stronger when there is something to live for.

Setting goals has many other significant benefits for the cancer patient:

1. **Setting goals prepares you mentally and emotionally to act out your commitment to regain health.** You are saying you *expect* to recover.

2. **Setting goals expresses confidence in your ability to meet your needs.** You are affirming that you are in charge of

your life and can make things happen. You are acting upon life rather than being acted upon by forces not under your control. The importance of this self-assertive stance is that it runs counter to the attitude of hopelessness and helplessness that contributes to the physiological conditions that permit cancer to occur in the first place.

3. **The stance that you are in charge of your life builds a positive self-image.** Setting goals and working to meet them affirm your own importance and the importance of your needs. By accepting and working to fulfill your needs, you are saying that you are a worthwhile person and that you matter to yourself.

4. **Setting goals provides a focus for your energy. It establishes priorities.** When life seems conditional, goals give you a direction and reasons to live.

We sometimes meet patients who are resistant to setting goals. They may doubt their ability to meet the goals and fear "failure." They may have known "goal-oriented" individuals who seemed cold and driven by their objectives. Or they may feel that it is pointless to establish goals because they don't expect to be around to meet them.

For these patients, we point out that the primary value of setting goals lies in being involved in your daily living and committed to worthwhile objectives, whether or not they are met. It is the *process* of striving to meet your goals, not their ultimate fulfillment, that gives meaning to life. Regarding the second objection, the driven individual is not cold and obsessive because he *has* goals, but rather because his goals are unbalanced; they may leave little time for human values. And finally, the belief that you won't live long enough to achieve your goals, as we have seen again and again in this book, can be a significant inhibitor to your recovery. (Later in this chapter, we'll give you some specific suggestions for affirming that you can live to meet your goals.)

Goals are simply tools to focus your energy in positive directions. They can be changed as your priorities change, new ones added, and others dropped. A goal is no more than a statement of your present needs, as you perceive them. *You* are responsible for understanding your needs and setting reasonable goals to meet them. And as you take action to achieve what matters to you, you are investing your own life with meaning—the single most important step toward moving in the direction of health.

DETERMINING YOUR GOALS: GENERAL GUIDELINES

Some people have a clear idea of what their goals are. For others, as we have said, asking the question, "What do *I* want out of life?" is quite literally a new experience. Many people spend so much of their lives meeting the expectations of parents, spouse, children, friends, and employers that they are not sure what they want for themselves. And people who may have been clear about their needs and wants in the past may be confused about their goals when circumstances change. No matter what your current situation is, the approaches below can help you define appropriate goals for yourself. Try each approach until you find the ones that work for you.

1. **Review the "benefits" of your illness.** In Chapter 10 we describe the benefits people derive from illness, such as permission to avoid resonsibility, work, or doing what other people want. The emotional needs implicit in each of these benefits are legitimate, but the patient's present problem is to develop a means of meeting these needs *other than through illness*.

If, for example, one of the benefits was that illness enabled you to spend time alone thinking, without the distraction of children, work, and so on, you might set a goal of putting aside a certain number of hours each week just for yourself. If illness brought you increased love and attention from friends, you might set a goal of having lunch or dinner or a tennis match with a friend on a regular basis or of asking for time from your spouse or lover or children more regularly. Use the benefits as a point of departure to help you discover what you really want for yourself.

2. **Ask "survival" questions.** Another way to identify what really matters to you is to consider the possibility that your goals, your reasons for living, may be the one thing making the difference between whether you live or die. Ask yourself "survival" questions like, "If I were hanging onto life by my fingernails, what do I want to do so badly that I would keep hanging on?" Or, "What do I want to do today that makes it worthwhile getting out of bed?" Whatever matters so much to you that it could determine whether or not you wished to survive is the ground level from which you can de-

velop your goals. But don't be surprised if no answers come to you immediately. Push yourself to continue asking questions aimed at revealing what you want your goals to be.

3. **Ask "growing-up" questions.** Dr. Art Ulene, in his book, *Feeling Fine,* suggests starting the process of goal setting by asking yourself, "What do I want to be when I grow up?" This question is valid no matter what your age. If people naturally grow and change but continue to play old roles without questioning them, these roles often become stale and unfulfilling. The intent of this question, then, is to force you to consider what *you* want out of life now, independent of past roles, social expectations, and so on.

SOME SPECIFIC SUGGESTIONS
FOR GOAL SETTING

Before you actually write your goals, we would like you to consider a few specific suggestions about goal setting that have helped our patients write satisfying goals that can be achieved.

1. **Write balanced goals for what you want to do—including activities that provide personal meaning as well as pleasure.** Of course, all goals depend on individual preferences, but the essential quality we look for in our patients' goals is *balance*—of physical, intellectual, and emotional needs.

We encourage you to include goals that address (1) your purpose in life: personal growth, your relationships with others, your career, and financial targets; (2) goals that are focused on pure recreation (but at least half of these should cost very little money); and (3) goals focused on physical exercise.

We have found that many people write too many work-oriented goals and tend to be "workaholics." Very often the underlying message in driven behavior is "I must justify my existence by the work I accomplish; I am not okay apart from my work." People also seem to set goals that clearly contradict the way they have been living. One of our patients, a successful attorney, was obsessive about his job; his "normal" work week was six days long, often eighteen hours a day. As he worked on his goals he came to realize that he needed to balance his work with some pleasurable activities. But when he set his goals they were: (1) sailing twice a week, (2) fishing once a week, (3) learning to ride a motorcycle. His new priorities provided as little balance as had his former way of living.

If you have completely neglected recreation for work, engaging in pleasurable activities should be one of your goals. If you have spent many years raising children and running your home, a newly satisfying activity might be an outside involvement in a political or charitable organization. Evaluate where your focus has been in the past and write goals that fill in the parts of your life you have disregarded.

2. Make your goals concrete and specific. When patients take the brave step of reinvesting in living, despite the fact of life-threatening disease, it is important that they achieve results that give feelings of accomplishment and affirm their control over their lives. Thus, goals need to be tangible so it is clear when they are met. Avoid loosely stated, general goals such as, "I want to have more money." Instead, state your goal in specific, concrete terms that you can carry out.

If your goal is "to have more money," add the specific activities that you see related to getting more money, such as "asking for a raise," "getting a part-time job," or "distributing my resumé to twenty-five prospective emloyers." If your goal is "becoming more aware of my feelings," you might set a goal of reading books about psychology, talking about your feelings with an intimate friend, or seeing a psychological counselor. Rather than stating a goal as "being more loving," you might set a goal of spending fifteen minutes a day alone with each of your children. As much as possible, make your abstract goals tangible so that you have the satisfaction of knowing when you have accomplished them.

3. Make your goals measurable. After you have defined a specific and concrete behavior for your goals, state how much must be done before you will feel a sense of accomplishment: for example, earning an additional $2,000; jogging three times a week; attending one adult education class per semester.

You can also give yourself a realistic schedule as an incentive. But keep in mind when you set it, that almost everything in life takes longer to accomplish than most of us think it will. Give yourself the gift of time.

4. Make your goals realistic. Just as you can set yourself up for failure if you establish goals that are unrealistic in terms of the time needed to meet them, you are apt to fail if you try to meet too many simultaneously. Your capabilities and training also need to be considered. Naturally, people's beliefs about what is possible differ, but it is important that you have some successes with realistic goals.

5. Make your goals within your power to make happen. One patient of ours set a goal of becoming a grandmother—delightful, but outside her power to make happen, since it was dependent on the actions of her daughter and son-in-law. This, too, is a setup for failure. Write goals that focus on *your* behavior rather than on the hoped-for behavior of others.

6. Don't be afraid to dream. A seemingly impractical idea may lead to a practical one. Think back on past pleasures and successes. Are there things you used to do that gave you great satisfaction, but that you've forgotten about? Are there mistakes from the past that could guide you in setting your goals now? Talking with friends about your goals may help you clarify them also, but be sure you don't get talked into adopting *their* goals or changing yours to meet their expectations.

SETTING YOUR GOALS AND DEVELOPING SPECIFIC ACTION STEPS TO MEET THEM

Now that you have some guidelines on how to determine your goals and make them satisfying, get a piece of paper and write some for yourself. We ask all our patients to write three, three-month goals; three, six-month goals; and three, one-year goals. The short-term goals should identify sources of immediate pleasure and gratification. The longer-range goals should express objectives that take longer to achieve and that affirm your expectation of living to meet them. The process is intended to help you start taking responsibility for meeting small, specific goals and then, after some successes, to help you broaden the scope of your personal responsibility.

Setting long-range goals can sometimes be frustrating and anxiety-provoking because you see a great gap between the desired objective and your present situation. Yet, listing the specific action steps needed to meet the goal will show you the precise activities you can perform to reach it. Breaking down even the longest-range goal into its component parts makes each step manageable, and the end-product within reach.

Action steps are not major acts or decisions but a series of modest, attainable steps. If one goal is to go to Waikiki for three weeks, for example, your list of action steps could include getting brochures from your travel agent about travel to Hawaii, opening a savings account for depositing money to make the trip, talking to friends who have gone to Hawaii about their trip, exploring group charter flights or other means of travel, getting vacation time scheduled at work, and so on. Each separate step establishes expectancy, direction, and ultimately will lead you to your goal. In other cases, if you do not know the precise steps necessary, your first action step might include investigating different ways of reaching the goal.

REINFORCING YOUR GOALS
THROUGH MENTAL IMAGERY

We have observed that the relaxation/mental imagery process is an effective way of strengthening patients' beliefs that they can meet their goals. You begin the process with the combined technique described in Chapter 11, only this time the mental imagery takes the form of visualizing a goal *as already met*—and then looking back in your mind's eye over the steps required to reach it.

Seeing the goal already met strengthens your expectancy that the desired event will occur, and reviewing the steps that led to meeting the goal may often suggest alternative paths by which a goal can be attained. As you discover such alternatives, you may wish to change your list of action steps to accommodate better ways of reaching your goal.

The mental imagery process for reinforcing goals is described below. Take the time now to select one of your goals and read through the steps slowly. As with the other mental imagery processes, it will help to tape-record the steps of the activity or to have someone read it to you the first few times you try it.

1. Use the relaxation process described in Chapter 11.

2. Select the goal you want to work on.

3. In your mind's eye, see yourself with the goal already met.

4. Experience the feelings you would have with your goal already met. What would people say to you? What would you be doing? What would you look like? Describe your surroundings. Add as many details as possible.

5. See other people who are important to you responding to your achievement.

6. Look back over any steps it took to reach your goal. What was the first step? Decide to take some action on this first step. Feel a sense of accomplishment for achieving each step. Add details about the action steps and your feelings.

7. Be happy and thankful for having reached your goal.

8. Gradually drift back to the present time.

9. Now open your eyes and take action on that first step.

Overcoming Problems in Goal Imagery

Sometimes, the mental imagery process will help you define the goal more clearly. One patient visualized herself at a famous resort, only to realize that she resented all the people she saw around her. This helped her understand that she needed time away by herself, not surrounded by others.

Occasionally, however, the mental imagery process identifies barriers to meeting goals. One of our patients discovered that when she visualized herself having completed her goal, she also saw a picture of her husband and children being very unhappy. She realized then that she feared her family's reaction to the personal changes she wanted to make, and she decided to discuss this openly with them.

Even though you normally have no difficulty creating mental images, you may find yourself unable to create a mental image of reaching your goal. This often means that you don't believe you are capable of meeting the goal. If this is so, continued practice of the mental imagery process will usually help strengthen your belief. If you cannot visualize achievement of the final goal, but you can visualize many of the steps along the way, the process will still begin to build a more positive belief in your own capabilities.

Similarly, you might discover during the mental imagery process that you have a negative expectancy about living long enough to achieve your goals. For example, if you are working on a goal to take a vacation with your family in a year, but you suddenly recognize that you have just thought to yourself, "I'll probably not live long enough to take that vacation," we suggest you stop the imagery activity. Then admit to yourself that you have expressed a possible negative expectancy and *balance* it with a positive one. You can remind yourself that you are getting appropriate medical care, that you've taken responsibility for influencing your own health, and that you have many more tools available to you now than you've had before, so that you may very well be alive to take that vacation—and in good health.

They key to changing this negative expectancy is not denying your feelings but becoming consciously aware of them and balancing them out with positive ones. You may not at first believe the positive expectancy that you are trying to substitute. That's not important. By asking yourself to remember that a better outcome is also possible, in time you will find yourself shifting to a more positive point of view.

Each time you find the goal imagery process interrupted by a negative belief, stop the activity and patiently balance the thought with a positive belief. Then return to the imagery process and visualize yourself reaching your goal.

After you have become familiar with the goal imagery process, begin to incorporate one or two of your more important goals into the regular relaxation/mental imagery process that you are doing three times daily.

As you continue to picture yourself achieving your goals, you will be increasing your expectancy that you can achieve them. You will also notice that you are beginning to act in ways compatible with bringing them about. Just as picturing your body's overcoming cancer and returning toward health helps you to respond and behave in ways that allow this to come about, so does regularly visualizing yourself accomplishing your goals help you to act in appropriate ways to give your life direction.

15

Finding Your Inner
Guide to Health

The unconscious mind contains priceless resources that can be mobilized for personal growth and healing. Indeed, throughout the history of psychological study, theoreticians have proposed the existence of a "center" in the psyche that directs, regulates, and influences the course of an individual's life.

This "center" has been called by various names. Freud was the first to call it the *unconscious*—the source of instincts and drives that influence behavior and yet are largely outside conscious awareness. Jung gave a different quality to the essence of the unconscious, proposing that an individual was not only driven by the unconscious but also led by it to increased personal growth and a sense of well-being. Jung proposed that the center of a person's psyche (which he called the *self*) also had a compensatory function. When a person was consciously fearful, for example, the self would attempt to provide him with the feelings of strength and courage required for dealing with the fearful situation at hand. Jung proposed that messages from the unconscious, or the self, were always conducive to the person's well-being.

The means by which the unconscious communicates with the conscious self is through feelings, dreams, and intuitions. Unfortunately, our culture seems to undervalue these messages. We are taught to value external events and objects—behavior, our bodies, material things, the logical output of our minds—but not our internal environment. Therefore, we tend to ignore feelings, dreams, and intuitions from our internal self, which are attempting to provide us with resources to meet the demands of the external world.

It has been hypothesized by several researchers that cancer patients may have been cut off from the resources of their unconscious processes. In our experience, many recovered patients have come to see their illness as, in part, a message to value and pay more attention to their unconscious self rather than to the demands of others. In addition, many patients have described having had specific insights, feelings, dreams, or images which provided valuable guidance in their efforts to regain their health.

The Inner Guide is a process we teach patients for tapping these rich inner resources of healing and strength. Visualizing your Inner Guide gives you access to the unconscious. It is a symbolic representation of aspects of the personality not normally available during conscious awareness. When you make contact with your Inner Guide—through a mental imagery process we will describe—you are connecting with important mental resources from which you are usually cut off.

The first major school of psychology to work with the Inner Guide as part of the therapeutic process was Jungian psychoanalysis. Jung reported that during meditation or reverie, spontaneous images sometimes formed that had an autonomous, life-of-their-own quality. In Jungian therapy, great emphasis is placed on establishing communication with these positive resources of the unconscious.

One process used for permitting this communication with the Inner Guide is called a "guided daydream," a form of mental imagery. Psychosynthesis, a recent psychotherapeutic process based on the work of Dr. Robert Assagiolli, also actively encourages the development of contact with the Inner Guide as part of a program of personal growth and discovery.

For many people, the Inner Guide takes the form of a respected authority figure—a wise old man or woman, a doctor, a religious figure—with whom the patient is able to carry on an internal conversation, asking questions and hearing answers that seem to be wise beyond the individual's conscious capacities.

Furthermore, patients are often more responsive to insights achieved in consultation with their Inner Guides than they are to the observations of a group leader or a therapist. Because the Inner Guide is an aspect of their own personalities, relying on such a guide is a healthy step toward taking responsibility for their physical and psychological health.

TAPPING YOUR INNER RESOURCES: EXAMPLES FROM OUR PATIENTS' LIVES

John

An eighteen-year-old patient of ours who had acute leukemia showed us the healing wisdom of the Inner Guide. John was a withdrawn and overly intellectual young man who believed that if he could not solve problems with his rational mind, they could not be solved. But one night he had a dream in which an "unorthodox doctor" appeared and indicated that he was a healer who had come to help him overcome his disease.

When he told us of the experience, we suggested that the doctor in his dreams might be an "internal healer" representing his own powers of recovery, and we encouraged him to see the internal physician in his mental imagery and to consult with him about his problems.

John had little difficulty reestablishing communication with the "unorthodox doctor" and conducted a mental dialogue around three major problems: his loss of weight on the hospital diet, his loss of muscle tone owing to a lack of physical exercise in the hospital, and his fear of girls and sexuality. From the dialogues, John came up with the idea of asking the hospital's head dietitian to give him a special 1,500-calorie protein drink every day. After beginning this regimen, he began to put on weight. He also recognized that he was not going to get the physical exercise he needed unless he was more assertive. Because his leukemia was advanced and unresponsive, the hospital staff assumed he was going to die and made no effort to get him into an exercise program. After consulting with his internal physician, John called in the physical therapist and insisted that she design an exercise program for him.

Regarding his fear of girls and sexuality, the internal physician recommended that rather than worrying about girls at the present time, he should try to become more responsive to people in general. John began wheeling himself around the hospital ward and talking to others. He was amazed at how friendly everyone was to him and slowly his fear of people began to diminish.

David

A second experience supported the effectiveness of using the Inner Guide as a pathway to the unconscious. David, who is now in his sixties, came to us shortly after he was diagnosed with multiple myeloma, a form of cancer that affects the bone marrow. During a therapy group, he told us a recurring dream he had had since childhood. He would dream of waking up in the middle of the night completely paralyzed, as in a spell. In the dream, he would struggle and struggle, convinced that if he could move one muscle he would break the spell, but he could never move. This nightmare had terrified him to the point that he insisted his wife make the bed with accordion pleats, believing that if the bed sheets were too tight around his feet, the dream would recur more frequently. Despite these efforts, the nightmare continued.

After his cancer diagnosis, we encouraged David to try to remember his dreams and record them, in the hope that something from his dream life would prove useful to his waking state. We suggested that any nightmare with as much potency as his was likely to contain powerful messages from the unconscious which might yield valuable psychological information.

Sometime after beginning to record his dreams, David had a series of nightmares, followed by a beautiful dream about two children playing delightedly in an open meadow. As dusk approached, the children came together to say goodbye, and one child said to the other, "Now that you're willing to play with me, I won't have to tie you down anymore."

Upon awakening and reflecting on the dream, David's intuition told him that one child in his dream represented his conscious self and the other—with the message about not tying him down—represented his unconscious.

As a successful executive who took a great deal of responsibility for his business, the welfare of his employees, and the growth of his community, David had for years ignored his feelings and emotional needs in the pursuit of his goals. He felt that his unconscious had been trying for years to get his attention with the recurring dream.

Believing that the child in his dream had told him how he could prevent his recurring nightmare, he continued to record his dreams, reading books on the meaning of dream symbols and seeking help from the group in interpreting their meanings.

In addition, David decided to take the image of his unconscious into his mental imagery three times a day. He asks the child what he has to say and promises to listen to him, so long as the child will not tie him down again. This Inner Guide has been a constant source of good advice, and David has not had a recurrence of his nightmare for two-and-one-half years.

He has since developed several other Inner Guides that appear to represent unconscious aspects of himself. One that spontaneously appeared in his mental imagery is a crying eight-year-old boy. David remembers that at age eight, he experienced a traumatic event that resulted in his making a decision to live his life so that people could not affect him emotionally. The image of the boy represented all the hurt and anguish that had led to his childhood decision to avoid close relationships. David soon realized that the crying child appeared in his mental imagery only when he was depressed and had bottled up his feelings. He learned to interpret the appearance of the child as a message that he was once again closing off his emotions.

Gwen

Gwen was a difficult patient to work with, and although she had shown a good physical response to our program, she often fought our efforts to help her confront psychological issues. She frequently resisted self-examination or consideration of alternative ways of relating to people. In the hope that we could find some way she would look at herself, we suggested that she use the Inner Guide mental imagery process.

Somewhat shyly she told us that a figure named Dr. Fritz had appeared spontaneously in her mental imagery two months earlier, but she had been too embarrassed to report it. When she had asked Dr. Fritz what he was doing in her imagery, he reported that he was there to help her regain her health. She then asked him a series of questions, and his answers indicated a deep understanding of the emotional issues Gwen had avoided facing in working with us.

She would listen to Dr. Fritz. She might, for example, have a telephone conversation with her daughter about an upcoming visit, a conversation which left her quite angry. She wouldn't say anything about the anger to her daughter, but later in the day she would begin having pain from her cancer. She consulted with Dr. Fritz about her pain, and he informed her that it resulted from not having dealt directly with her daughter. She was feeling resentful of her daughter's demands on her time, Dr. Fritz stated, and if she wanted to get rid of her pain she needed to phone her daughter and tell her that she was not coming for the weekend. When Gwen called her daughter and cancelled the visit, her pain began to go away. She reported a number of such incidents—perhaps thirty or forty over a period of six months—and her health improved steadily.

Janet

Some patients have received valuable insights and information by having mental dialogues with the symbols in their cancer imagery process. Janet was diagnosed with breast cancer that had spread to her abdominal cavity. She began using visual imagery when she entered therapy with us. Despite her serious prognosis, she had a remarkably good response and was able to return to work and resume her normal activities for two-and-one-half years.

Janet then began to experience some emotional upsets and after several months of unusual stress her disease flared up again. During an imagery session shortly thereafter, she called up the image of her white blood cells and asked them mentally if they would work overtime in a specific effort to regain control of her tumor. They replied that they would not work alone, but that she would have to work, too. They indicated that if she were to regain her health, it was important that she get in touch with the emotional reasons why her disease was recurring and do something about them, in addition to practicing her imagery three times a day. Then they reassured her that they would continue to work diligently on her cancer and to reproduce so there would be a continuous source of new white blood cells to fight her disease.

As a result of this dialogue, she returned to our center for a follow-up therapy session where she began to uncover and deal with her recent difficulties. During the session, her tumor began to diminish and she returned home, again on the road to recovery.

Frances

Frances is another patient who reported engaging in an internal dialogue with her visual imagery. Frances came to us after being diagnosed with a recurrence of lymphoma, a cancer that affects the lymph system. As part of her imagery, she imagined her cancer being destroyed by her chemotherapy and her white blood cells. Then she would imagine her bone marrow remaining healthy and producing more white blood cells to combat the cancer.

Frances is a poet and keeps a journal of her ideas, intuitions, and dreams. The following is a poem written from her journal, which is now part of her book entitled *Any Time Now*. She describes her first contact with a source of internal guidance which took the form of her bone marrow:

JOURNAL ENTRIES

May 15, 1976

4 P.M. Read new snake poem to Mark. His suggestions make it a better poem and they make me sad.

8 P.M. Meditating, visualizing. Suddenly couldn't see my bone marrow. Couldn't see it at all. Asked myself what is this all about? Why am I punishing myself?

Instantly an answer: I let Mark change *my snake poem*. I let him say *This is what you mean, it's not about that*—he took my meaning out of my poem.

I understood: my bone marrow was saying *I* am the source—of all creativity, all good—the white cells that cure come from me—I am the center—the generator, in this body—of the life force—

I promised I would restore my poem to its meaning.

I saw white cells pour from the bone marrow into the blood, thousands—moving with that cellular shimmer, that movement-in-liquid that we recognize as LIFE.—They softened, soothed, and brought nourishment. And they killed the abnormal cells.

And I could see again into my bone marrow— glistening—in its aura of wet and gold—

Suddenly—I remembered the snake under the Acropolis (in *The Bull from the Sea*)—Theseus trying to save besieged Athens—an old woman, guardian of the Goddess' snake, shows him the secret way out— a path, through the depths of the hill. They stop and look into a deep pit—the snake, ancient, sacred to the Goddess—the old woman feeds it—it eats—a good omen, his enterprise will prosper.

Now I understood—my shimmering bone marrow is the repository—in me—of the force of the universe—and I suppose the autonomy I am trying to achieve must stem from that knowledge—

I must respect the life force AS IT IS IN ME—and IT IS IN ME generated from the bone marrow, the source of blood, and holder of the codings of the genes—

In the weeks and months ahead, Frances received much valuable information concerning her emotional response to daily events through the presence or absence of the image of her bone marrow when she practiced visualization.

ANOTHER APPROACH TO THE INNER GUIDE

In our experience, most patients' Inner Guides take the form either of a respected authority figure or of some other serious figure with a great deal of symbolic value. Drs. David Bresler and Art Ulene, however, report much success using lighthearted fantasy creatures as Inner Guides.

Bresler, of the UCLA Medical School Pain Clinic, has

patients use mental imagery to contact their Inner Guides as a source of information about their pain. He frequently suggests the guides take the form of humorous animals—"Freddy the Frog," as one example. Despite their whimsical qualities, these creatures help patients identify the things going on in their lives that may be contributing to their pain.

Ulene, who offers advice on health on the "Today Show," described in his book, *Feeling Fine,* an approach similar to Bresler's. Ulene encourages developing a "creature-advisor" that will allow you to call on the right brain—the hemisphere concerned more with symbolic, intuitive functioning than with the logical, rational thinking associated with the left hemisphere—for help in problem solving. He describes the creature and the mental imagery process:

> The animal, of course, is nothing more than a symbol for your inner self, and talking to the animal amounts to talking to yourself, but on a brain wavelength you don't often use.
>
> Recently I used my own personal creature—a rabbit named Corky—to solve a work-related problem I had. For days I had been trying to seek a way out of a situation. No solutions. Lots of frustration. Lots of stress. Then one day I thought, "Let's see what Corky has to say about this."
>
> I closed the door to my office, drew the blinds, and sank into my chair. Quickly I imagined myself at my relaxation spot—a ski slope at Mammoth. Within seconds Corky popped up. I stated my problem and asked him, "What should I do?"
>
> "*You* shouldn't do anything," the rabbit answered unhesitatingly. "Let Frank handle it. That's not your problem."
>
> Why hadn't I thought of that? It was the right answer, although it had escaped me for days while I pondered the problem.
>
> I got on the phone to Frank (who handles administrative matters for my television show) and told him about my conversation with the rabbit. Frank agreed to take care of the problem. Within seconds I felt better.
>
> I admit the solution should have been obvious all along. But that's just the point. It wasn't obvious

to the verbal side of my brain. Only when I called in my creature-friend was I able to move into a fresh area for the solution.

Ulene's approach is simple and straightforward and has the advantage of demystifying the process so that there are no barriers presented by your having to assume any mystical or religious beliefs to consult with an Inner Guide.

THE INNER GUIDE MENTAL IMAGERY PROCESS

We have found this experience uniformly valuable in aiding our patients' recoveries and encourage you to try it. The steps described below are designed to help you establish initial contact with an Inner Guide, whatever form it takes. Once you have found it, you may call upon it whenever you wish during your regular, three-times-a-day mental imagery.

1. Sit in a comfortable chair, feet flat on the floor, eyes closed. Use the relaxation process (Chapter 11) to get very comfortable and relaxed.

2. In your mind's eye, see yourself in a natural setting that gives you a feeling of warmth, comfort, peace, and serenity. Select the spot from your memory or your fantasies. Concentrate on the details of the scene. Try to experience it with all your senses—as if you were really there.

3. Notice a path emerging near you, which winds toward the horizon. Sense yourself walking along this path. It is pleasant and light.

4. Notice that in the distance there is a radiant blue-white glow, which is moving slowly toward you. There is nothing threatening about the experience.

5. As the glow comes closer, you realize it is a living creature—a person (whom you do not know) or a friendly animal.

6. As the person or creature comes closer, be aware of the details of its appearance. Is the creature masculine or feminine? See its shape and form as clearly as you can. If your guide is a person, notice details of face, hair, eyes, bone structure, build.

7. If this person or creature makes you feel warm, comfortable, and safe, you know it is an Inner Guide.

8. Ask the guide's name, and then ask for help with your problems.

9. Engage the person or creature in a conversation, get acquainted, discuss your problems as you would with a very close friend.

10. Pay careful attention to any information you receive from your guide. It may come in the form of conversation or through symbolic gestures, such as the guide's pointing toward something or producing an object that represents its advice.

11. Establish an agreement with your guide about how to make contact for future discussions.

12. Then when you are ready, let your consciousness come back slowly into the room where you are sitting and open your eyes.

Do not be discouraged if you do not make contact with your guide or receive information from it on your first attempt; it is not uncommon for it to take several attempts before making contact. Because this is a part of yourself that you may not have paid attention to for years, reestablishing communication often takes time and patience.

If you feel uncomfortable or embarrassed consulting an Inner Guide, remember that the figure you are calling upon is merely a symbol for your inner self, an intuitive, wise, responsive part of your personality with which you are generally out of touch. If you can establish a strong relationship with your Inner Guide, you may receive an extraordinary amount of information and advice about your feelings, motivations, and behavior. The guide can tell you when you are making yourself sick and suggest what you can do to help yourself get well. This is just one more ability you have that you can mobilize toward health.

16

Managing Pain

Medical researchers still do not know precisely what causes pain, nor do they fully understand its pathways of communication between body and mind. And if pain is difficult to explain on a simply physiological level, it is even more difficult to understand when we consider a complex, interdependent system of mind, body, and emotions. While pain can have physiological causes, it can also be caused by emotional stress alone. To deal with pain, then, we must take into account not only the patient's physical state but his or her emotional state as well.

To the cancer patient, pain is often the most frightening aspect of the disease. A stiff back from tension or a "crick" in the neck from sleeping on an unfamiliar pillow would be largely ignored by most people, but once someone is diagnosed as having cancer, every ache and pain takes on new meaning. Any discomfort is focused on with the greatest attention, for fear that it might be a sign the cancer has recurred or metastasized to a different part of the body.

In addition, it is almost impossible to know what causes pain or to distinguish which elements are physical and which may be psychological. We have seen cases in which two patients have virtually identical tumors in location and size, yet one patient is in excruciating pain and the other experiences

179

none. The differences may be physical on a level we do not perceive. Unquestionably, though, they may also be psychological.

THE EMOTIONAL COMPONENTS OF PAIN

Pain also has a close relationship to emotional states. We had a vivid example of this with a patient who came to us very close to death. Frederick was a physician in his midforties who had bowel cancer with massive liver metastases. The bowel cancer had been surgically removed, and he had received chemotherapy for the liver metastases, but his doctors considered the chemotherapy a failure and discontinued treatment. Despite the seriousness of his illness and his intense pain, Frederick was extremely disciplined, convinced he would recover, and fought hard to stay alive.

During our work with him at the center, he became aware that many of the problems and stresses in his life were related to an extremely judgmental part of his personality, which held him to almost impossible standards of professional competence and acceptance by his colleagues. One of the "benefits" of his illness, was that it gave him comfortable disability payments from his insurance and, as a result, freed him from the constant pressure of proving himself professionally.

Although Frederick had been very close to death, he began to show signs of recovery. With his highly disciplined practice of the relaxation/mental imagery process, the size of his grossly distended liver diminished, and with it, so did the intense pain. Soon he was able to resume a number of his normal activities, and five months after we first saw him, he reopened his medical practice. Shortly thereafter, his insurance company notified him that they were discontinuing his medical disability payments. During this conversation, Frederick's liver pain returned. From then on, his condition steadily declined and he died within three months. The fact that the pain recurred *during* the disturbing conversation with the insurance company suggests the connection between Frederick's pain—real, tangible, physical pain—and his emotional state.

Pain and Dreams

More evidence of the emotional component of pain is the fact that patients often report being awakened from a deep sleep by intense pain. We believe the reason for this is as follows: The unconscious tends to deal with unpleasant issues during sleep that may be too threatening to confront while awake. The content of these unconscious thoughts is so distressing that it results in physical pain. Sometimes patients have clues to this content through dreams they remember. In such cases, we recommend that they try analyzing the threatening dream by having a dialogue with the dream figures during their mental imagery exercises, treating them as if they were Inner Guides trying to give important advice.

THE "REWARDS" OF PAIN: LEARNING NOT TO USE PAIN AS A JUSTIFICATION

Physical pain serves a number of important psychological functions. A cancer patient may find that many "benefits" of the illness—being taken care of, receiving more love and attention, getting out of a difficult situation, and the like—are derived more from the patient's suffering from pain than from the malignancy itself, for the pain overtly reminds everyone of the disease. We call these the "external rewards of pain," because they serve to influence the external environment—that is, other people and their behavior toward the patient.

Just as cancer can sometimes give people the justification they need to acknowledge their own importance and demand that their needs be met, so can pain. If you can give yourself permission to request love and attention, relaxation, and release from undue stress without using pain as a justification, you will be able to reduce your pain.

Pain also has "internal rewards." For example, some of our patients appear to use physical pain as a diversion, an excuse to avoid looking at the emotionally painful conflicts in their lives. In these cases, physical pain may be unconsciously substituted for emotional pain because the physical pain is often the more bearable, particularly if the patient fears that he or she does not have the skills to deal with the emotional pain or has given up hope of resolving the conflicts.

At the same time that you explore the physical causes of pain, then, we urge you to examine the possible "rewards" you may be getting from it. This self-examination alone may help you begin to alter the thoughts and behaviors that are contributing to your pain. Ask yourself: "Why do I need this pain? What purpose is it serving? What does it allow me to do, or not do? What am I getting from it?" Answering these questions is often difficult. Your conscious mind tends to reply: "I don't want this pain. It serves no purpose. It keeps me from doing what I want to do." But it is important to move on past that point. You might get help in answering these questions from people close to you who will be very honest, or from a professional counselor.

APPROACHES TO MANAGING PAIN

Because pain is so often linked closely to tension and fear, many of our patients experience a decrease in pain after beginning to use the relaxation/mental imagery process regularly. We believe this occurs for two reasons. First, the relaxation activity reduces muscle tension, which reduces pain. Second, as the mental imagery process helps the patient develop an increased expectancy that he can recover, his fear is lessened, reducing tension and further decreasing pain.

In this chapter we describe our approaches to managing pain. We begin by helping patients understand its emotional components: when and why it occurs, in what intensity, and under what circumstances the patient is entirely or nearly pain-free. Then we describe the techniques that may lessen the pain.

Recognizing How You May Be
Contributing to Your Pain

Pain is never constant, although patients frequently describe it that way. If you were to keep a careful record of your pain, you would probably see that there are times when you are pain-free, when the pain is minimal, and when it varies in intensity. It will help you to become aware of what you are thinking and what is going on in your life at each of these times.

For instance, a patient might tell us that on awakening he is free of pain. But when he begins to think about getting out of bed, the pain begins. Upon examining his thoughts at this time, he may report suddenly remembering he is ill, that he cannot function as he used to, that he doesn't feel like "his old self." Once up and about, he may experience low-intensity pain until the phone rings, at which time there is a sudden, dramatic increase.

To us such a report would indicate that this patient's overall negative expectancy is contributing to his pain. Instead of seeing himself as potent and capable of dealing with daily living, he reminds himself of his illness, he expects not to be able to function easily. In addition, he seems to anticipate a troublesome telephone conversation. In such a case we would ask him whom he imagined was calling, what he expected the conversation to be, and why he felt incapable of handling the situation.

Once he became aware of the expectancies that may be influencing his pain, he would have the ability to modify these thoughts. He could practice the relaxation/mental imagery process more regularly to reinforce a positive expectancy. He could limit his exposure to anticipated stressful situations or work on changing his way of responding to unavoidable situations. This awareness of how he may have contributed to his pain is an important first step in reducing it.

MENTAL IMAGERY FOR COPING WITH PAIN

In addition to seeking out the possible emotional components with our patients, we use three mental imagery processes specifically designed for managing persistent pain: visualizing your body's healing resources, communicating with the pain, and visualizing the pain. (These are adapted from the work of Drs. C. Norman Shealy of the Pain and Health Rehabilitation Center in La Crosse, Wisconsin, and David Bresler of the Pain Clinic at the UCLA School of Medicine.) Try all three until you find those that work best for you. Do the imagery as often as you need it. There is no limit to the number of times it can be practiced and still be effective. We hope these activities will stimulate you to find additional creative ways of dealing with your pain.

Visualizing Your Body's Healing Resources

The purpose of this activity is to make you an active participant in mobilizing your body's healing resources to the area of pain and encouraging those potent forces to correct the abnormality so that the pain will decrease. By practicing the activity you strengthen the belief in your ability to take control over your pain and your body's processes—and thereby decrease the fear which is often a component of pain.

1. Prepare yourself by using the relaxation activity described in Chapter 11.

2. Visualize an exploratory mission by your body's white cells (or another image of your body's healing forces) to discover the difficulty. Try to see the image very clearly. Send the healing resources to the part of your body experiencing the pain.

3. If the white blood cells (or your own mental image) find cancer cells, visualize the white cells attacking and destroying the cancer, leaving the area clean and healthy and free of pain.

4. If the white blood cells (or your own mental image) find no cancer, but instead aching, tense muscles or ligaments, see these muscles relaxing, feel the relaxation in the area, see the muscles relaxing like tight rubber bands going limp.

5. Notice that as you hold this image of the muscles and ligaments relaxing, the pain diminishes and may even leave the area.

6. Give yourself a mental pat on the back for participating in relieving your pain and then go about your usual activities.

Communicating with the Pain

Carrying on a mental dialogue with your pain is similar to consulting your Inner Guide—both processes can tell you a great deal about the emotional components of your pain and illness. Gwen, for example (discussed in Chapter 15) consulted her Inner Guide, "Dr. Fritz," when she had pain. He told her the reason for her pain was having made a commitment she didn't want to keep. When she followed his advice (her own good judgment), and cancelled the commitment (a visit to her daughter) the pain went away. No one is better able than you are to tell you what is causing the trouble.

1. Prepare yourself by using the relaxation process described in Chapter 11.

2. Visualize the pain as a creature of some sort. Try to see the pain-creature very clearly.

3. Establish a dialogue with the pain-creature. Ask it why it is there, what message it has, what purpose it serves. Listen very carefully to its answers.

4. Now ask the pain-creature what you can do to get rid of it. Listen carefully to what it has to tell you.

5. Open your eyes and start to follow its advice. Notice whether or not your pain is reduced.

6. Congratulate yourself for helping to relieve your pain and resume your usual activities.

Visualizing the Pain

Another pain-reduction method involves imagining what your pain looks like. This, like the first visualization, reinforces your belief that you can control your body processes.

1. Prepare yourself by using the relaxation process described in Chapter 11.

2. Focus on the pain. What color is it? See its color and shape and size clearly. It may be a bright red ball. It may be the size of a tennis ball or a grapefruit or a basketball.

3. Mentally project the ball out into space, maybe ten feet away from your body.

4. Make the ball bigger, about the size of a basketball. Then shrink it to the size of a pea. Now let it become whatever size it chooses to be. Usually it returns to the original size you visualized.

5. Begin to change the ball's color. Make it pink, then light green.

6. Now take the green ball and put it back where you originally saw it. At this point, notice whether or not your pain has been reduced.

7. As you open your eyes, you are now ready to resume your usual activities.

SUBSTITUTING PLEASURE FOR PAIN

A number of our patients have discovered perhaps the most satisfying approach—substituting pleasure for pain. By engaging in some pleasurable or gratifying activity when they are suffering from pain, they have found they could alleviate or even eliminate the distress.

For instance, Tim, a young plastic surgeon with Hodgkin's disease, was in such intense pain that he had difficulty walking. During a group session held at a retreat, we suggested that Tim go fishing. Although the fishing hole was about a half-mile walk and Tim was not sure he could make it, he did so with the help of another patient.

Once there, he also had to be helped to prepare his line, but as soon as he threw in his hook, Tim caught a trout. His pain immediately diminished. The two men fished for about forty-five minutes, and during that time Tim experienced no pain. Moreover, he was so eager to get back and show the fish to the others that he walked back easily.

As a physician, Tim was aware that such things happened, but he hadn't acknowledged that they could happen to him. The next day, we suggested a game of tennis, knowing that Tim had been an excellent player but had not played in the two years since his diagnosis. We hit the ball so that he could return it without having to move around much. After about thirty minutes, Tim quit at a comfortable level of fatigue, and told us that during the game he had experienced no pain. To his further surprise, he remained nearly pain-free for two days.

Tim's experience of substantially reduced pain following pleasurable exercise may be a function not only of his being involved in an enjoyable activity but also of getting the exercise he had been denying himself because of the pain. The interrelationship of mind, body, and emotions works so that improved physical state contributes to improved physical state, and so on.

Obviously, we cannot promise that if you rush out and engage in intense physical activity your pain will go away. But we have observed many times that patients withdraw from pleasurable activity when they are in pain. At times, they almost seem to punish themselves for having pain by avoiding even those activities that they can handle. Our experience has shown that participation in gratifying activities is rewarded by a reduction in pain.

If, however, you still find your pain persists, the same approaches that we use to treat cancer in general apply to treating pain. Understand the emotional components of your pain, examine the possible underlying reasons for it and then give yourself permission to act in emotionally satisfying ways without using pain as a justification. Then, once you reassert your control over your body's processes and reinforce your positive expectancy for recovery, chances are good that your pain will disappear.

17

Exercise

We began to think seriously about including exercise in our treatment program after meeting Dr. Jack Scaff in 1976, a prominent cardiologist who uses exercise as a major element in treating heart patients. Scaff's vigorous exercise program was one that physicians ten years ago thought would kill rather than help a heart patient. As we discussed the potential such a program might hold for cancer patients, we realized that a significant number of our most successfully treated patients had maintained a program of vigorous physical exercise after their diagnosis, and they all had slim, wiry builds.

After making these preliminary observations, we began to research the medical literature to seek out the reasons that vigorous exercise might have great advantages in assisting the recovery of heart and cancer patients. One of the first observations we came upon was that the rates of heart disease and cancer have both paralleled the degree of industrialization in a society. The incidences of heart disease and cancer have both increased dramatically as life has become more affluent (allowing the population to overeat), more sedentary (decreasing the amount of physical exertion)—and much more stressful.

We found that as early as 1911, James Ewing, one of the early great names in cancer research, observed that cancer was much more likely to occur in the "well-to-do and indolent" than in the "poor and overworked." Ewing believed that a lack of exercise in the higher socioeconomic classes was a factor. In 1921 when I. Silvertsen and A. W. Dahlstrom analyzed the case histories of 86,000 deaths, they discovered that death rates from cancer were highest among those having occupations involving the least muscular effort, and lowest among those having occupations involving the greatest muscular effort. Observing that cancer seemed to be a product of the Machine Age, these researchers pointed out that relatively "uncivilized" societies were also relatively cancer free.

Animal studies supported this idea. In 1938, Silvertsen found that the incidence of cancer in a strain of cancer-prone mice was reduced to 16 percent by a program of restricted caloric intake and daily exercise. Mice in the control group, which had unrestricted diets and little exercise, had a cancer rate of 88 percent. Other studies such as those by H. P. Rusch and B. E. Kline similarly showed decreased tumor growth in laboratory animals that were exercised.

In one ingenious study reported in 1960, S. Hoffman and K. Paschkis took an extract from fatigued (exercised) muscle tissues of mice and injected it into mice in which they had also transplanted cancerous cells. They discovered that the muscle tissue extract led to decreased tumor growth and, in a few cases, to disappearance of malignancy. An injection of extract from nonfatigued muscle had no effect.

The work of Dr. Hans Selye and other stress researchers suggests that the correspondence between exercise and reduced incidence of cancer may be related to the appropriate channeling of stress. A number of animal studies have shown that when animals are stressed again and again and not permitted a physical outlet for releasing the stress, there is a steady deterioration of their bodies. But if animals are stressed and then allowed to physically act, the amount of damage is minimal.

These findings, coupled with the information from other animal experiments that vigorous exercise tends to stimulate the immune system, indicate that regular physical exercise is one of the best tools for appropriately channeling the physiological effects of stress, and may also stimulate the body's natural defenses to do battle with malignancy.

Exercise has more than physical benefits; it can produce significant psychological changes as well. Several studies have observed that people on regular exercise programs (specifically, a combination of walking and jogging) tend to be more flexible in their thinking and beliefs, they tend to have an increased sense of self-sufficiency, a strengthened self-concept, improved self-acceptance, less tendency to blame others, and less depression. The overall picture is that people engaged in regular exercise programs tend to develop a healthier psychological profile in general—one often identified with a favorable prognosis for the course of the malignancy.

This information is particularly important to us for, as we have seen, mental depression is one of the most significant emotional issues affecting malignancy, both before and after diagnosis. Since recent studies have also found a correlation between depression and impaired functioning of the immune system, exercise as one of the most effective ways of reversing depression becomes a potent factor in getting well again.

In addition, the changes in our patients' psychological profiles that we have come to recognize as positive indicators of the probability that they will outlive their predicted life expectancies are highly similar to the psychological changes researchers have seen occurring in people who exercise on a regular basis. In fact, those of our patients who have far outlived their predicted life expectancies underwent just such psychological changes in our treatment program.

Regular exercise contributes to positive personality changes in other important ways. Setting aside the time for regular exercise requires taking firm control of your daily schedule. Taking charge of your schedule will give you the feeling of being in charge of your life. This assertive attitude helps create the emotional climate conducive to recovering from your disease.

Finally, exercise teaches you to pay attention to your body's needs. The feeling of vitality and health that you get from regular exercise helps you see your body as a friend, a source of pleasure, something deserving of your care and attention. Asserting your needs through a program of regular exercise is a way of saying that you are important.

If exercise can help bring about physical changes in your immune system and the psychological attitude that contributes to your quality of life and possibly even to your recovery, then establishing a regular program of exercise will be well worth the effort.

To our knowledge, exercise has not previously been included in a cancer therapy regimen. While some specialists might consider it inadvisable for patients with cancer that has spread to the bone, for those with low platelet counts (the mechanism that assists in blood clotting), or for those with other limiting conditions, we believe that most patients, even those with these special conditions, can maintain an exercise program. Our primary caution is that they should proceed at a slower pace, recognizing that it is possible to injure themselves, and carefully observe any warning signals of pain or stiffness.

OUR EXERCISE PRESCRIPTION: ONE HOUR, THREE TIMES WEEKLY

The exercise program we have devised is based on the one determined to be effective for heart patients. We ask all patients to begin a program consisting of *one hour of exercise three times a week*. Please note that the one-hour time frame is important. Studies suggest that shorter exercise periods do not produce beneficial effects as consistently.

If you are bedridden and hardly able to move, we suggest you use the mental imagery process to visualize yourself engaging in physical exercise. This begins to build the expectancy of greater physical ease and establishes a commitment to recognizing the needs of your body. If you are able to move your arms and legs, we suggest you exercise in bed. And if you are able to walk around your room or home, we encourage you to take that walk.

Let's take the example of a person with leukemia who is currently in the hospital undergoing chemotherapy, has a significant amount of pain requiring narcotics, and is receiving intravenous feeding. Generally, this person's only activity is to go to the bathroom with help. The first step for this patient in beginning an exercise program is to decide when the exercise periods will be. It is important that the exercise hour be at a time when there are few interruptions—let's say from three to four o'clock in the afternoon when the nurses are changing shifts.

This person could begin exercising by moving his hands and feet around in the bed as much as possible without causing severe pain (even the fingers and wrist of the arm with the intravenous tubes in place are probably sufficiently free to be moved) and raise his head up off the pillow and down again for about four to five minutes. Next, the patient could use mental imagery to picture himself doing a favorite activity—playing tennis, swimming, walking at a pleasant pace through the woods. Whatever the activity, the important thing is that it be physically taxing and enjoyable. Picture doing the activity for five to ten minutes, then repeat the physical exercise for another four to five minutes, moving legs, arms, head, and so on. Again, picture a favorite activity for five to ten minutes.

By repeating the combination of physical activity (five minutes) and visualization (ten minutes) four times, and then calling the nurse and going to the bathroom (if only for the exercise), the patient has completed the equivalent of one hour of exercise. He should repeat this program three times a week, until he no longer needs the intravenous tubes—at which point he can increase the amount of physical activity.

When the patient is released from the hospital, he already has a regular schedule of one hour of exercise three times weekly to fill with appropriate activities. The idea is to work toward a program of walking for a full hour then a combination of walking and running. This program will need to be adjusted according to the person's physical condition at various times.

If you are fully ambulatory but not used to exercising and wonder how to begin, the research discussed earlier suggests that a combination of walking and jogging for one hour, three times weekly, is probably the best form of all-around exercise. However, more important than the form of exercise is its regularity. And if you are enthusiastic about the exercise you choose, you are more likely to do it regularly. So if you enjoy swimming and tennis, and are physically able to manage them, we suggest you do so—remaining within the limits of "safe" activity.

The best criterion we have found for "safe" activity is one employed with cardiac patients; the upper limit of physical exertion we use is when the pulse rate is 24 to 26 beats per ten seconds, which is 144 to 156 beats per minute. Since it is hard for most people to determine their pulse rates, particularly while exercising, we have established a rule of thumb: *exercise is safe so long as you are able to maintain a conversation,* even if somewhat halting, while exercising.

Anytime you become sufficiently winded, whether exercising in bed, walking, or running, so that you cannot maintain a conversation, you should reduce your level of activity. If you are running, slow down or walk; if walking, stand or sit down. Since the ability to carry on a conversation will usually cease before you reach the pulse rate of 26 beats per ten seconds, the rule will keep you within the safety limits.

We are convinced that this exercise program can contribute to both your physical and your mental health. But we want to state clearly that *you* are responsible for protecting yourself from injury or overexertion. If you pay attention to the criterion for safe activity, there is no reason you need injure or overexert yourself. We ask you to accept responsibility for your own behavior so that you exercise in a reasonable manner. We ask all our patients to accept responsibility for their exercise programs, and they rarely injure themselves.

Our experience with this program has shown us that cancer patients are capable of far more physical activity than most people usually assume. For example, recall the case of Tim. Exercise, which he had denied himself for two years, improved his health and helped relieve his pain. One of our patients with extensive bony metastases completed a minimarathom (6.4 miles), while another with an inoperable pelvic cancer recently completed a half-marathon run (13 miles). Still another who is both a patient and consulting staff psychologist recently completed a 26-mile marathon with us. He has had lung metastases from a cancer of the kidney for four years, yet he had no breathing problems in the race. As a matter of fact, he went out to dinner the evening after the race while we went to bed. To our knowledge, it is the first time anyone with advanced cancer has completed a marathon.

Perhaps the most convincing observation that we have made is that over half the patients in our research population—all of whom have been declared medically incurable—remain 100 percent active, as active as they were before the original diagnosis of cancer. When the quality of life improves so do people's commitments to living and beliefs that they can recover. Although no single component of our program can be singled out as the cause of this improved quality of life, a regular exercise program is unquestionably part of it.

While we strongly believe in the benefits of regular exercise, we are not comfortable in suggesting dietary guidelines for cancer patients. The research on diet and cancer is highly confusing and contradictory, although it does show a consistent correlation between decreased caloric intake in laboratory animals and decreased incidence of malignancy, as well as a slower course of tumor growth. But this research has been done under laboratory conditions with animals, not with humans.

As a result, all we can advise in relation to nutrition is a gradually decreased caloric intake for patients who are overweight—until they reach their proper weight. In addition, we suggest they avoid excessive use of alcohol.

Our experience has shown us that there is a great deal to be gained from regular physical exercise, so we urge you to begin a program now, regardless of your physical condition. The psychological and physical benefits can be immediate.

18

Coping with the Fears
of
Recurrence and Death

Virtually all of our patients in the research project at the treatment center in Fort Worth have been diagnosed as medically incurable, with a prognosis that indicates that they can expect to live only one more year. Although most of those taking part in our program have outlived their life expectancy and many now show no signs of disease, the possibility of a recurrence and the likelihood of death are ever-present for them.

All cancer patients fear the possibility of a recurrence—and indeed it is not unusual for a patient to begin treatment, improve significantly, and then experience a flare-up. For patients using our approach to treatment, however, it seems particularly distressing for it tends to cast doubt on the effectiveness of the treatment and on their ability to make the psychological changes necessary to maintain health. To cope with this situation, we have learned to balance our patients' hopes of recovery with an open discussion of how to deal with their fears of recurrence and death. It is important for patients to understand that the psychological change that makes recovery possible is not usually a straight uphill course but a dynamic process with ups and downs along the way.

In addition, all change takes time, but there are as yet no

scientific data on the precise time lag between psychological change and the resultant physiological change that could lead to recovery. Therefore, patients should recognize that each change in their health—whether positive or negative—in the months ahead is valuable feedback from their bodies and contains information that can help direct their path toward the ultimate goal of recovery.

RECURRENCE: THE BODY'S FEEDBACK

Being prepared for a recurrence is one of the best ways to reduce the fear surrounding it. When our patients first come to us, we explore together their worst fears about a recurrence and develop a strategy to deal with it, should it happen. We describe to them what typically happens when patients are told their disease has recurred. Usually the news is followed with a period of confusion and emotional turmoil, a sense that "the bottom has dropped out." Many have described this period as a roller coaster experience that lasts anywhere from one to four weeks, depending on the amount of emotional support a patient has. During this time there may be a reevaluation or change of medical treatment. We encourage patients not to expect a lot of themselves at this point. They need their energy just to hang on.

We ask patients to remember two points. First, they must reach out to everyone in their support system—family, friends, the health-care team—for love, understanding, and acceptance of their mood swings. Their energy to fight the despair they may feel will come from this support. Second, they should not make any major decisions about what they think the eventual outcome of their disease will be. If patients decide that the future is going to be as painful as the present, they may give up emotionally, which can further hasten their physical decline. During a recurrence, we ask them to remember that this is a frightening and painful but *temporary* period. The shock and confusion will pass. When it has, they can begin to make a calm evaluation of what has occurred and what the future holds.

As soon as patients indicate that this difficult period is over and that they have the energy and perspective to examine the meaning of their recurrence, we begin our exploration together. We view the recurrence not as failure but as a physiological message from the body that has meaningful psychological implications. Some of the possible messages are:

1. Patients may have unconsciously surrendered to the emotional conflicts they face. The recurrence transmits the message that they need the help of a therapist either to resolve the conflicts or find better ways of coping with them.

2. Patients may not yet have found ways of giving themselves permission to meet their emotional needs except through illness. Carefully reviewing the "benefits" of illness to ascertain whether they can find other ways to meet their needs may be helpful at this time.

3. Patients may be trying to make too many changes in their lives too fast—in itself a physical stress. Their bodies tell them to slow down and not drive themselves so hard.

4. Patients may have made important changes but have since slacked off and become complacent. Many patients have described the difficulty of maintaining the unstressing activities once the immediate threat of their illness has passed. That is certainly understandable. People tend to respond quickly only to immediate needs, and a new regimen can become a habit only with disciplined practice.

5. Patients may not be taking care of themselves emotionally; their behavior may be self-destructive. Their bodies remind them to put a priority on their own needs and health.

This list is only a partial one, of course. A therapist can be very helpful in discovering what message a recurrence holds, but patients must actively explore their own minds to understand the meaning of the message.

Consulting your Inner Guide, as described in Chapter 15, can be very useful during this process. We encourage patients to call up the image of their guide at least once a day in their visual imagery process and ask it, "What is the meaning of my recurrence? What message does it hold for me?"

Another valuable exercise is for patients to examine the period of time just prior to the recurrence. What events or changes were going on then, what behaviors or activities were they engaging in that were different? Again, the objectivity of friends, family, or therapist can be of great assistance in this exploration. These procedures for exploring the meaning of any flare-up or recurrence of cancer often turn up valuable information that has positive results in patients' overall efforts to regain their health. This can also be a time for patients to reevaluate their efforts to regain their health and decide whether or not to change direction.

DEATH: A REDECISION

Possibly the most emotion-laden, fearsome, difficult fact of life to face is death. It is so awesome that the subject of death is a virtual taboo in our society. The failure to discuss—even to acknowledge—death gives rise to its fearful hold over us and uncertainty in our approach to it. As we have mentioned before, most cancer patients are less afraid of the fact of death than of its quality. They fear a lingering death that will drain family and friends emotionally and financially. They dread the prospect of months in a hospital, away from loved ones, leading a lonely, painful, and empty life. Their families often try to avoid the subject of death entirely. When the patient tries to discuss the possibility of dying, the most frequent response is, "Don't talk like that! You're not going to die!" Because patients cannot talk about death even with those who matter the most to them, their fears are unrelieved and may continue to grow. (In the next chapter, we will discuss the importance of communicating openly about death.)

Despite everyone's reluctance to discuss it, Dr. Elizabeth Kubler-Ross, one of the foremost authorities on death and dying, has observed that both adults and children instinctively know when their death is imminent. She has also stated (and we have seen it in our own experience) that frequently people will not let themselves die, lingering on because a loved one or even their medical team cannot accept their dying. These people bear the double burden of knowing they are dying and having to keep up a front for others.

In the early phase of our work, several experiences that were painful both for us and for our patients made us reexamine our view of death, and taught us the necessity of specifying to our patients their right to take charge of their death as well as their life.

Some of our early patients felt we had given them the key to certain recovery and thought, "Yes! I can do it!"—and then, as we discovered later, felt guilty if they failed to recover. These patients would come to Fort Worth approximately three to four times a year for one-week sessions and then return home. Between sessions they would keep in contact with us by phone, and occasionally we visited them in their homes on one of our trips around the country. Suddenly all communication would cease for several weeks, and later their families would inform us that they had died.

Because of our involvement with these patients, we were bewildered and hurt at our exclusion from their final days. Eventually, their families brought us these last words: "Tell Carl and Stephanie that the method still works," or "Tell them it isn't their fault." Finally, we understood. Our patients had felt that our assistance in their efforts to regain their health obliged them to stay alive to prove the value of our program. Dying meant that they had failed themselves and us. With time we recognized that since patients could direct the course of their recovery, we also had to admit that they could—and should—direct the course of their dying, if that was the direction in which they wished to move.

Opening a Discussion of Death

Now, as part of our program, we seek to free patients from such guilts and help them to confront their fears and beliefs about death. A square look at the possibility relieves patients of a great deal of anxiety and seems to reduce the physical pain of dying. In fact, it is now rare for our patients to suffer a lingering or painful death. Many are very active up to a week or two before their death, and they often die at home with loved ones or at the hospital following a stay of less than a week. We attribute this improved quality of dying to the ability to face fears with honesty and understanding and to acknowledge when one is dying.

We introduce the topics of recurrence and death to our patients at the center in a group discussion during the first week of each treatment session. We bring up the possibility that sometime in the future they may come to a decision that it is time for them to move toward death, and we ask that they tell us of such a decision. We assure them that we will be as supportive and caring through their dying as through their struggle to regain their health. They have the right to give up the struggle and let go of life.

We point out one important thing to our patients: Whether or not they recover from the cancer, they have succeeded in improving the quality of their living—or the quality of their dying—and have exercised great strength and courage.

OUR PATIENTS' EXPERIENCES

The following case histories show the range of experiences our patients have had in dealing with death.

Frederick

Frederick whom we spoke of in Chapter 16, was extremely close to death when we began working together. He was very cooperative and showed significant emotional improvement during his initial week at the center. By the end of the week, however, it was clear that many issues remained unresolved, and we anticipated that Frederick might face stormy physical and psychological weather at home.

His first call to us came forty-eight hours after he had arrived home, and he continued to call every two days. He was feeling intense anxiety and depression and his physical condition was steadily deteriorating. Our fourth conversation with him after he had been at home for approximately ten days found him quite weak and close to death. He was not eating and was emotionally distraught and exhausted. He had been making great psychological demands on himself and he was going rapidly downhill, so we advised him to stop fighting, to put himself into neutral, and see what would happen. We recognized, of course, that by easing the struggle he might accelerate his movement toward death, but he was already headed very rapidly in that direction.

During the next three days Frederick was semiconscious and slept almost continuously. He later told us that during this time he knew he was very close to death, yet he felt more calm than he had before. In his semiconscious state, Frederick had what he described as a dreamlike experience in which he had to make a conscious choice to live or die. In this dreamlike state he made the decision to live, and as he did so he regained consciousness, turned to his wife, and spoke to her clearly for the first time in three days. He asked her to turn on the tape recording of the relaxation/mental imagery process and began once again to practice the technique. The following day he was a bit stronger and began to eat. We continued to communicate regularly as he became more active, going to church and swimming in the family pool.

Just four months after approaching the point of death, Frederick resumed his medical practice. Several weeks later, however, he received an upsetting telephone call about the cancellation of his disability insurance. This call and the anxiety it provoked seemed to trigger the recurrence of his cancer. His health rapidly deteriorated, his malignancy recurred, and shortly thereafter he died.

Kim

Kim was a woman in her late thirties with breast cancer and widespread metastases. She had been very open to doing important emotional work with us, and her health had gone along well for about a year. Suddenly she had a recurrence of her malignancy. She returned to our office on a regular follow-up visit and again addressed the psychological issues related to her illness.

On her return home this time she was unable to muster up energy to engage in the activities she felt would be helpful to her health. The weather was extremely cold and stormy, making it very difficult for her to get out of the house to exercise. She lost contact with most of her friends. As her disease continued to grow, so did her frustration. She telephoned us one day to say that she was extremely discouraged. She had forgotten what it felt like to *be* well, so how could she maintain the hope that she could *get* well? We suggested to Kim, as we had to Frederick, that perhaps it was time for her to stop the struggle and put herself in neutral. She told us that our suggestion was a source of relief.

During the phone conversation, we had also openly discussed the possibility that she might die if she stopped fighting. The day following the telephone conversation was a rather full one. She did her routine housework, fixed dinner, and ate with her family. After dinner she told her family she had a headache and was going upstairs to bed. One of the family checked on her later and found that she had died quietly in her sleep.

Celeste

Celeste is a thirty-two-year-old woman who presents one of the most involved examples of our experience with the death process. We have been working with Celeste for two-and-one-half years, ever since she was diagnosed as having an advanced leiomyosarcoma. Celeste's time with us has been punctuated with psychological ups and downs, with periods of remission and recurrence.

Approximately one year ago, she received the news that she had advanced lung metastases. Celeste contacted us, informed us that she was in great pain and was ready to move toward death. She stopped all efforts to alter the course of her disease and began to prepare herself to die. She lay in bed for several days taking painkillers while many of her friends came to say goodbye.

Then one day she became aware that the glorious picture she had painted of her death was not coming about. Instead, she was lying around in a semistupor, taking painkillers but still experiencing much pain, constipated, uncomfortable, and dopey. Suddenly Celeste was very much aware of not wanting her four-year-old son to watch her die in this condition. She recalls saying to herself, "Hell, this is not the way I want to die," whereupon she stopped all medication, got out of bed, began to resume her activities, and made plans for a one-week trip alone to Mexico. Within several days she was on the airplane, essentially free from pain.

Celeste returned home to enjoy relatively good health for four months. Then her disease flared up again. Shortly before the flare-up her father had suddenly died. The loss and the accompanying problems of settling his estate were very difficult for her to deal with. Shortly thereafter she received news that her mother had been diagnosed with cancer.

Recently Celeste telephoned to let us know that she was again ready to move toward death. She added that she still believed she could regain her health but hadn't the energy to do so. She thanked us for the work we had done with her and said that her emotional growth from our experience together now allowed her to die in peace. After we had exchanged our feelings and goodbyes, she concluded our conversation with, "But I want you to know I am still open to a razzle-dazzle miracle—I wouldn't be opposed to suddenly getting well again!"

GAINING A PERSPECTIVE ON LIFE AND DEATH

These three patients learned that they could struggle successfully to maintain life or cease the struggle and move toward death. The important point is that each of them confronted the possibility of death openly and seemed to decide when they were ready to die.

To help you formulate your ideas about death and dying, we have developed a mental imagery process (actually a "guided fantasy") that encourages you to gain a larger perspective on life and its ultimate consequence. The purpose is not to "rehearse" your death but rather to stimulate a "life review" that can point out important goals that you can still accomplish. The activity can help you decide to let your old attitudes, beliefs, and personality traits die off and can give birth to new beliefs, new feelings, and new ways of responding to life.

This mental imagery process is used in other psychotherapeutic settings than that of life-threatening illness. Even if you do not have cancer, we invite you to participate in the process. The exercise will help you clarify whether you believe that recurrence is synonymous with death, whether you have a particular image of how you will die, how you think your family and close friends will react to your death, and what you believe will happen to your consciousness when you die.

Because ideas about death involve religious beliefs for many people, we have tried to write the instructions for the mental imagery process in a way that neither imposes nor presupposes any particular faith. Translate our language into the framework of your own beliefs. As with the other mental imagery activities, it will be helpful for you to read the instructions slowly or prerecord them on a cassette.

1. Sit in a comfortable chair in a quiet room and begin the relaxation process to become more relaxed.

2. When you feel relaxed, picture your physician informing you that your cancer has recurred. (If you do not have cancer, imagine being told that you are dying.) Experience the feelings and thoughts you have in response to this information. Where do you

go? Whom do you talk to? What do you say? Take
your time to imagine the scene in detail.

3. Now see yourself moving toward death. Experience whatever physical deterioration takes place.
Bring into sharp focus all the details of the process
of dying. Be aware of what you will lose by dying.
Allow yourself several minutes to experience these
feelings and to explore them in detail.

4. See the people around you while you are on your
deathbed. Visualize how they will respond to losing
you. What are they saying, and feeling? Allow yourself ample time to see what is occurring. Imagine the
moment of your death.

5. Attend your own funeral or memorial service.
Who is there? What are they saying? What are people feeling? Again, allow yourself plenty of time.

6. See yourself dead. What happens to your consciousness? Let your consciousness go off to wherever you believe your consciousness goes after
death. Stay there quietly for a few moments and experience that.

7. Then let your consciousness go out into the universe until you are in the presence of whatever you
believe to be the source of the universe. While in
that presence, review your life in detail. Take your
time. What have you done that you are pleased
with? What would you have done differently? What
resentments did you have and do you still have?
(Note: Try to review your life and ask yourself
these questions no matter what you believe happens
to your consciousness after death.)

8. You now have the opportunity to come back to
earth in a new body and create a new plan for life.
Would you pick the same parents or find new parents? What qualities would they have? Would you
have any brothers and sisters? The same ones? What
would your life's work be? What is essential for you
to accomplish in your new life? What will be important to you in this new life? Think your new prospects over carefully.

9. Appreciate that the process of death and rebirth is continuous in your life. Every time you change your beliefs or feelings you go through a death-and-rebirth process. Now that you have experienced it in your mind's eye, you are conscious of this process of death and renewal in your life.

10. Now come back slowly and peacefully to the present and become fully alert.

IMPLICATIONS OF THE DEATH-AND-REBIRTH FANTASY

Although responses to this imagery process are, of course, very personal and different, we have observed some general reactions. One of the most frequent reactions patients report is that their fantasy of their own death was not nearly as difficult or painful as they had feared it would be. They often gain valuable insights into what they would say to their loved ones to ease the inevitable pain and sadness of loss. When they imagined their own funeral, they were reassured that their friends' and family's lives would continue after they were gone. They also formulated an idea of how they wanted their funeral to be conducted.

The life-review aspect of the fantasy is probably one of the most helpful for patients—as well as for others we have taken through the process—in clarifying the changes they would like to make in their lives. We point out to people that after going through the process and coming to important recognitions, they have time now to make the desired changes so that when they die, they will not feel the regrets and resentments they may just have imagined. And by fantasizing the kind of person they would be if given an opportunity to create a new life, they have actually decided how they want to be different. We encourage patients to explore ways to become that kind of person *now*—in *this* life.

Through this imagery activity we hope you will see that the pathway to health is really a process of rebirth. As you explore yourself and your participation in health, you are permitting the unconstructive old beliefs to die off and creating positive new attitudes and a new life—allowing yourself to become more the person you would like to be.

19

The Family Support System

At our treatment center in Fort Worth, we have made it a firm policy that all patients entering our program must be accompanied by a spouse or, if they are unmarried, widowed, or divorced, we encourage them to bring their closest family member. On occasion, we have also worked with patients' sons and daughters or brothers and sisters. There are two very important reasons for this policy. First, when patients are being asked to modify attitudes about their disease or to adopt programs of regular mental imagery or exercise, the support of spouse and family can determine the degree to which patients carry out these directions.

Second, and no less significant, spouses and family members frequently need as much support and guidance in coping with feelings as patients do. No experience is more certain to make you feel at times confused, inadequate, and lacking in compassion and understanding than watching someone you love go through a life-threatening disease. Yet this experience can also leave you feeling enriched and human in ways not normally experienced in everyday living. Some days you may feel a rare love and intimacy; other days you may feel an inarticulate frustration and rage.

ACCEPTING THE PATIENT'S FEELINGS— AND YOUR OWN

If there is one message we want to convey in this chapter, it is the necessity for accepting this kaleidoscope of feelings. This will be a time charged with emotion for you and your loved one, and many of these feelings may seem "unacceptable" or "inappropriate" to you. You may feel angry, you may find yourself wishing he or she were dead or imagining yourself running away from it all. The difficult lesson to learn is not to judge yourself for having these feelings. Instead, accept the fact that you are experiencing them and attempt to suspend judgment.

In the case of a life-threatening disease like cancer, there are no "appropriate" or "inappropriate," "mature" or "immature" feelings; there are only feelings. Thus it is futile to tell yourself what you "should" or "ought" to be feeling. The object is to discover how you can respond most beneficially for yourself and the person you love. And the first step is to accept your feelings and those of the patient and to understand that these emotions are necessary and right in coming to grips with the possibility of death.

Everyone is aware of the need to be understanding, tolerant, and accepting of the patient. Apply the same principle to yourself. Just as you can understand the fright, the terror, the hurt of your loved one, be aware of your own fright, terror, and hurt, and be understanding with yourself as well. No one ever faces the death of someone they love without also facing their own eventual death. Accept yourself and be gentle.

Individuals vary widely in how they deal with crises. The way you handle a diagnosis of cancer in your family is likely to be similar to the way you have dealt with crises in the past. This chapter is intended to offer support and some potential coping strategies for the families of cancer patients. It is not meant to create an unrealistic expectation of how a family "should" handle a loved one's diagnosis or to cause guilt over how a previous family illness might have been handled. It is highly unrealistic to expect yourself to learn entirely new coping styles in the face of great turmoil. What follows is meant to encourage families to accept and appreciate the difficulties they face and to offer some tools they may find helpful.

ESTABLISHING OPEN, EFFECTIVE, SUPPORTIVE COMMUNICATION

People diagnosed with cancer or other life-threatening disease go through great swings of mood. They experience fear, anger, self-pity, a sense of loss of control over their lives—and their emotional ups and downs usually frighten them. At first, the family is also likely to react with fear at such great fluctuations in their loved one's emotional state. You may find yourself wanting to avoid communication because it may be painful and confusing.

But even if the emotions are painful, it is important during the first weeks following the diagnosis of cancer to establish a basis for honest, open communication. The patient needs to be allowed—and encouraged—to express feelings. You and all members of the family must be prepared to listen, even though there may be a large part of you that doesn't want to. If the patient is denied the opportunity to discuss what is most troubling—fear, pain, death—he or she will feel isolated. When what really matters to you is precisely what you cannot discuss, then you are very lonely indeed.

One key to easing this time is to encourage open expression of feelings, listen without judging, and accept your feelings and the patient's as natural and necessary. Then try to interpret the real meaning of a request, and honor as much of the patient's needs as you can without losing your own integrity or sacrificing other members of the family in the process. There is no doubt that this will require unusual amounts of patience, sensitivity, and understanding on the part of the entire family, but knowledge of what to expect and some advice on how you might cope can help get all of you through the experience.

Encourage the Expression of Feelings

After hearing the cancer diagnosis, patients may cry a great deal. They are mourning the possibility of their own death and the loss of the feeling that they will live forever. They are mourning the loss of their health and their image to themselves as vital, powerful people. Grief is a normal sponse; the family must try to accept it. Holding in feelings and maintaining composure in the face of death does not define bravery. Bravery is being the human being you are, even when others would impose external standards on how you "should" behave.

The single, most important thing the family can offer is the willingness to go through this experience with their loved one. Unless the patient asks to be alone, stay with him or her; provide lots of physical touching, hugs, and closeness. Share feelings without thinking you have to change them.

So-called inappropriate feelings will change in time as your understanding or perception changes, but they will change far more quickly if you permit yourself and the patient to experience them than if either of you denies them. Denying feelings short-circuits the potential learning they offer, for feelings provide a base of experience from which new understanding can develop.

Moreover, nothing will ensure your continuing to have a feeling you might consider inappropriate more than trying to deny it. When your conscious mind denies a feeling, it goes underground and continues to affect your behavior in unconscious ways that you have little control over. You hang on to it. But as feelings are accepted, they are much more likely to change and be released.

Whatever you and your family feel is okay. Whatever the patient feels is okay. If you find yourself trying to change how others feel, stop yourself. It will lead to pain and blocked communication. Nothing can hurt a relationship more than for people to feel they cannot be themselves.

Listen and Respond While Maintaining
Your Own Integrity

When your loved one is emotionally distraught, you may want desperately to do something, almost anything, to help. When this happens, the best course is to ask the patient, "Is there anything you would like me to do?" Then listen carefully. This is a time for a great deal of potential misunderstanding, so try to hear the real meaning of the patient's request.

If the patient is feeling self-pity, he or she may say something like "Oh, just leave me alone; everything that could possibly happen to me has already happened!" Since this is a confusing message, you might repeat what you think you understand—"You'd like me to leave you alone?" or "I'm not sure whether you want me to stay or go"—to be certain you have the message right, and so that the patient knows how you understood the request.

At other times, you will receive some requests that are not possible to fulfill, or you might get an explosion of bottled-up feelings. In response to your question, "Is there anything you would like me to do?" you might get a reply such as, "Yes, you can take on this damned disease so I can have a normal life like you!" Such a response leaves you feeling hurt and angry. You believe you have made a gesture of love and understanding, only to be lashed out at. Your tendency might be either to strike back in anger or to withdraw.

Withdrawal is the most destructive response of all. If you withhold your own hurt and pain, you'll almost inevitably begin to withdraw emotionally from the relationship, which will produce even more hurt and pain. Even a forced response, keeping communication open, will be better for both of you in the long run. For example, try the following response: "I'm aware that you must be feeling a lot of frustration and anger, emotions that I can't begin to anticipate. But I really feel hurt when it comes out that way." This response communicates acceptance for your loved one's feelings as well as honesty about your own.

It is important that you strive to maintain your own integrity. If you offer to help and receive unreasonable requests, then you will have to communicate your limits: "I want to help, but I'm not able to do what you ask. Is there any other way I can help?" This keeps communication open and indicates your continued love and caring, but still defines limits to what you are able and willing to do.

Another problem that may arise is a request that would require sacrificing the needs of other members of your family. This problem, too, can often be solved through careful communication, until both parties are clear about the implications of the request.

Take the following conversation as an example. A grown son is visiting his father in a hospital 300 miles from home:

> **Son:** Dad, is there anything I can do to help?
> **Father:** Yes, if you would come and visit me more often that would help a whole lot. I feel so much better when you're here.

The son may want to honor this request, yet he also recognizes the strain on himself of the long drive and the strain on his family of his frequent absences. In addition, in nearly every parent-child relationship unresolved feelings of guilt or hurt complicate a clear resolution of the issue. The next step in this case is for the son to share his dilemma with his father:

> **Son:** Dad, I'm pleased that my coming is important to you, and I'm glad you feel better when I'm here. I'd like to know how often you want me to come back. I want to visit you, but it causes some hardship on my family, and I'm trying to balance those out.
>
> **Father:** Oh, I don't want to be too much trouble to you. You just go about your life and forget about me. I'm an old man and probably won't live much longer anyway.

At this point it would be easy for the son to get diverted from the central issue and either try to reassure his father that he is indeed loved or get angry at this apparent effort to manipulate him and make him feel guilty. His getting involved in either issue would prevent resolution of the basic dilemma. The son should stay with the essential question:

> **Son:** *(Gently)* Dad, you asked if I would visit you, and I'd really like to do that. But it would help me a lot if you could tell me how often you'd like me to come.
>
> **Father:** Oh, well, however often you can. You know how often you can.

The conversation could end here, with neither person feeling satisfied. Instead, it is important for the son to go back to the central issue:

> **Son:** *(Firmly, but gently)* Dad, how often do you want me to come and visit? It's important that I know. It does take some effort to get out here to visit you, so I want to feel good about any commitment I make. It would really help me if you would tell me how often you want me to visit.
>
> **Father:** Well, I'd like to see you every chance you

get. I'd like to see you every weekend. I know
you're awfully busy, and maybe just once a month
. . . I'm not sure . . . I guess if you'd come to see
me once a month that'd be better than nothing.

Son: It is a long trip, so I don't think I can comfort-
ably make it every weekend. But I would like to see
you more than once a month. Why don't we plan on
every other weekend? I think that's reasonable while
you're as sick as you are. We can check again in a
month. I expect you'll be much better by then. But
for the next month I'll be here every other weekend.

Father: Well, O.K. I don't want to be a burden on
you. I hate being sick and putting you out.

Again, the conversation could end here, though it would
still leave things a bit unresolved. But it is clear now that
some of the father's querulousness and self-pity comes from
the difficulty accepting his weakness and poor health. Still, he
continues to need some reassurance that he is loved. The best
reply for the son might be:

Son: Dad, I'm sure it's tough being sick like this,
but I just want you to know that I love you and
want to be with you. It's very important for me and
my family to be around you during this illness. It
may be an inconvenience, but that's what families
are for. I just want you to know that I love you and
want you to get well.

The conversation ends with both people feeling good,
with no loose ends of guilt or misunderstanding.

Open and supportive communication requires sensitivity
to what you say and hear. The suggestions that follow may
help you to help your loved one.

As best you can, try to avoid phrases that deny or reject
the patient's feelings, such as, "Don't be silly, you're not going
to die," or "You've just got to stop thinking like that," or
"You've got to stop feeling sorry for yourself." Remember that
you do not have to do anything about the patient's feelings
except listen to them. You do not need to understand them or
to change them. If you try to change them, you'll only make
your loved one feel worse because you'll communicate the
idea that his or her present feelings are unacceptable.

You do not have to find solutions for the patient's problems, to "rescue" your loved one from depressing feelings. Simply let him or her express such feelings. You do not have to provide therapy, since your efforts will probably communicate lack of acceptance and the message that the feelings ought to be different from what they are. The best you have to offer is acceptance and acknowledgment of what your loved one is feeling. If you can, briefly summarize your interpretation of his or her feelings, such as, "You're upset with the way this whole thing came about," or "It just doesn't seem fair." Even a nod or saying, "I understand," may be better than saying things that could imply nonacceptance.

Ask yourself whether you are doing more talking than listening or whether you are finishing the patient's sentences. In either case, consider whether your own anxieties are speaking and whether it might be more helpful to let the patient lead the conversation.

If you talk less, you may encounter long periods of silence. There is a great deal of introspection necessarily going on during this time, so it is perfectly natural that both you and the patient will be deep in thought at times; it does not mean a rejection of each other. The silence may even serve to encourage a normally withdrawn person to begin to share long pent-up feelings.

If you are not used to allowing periods of silence in your conversation—and most of us feel obliged to fill any pauses in a conversation—you may find them anxiety-producing. Try to become comfortable with the silences. Two people who are at ease with such pauses may come to value their conversation all the more because they don't feel they have to talk except when they really have something to say. A way to handle your anxiety is to talk about it. Discuss how you feel about the silence, then listen closely for his or her response.

Be aware that many of your feelings may be very different from those of your loved one. You may be trying to cope with the pragmatic fact of holding daily living together, while the patient may be engrossed in fears of dying and reviewing the meaning of his life. At some point, you may think you have begun to understand the other's feelings, only to find that his mood has swung radically to one that is again incomprehensible to you. This stands to reason: you are having two very different experiences, and you will naturally have different responses to them.

In many families, it has become virtually a test of love and loyalty that everybody have the same reactions to experiences. Wives tend to feel their husbands growing away from them, or children may be seen as rebellious, if they have substantially different reactions to an experience. The requirement that everybody have the same "acceptable" feelings is a drain on a relationship at any time, but it raises a nearly insurmountable barrier to communication during this period of great emotional swings. Try to allow for differences.

SUPPORTING THE PATIENT'S RESPONSIBILITY AND PARTICIPATION

Every family of a cancer patient feels both the desire and the responsibility to be as supportive and caring as possible. At the same time, it is essential that family members attend to their own needs while allowing the patient responsibility for his own health. As you well know by now, our treatment is based on the premise that every patient can actively participate in his own recovery. Therefore, it is essential the patient be treated as a responsible person, not an irresponsible child or a victim.

Be Supportive without "Babying" the Patient

How supportive should you be with a loved one who has cancer? The best approach is to be supportive without "babying." The babying response is made from the position of a parent talking to an irresponsible child: the parent does not believe the child is capable of making a decision and may even mislead the child. The following is an example of using this approach in your relationship with a cancer patient:

> **Patient:** I'm afraid of that treatment. I really don't want it. I don't think it will help me.
> **Babying Reply:** Now, you know you've got to take it. It won't hurt you. It's good for you. And that's all we're going to hear about that.

The treatment may very well be painful, so a babying response misleads and diminishes the patient. It communicates that we don't believe the patient can deal with life as it is.

When either the patient, the spouse, or another family member is afraid, it is important that they communicate as one adult to another, realistically and openly acknowledging the potential risks and pain involved. An appropriate response to the fears of the patient above, then, might be as follows:

> **Supportive Reply:** I can understand your fear. The treatment scares me some, too. And I don't really understand all that's involved. But we're in this together, and I'll go through it with you and be as supportive as I know how to be. I think it's important that you have the treatment and that you expect it to do what we all hope it will do.

A supportive rather than babying stance is equally important with children who are cancer patients. Just because a child is sick does not mean he or she wants or needs to be treated like a baby. In addition, children are often able to cope more effectively with their feelings than are adults, because their feelings are closer to the surface, and they are less likely to judge themselves for what they feel. By not babying children, you are communicating recognition of their own resources. So, if a child is frightened when facing treatment, the communication might be as follows:

> **Supportive Reply:** Yes, it may hurt, and it is scary. But it's the kind of treatment that you need to get well, and I'll be with you through it all.

This last message, "I'll be with you," is essential. All the fine words and phrases are of less help than your being with your loved one, whatever the age.

Be Supportive without Trying to Rescue the Patient

A problem related to babying the cancer patient is being supportive without becoming a "rescuer." The so-called rescuer role, which people adopt unconsciously, is based on the theories of Dr. Eric Berne, the father of transactional analysis, and developed further by Dr. Claude Steiner in his books, *Games Alcoholics Play* and *Scripts People Live*. We are likely to assume this role when dealing with people who are weak, helpless, powerless, or unable to take charge of their lives. "Rescuing" may look as if you are helping someone, when in fact you are reinforcing weakness and powerlessness.

The families of cancer patients easily slip into the rescuer-role trap with their loved ones, because the patient often adopts the stance of victim, taking the position, "I am helpless and hopeless, try and help me." The rescuer's position is, "You're helpless and hopeless; nevertheless, I will try to help you." At other times, the rescuer may play the role of a persecutor, taking the position, "You are helpless and hopeless, and it's your fault."

Steiner has called such interactions "the Rescue Game." In the game, the participants can continue switching roles almost indefinitely. Anybody who knows how to play one of the roles also knows how to play the others. The problem is that, like most psychological games, this one is destructive. It exacts a heavy price from the victims, robbing them of the power to solve their own problems and keeping them in passive positions.

From our point of view, nothing could be more destructive of the patient's need to take charge of his own health. The interaction might begin with the victim's complaining about his or her pain, lack of energy, and inability to engage in normal activities. The rescuer is then likely to try to help, doing things for the victim, rescuing the victim from having to take care of himself. The rescuer may bring the patient food or drinks, even though the patient is perfectly capable of getting these for him- or herself. The rescuer may offer a steady stream of advice (which is usually rejected) and may perform unpleasant tasks without being asked to do so.

The rescuer may appear loving and caring, but actually contributes to incapacitating the patient both physically and psychologically. Eventually, the patient may get angry and resent having been manipulated. In addition, the rescuer, who has been denying his or her own needs while tending to the patient's, may begin to feel hostile toward the patient, and then feel guilty for being angry. Clearly, no one benefits from the interaction.

Instead, such interactions serve to isolate the patient. When someone who is in the position of power tries to protect the patient (and other family members) from having to deal with painful subjects—especially death—the result is a cutting off of the patient's channels of communication about the subjects most important for him—and for the family—to confront. Further, this tactic inhibits family members' abilities to express their feelings.

It is also damaging to try to protect the patient from other family problems, such as a child's difficulties in school. Taking the attitude that the patient "already has so many problems" isolates him or her from the family precisely at the time when it is most important for the patient to feel committed to and involved with life. Closeness comes from sharing feelings: the moment feelings are withheld, closeness begins to be lost.

The patient can also assume the rescuer role, most frequently by "protecting" family members by not expressing his or her fears and anxieties. In the process, the patient becomes increasingly isolated from the family. Rather than protecting, the patient is actually excluding the family and communicating a lack of trust in his or her loved ones. When people are "rescued" from their feelings, they don't have an opportunity to experience and resolve them. As a result, family members may continue to have unresolved feelings long after the patient has recovered or died.

Just as the family needs to avoid trying to rescue the patient from the joys and pains of everyday family life, patients need to avoid trying to rescue their families from painful feelings. In the long run, everybody's psychological health is improved when feelings are openly dealt with and resolved.

Helping, Rather Than Rescuing

It is easy to see how the Rescue Game could get started between a cancer patient and a spouse. All our cultural conditioning says that the way loving people should respond to illness is by taking over for the patients, doing everything for them, helping them to the point that they need do nothing. This gives patients no responsibility for their own well-being. The key is to be helpful instead of smothering. However, there is sometimes a fine line between the two. The critical element in helping is that it is something you *want* to do because it makes you feel good, not because of something you expect from the person you helped. Anytime you find yourself getting resentful or angry, you can be sure you did something with an expectation of how the other person should respond. And the habit may be deeply ingrained. In order to break it, you need to pay close attention to your feelings.

Steiner suggests three other clues that will help you identify rescuing behavior. You are rescuing if:

1. You do something for someone else that you don't want to do, without communicating that you don't like doing it.

2. You start out to help another person and find that he or she has left you with most of the task.

3. You are not consistently letting people know what *you* want. Of course, letting them know does not mean you will always *get* what you want, but you are preventing others from having reactions to your needs if you won't express your needs openly.

If you find yourself rescuing instead of helping, remember that patients' lives may depend upon their using their own resources.

REWARDING HEALTH, NOT ILLNESS

As essential as it is for patients to assert control over their lives in order to recover health, it is not unusual for spouses and friends to reward illness unconsciously. Families are often most loving, supportive, and caring when patients are weak and helpless; they begin to remove these rewards as soon as patients regain health.

It is imperative that spouses, family members, and friends encourage patients to do what they can for themselves and give them love, support, and affection for independence, not for weakness. If all the rewards come from being weak, patients have a stake in illness and less incentive for getting well.

Rewarding illness instead of health is most likely to occur when the family members consistently subordinate their own needs to the patients'. An atmosphere in which everyone's needs are important—not just the patients'—encourages patients to use their own resources to move toward health.

These suggestions will help you reward health:

1. **Encourage the patient's efforts to take care of himself or herself.** Many family members rush in and take over for patients, virtually denying them the opportunity to take care of themselves. Usually this is accompanied by such comments as, "You're sick, you shouldn't be up and around like that. Let me take care of it." This simply reinforces illness. Patients should be allowed to do things for themselves, and family members should comment on their loved one's strength: "I

think it's great the way you're taking care of yourself," or "We really enjoy it when you join us in family activities."

2. Comment when the patient looks better. People sometimes are so aware of illness that they fail to comment when the patient shows signs of improvement. Be sure to observe signs of improvement and let your loved one know how pleased you are.

3. Spend time with the patient in activities unrelated to illness. Sometimes it can seem—between visits to the doctor, treatments, obtaining medication, coping with physical limitations—there is nothing but illness-related activities. But to build an emphasis on life and health, it is important to take time to do pleasurable things together. Having cancer does not require that you stop enjoying yourself. Quite the contrary: the more enjoyable life is, the greater the investment the cancer patient has in staying alive.

4. Continue to spend time with the patient as he or she gets well. As mentioned, many families offer support and attention to the patients as long as they are sick and ignore them when they begin to get well. Since all of us like attention, this means we receive the reward of attention while we are sick, only to lose it when we get well. So be aware of offering continuing attention and support during the recovery.

To make sure you are rewarding health and avoiding rescuing, every member of your family must pay attention to his or her emotional needs. There is no question that this is difficult, and it certainly runs counter to the "selfless" role that society encourages as a response to illness. But if you give up your needs to meet someone else's, it ultimately breeds resentment and anger. You may not be aware, or not wish to acknowledge, that you are experiencing such feelings. In fact, a spouse will often harshly admonish children for complaining because they have to change their lives because of a parent's illness, but some of the harshness stems from avoiding one's own feelings of frustration and resentment.

Many families put the patient's needs first because they expect, perhaps unconsciously, that the patient will die. This expectation is heard in such a comment as, "These may be my last few months with her, so I want to be sure that everything is perfect." This attitude has two serious consequences: resentment and communicating the negative expectation. As we have said, the family eventually begins to resent the unnecessary self-sacrifice, and the patient resents the subtle demand for gratitude for his family's self-sacrifice. The family's ability to maintain more-or-less normal interests without fawning over the patient will reduce resentment on all sides.

Furthermore, the family's self-sacrifice communicates the belief that the patient will die. Putting off discussions or making long-range plans or avoiding references to the serious illness or death of an acquaintance also communicate the expectation of death. That which is avoided is usually that which is feared, so by omission, families express their expectancies. And because of the role expectations can play in the outcome of cancer or other diseases, the family's negative expectations severely undercut the patient's ability to maintain hope.

Thus, treating the patient as if you expect him or her to live is essential. The family need not believe the patient *will* recover; they need only believe that he or she *can* recover.

Other beliefs families may be communicating to patients, either overtly or subtly, involve their evaluation of treatment and the competence of the health care team. Again, since the patient's positive belief in the effectiveness of the treatment and trust in his or her physicians play an important role in recovery, you may need to reexamine your own expectancies and attempt to alter your beliefs so that they will be supportive. You are part of the patient's "support system," so it is important that you support health and recovery.

The ideal is for the family to have a positive belief both that the patient can get well and that the treatment is a strong, powerful ally. We realize that this is asking a great deal when the family, like the patient, has received all the societal programming that says cancer equals death. But your beliefs matter enormously.

MEETING THE DEMANDS OF LONG-TERM ILLNESS

The suggestions we have made—to establish clear, honest communication and to avoid putting aside everyone's needs but the patient's—are based on the realities of living with a cancer patient for many months or years. The price of less-than-open communication or of constantly trying to rescue the patient is to have to live your life playing a false role. It is a tremendous energy drain to try to act positive when you do not feel it. Dishonesty over the possibility of recurrence or death will create distance and awkwardness in your relationship.

Dishonesty will also be reflected in the physical health of the family members. The stress of dealing with a long-term and life-threatening disease can threaten your own health, unless you confront the problem openly. Certainly, there is pain in honesty, but in our experience it is minor compared with the pain of inevitable distance and isolation that occurs when people cannot be themselves.

The family may also find it difficult to provide all the emotional support the patient needs, due to the intensity of the relationship at this point and the fact that the family members have their own needs. However, there is no rule that limits warm and supportive relationships to just the immediate family, and many patients benefit by establishing friendships and forming attachments with people outside the family who can give them some of the recognition and support they need. The patient's effort to reach outside of the family should not be viewed as a sign that the family has failed. It is unreasonable to expect that family members can meet all the patient's emotional needs and still pay attention to their own.

Both patient and family members can benefit from periodic counseling to resolve difficulties or gain support in learning how to meet their needs in a situation that is potentially guilt-inducing for everyone. A number of oncology departments offer family counseling services as part of the treatment program. Also, an increasing number of psychologists, psychotherapists, and counselors are being trained in counseling cancer patients and their families, and most communities have qualified ministers and therapists.

Family counseling is often helpful for opening up communication and for providing a safe climate in which to face anxiety-producing issues. It can also help patients deal with some of the factors that may have contributed to their susceptibility to cancer in the first place.

The almost inevitable financial burden prolonged illness places upon a family is another difficult area that requires openness and honesty. Typically, the financial burden can make family members feel guilty about spending money to meet their own needs. Our social conditioning suggests that whatever available money is not already committed to necessities should be set aside for the patient's needs. Yet patients also feel guilty about spending money, since it is their illness that has placed the financial drain on their families in the first place.

All of these feelings become exaggerated if both patient and family come to believe that death is inevitable. The family will often push the patient to spend money, while the patient may feel the expenditures are being "wasted" on him and should go to family members "who still have a life ahead of them." Few families find it easy to balance everyone's financial needs. Doing so requires creative problem solving and open discussion.

LEARNING AND GROWING

Despite the very serious problems you are facing, if you are willing to confront openly and honestly the experience of dealing with the life-threatening disease of your loved one, the experience may contribute to your own personal growth. Many of our patients and their families have reported that the communication opened up during the illness led to greater closeness and depth in their relationships.

Another frequent consequence of facing the possible death of a loved one is coming to terms with your own feelings about death. Having faced death indirectly, you find it no longer holds the same terror.

We observed in earlier chapters that some patients who have faced cancer and have worked to influence the course of their disease develop a psychological strength greater than that they possessed before the illness—the feeling of being "weller than well." The same is true of their families. Those that face cancer with honesty and openness also can become "weller than well." Whether or not the patient recovers, the family can develop a psychological strength with which to live the rest of their lives.

Bibliography

References in **bold type** are of special interest to the layman.

Abse, Dr. W.; Wilkins, M. M.; Kirschner, G.; Weston, D. L.; Brown, R. S.; and Buxton, W. D. Self-frustration, night-time smoking, and lung cancer. *Psychosomatic Medicine*, 1972, *34*, 395.

Abse, D. W.; Wilkins, M. M.; VandeCastle, R. L.; Buxton, W. D.; Demars, J. P.; Brown, R. S.; and Kirschner, L. G. Personality and behavioral characteristics of lung cancer patients. *Journal of Psychosomatic Research*, 1974, *18*, 101–13.

Achterberg, J.; Simonton, O. C.; and Simonton, S. **Stress, Psychological Factors, and Cancer.** Fort Worth: New Medicine Press, 1976.

Ader, R., and Cohen, N. Behaviorally conditioned immunosuppression. *Psychosomatic Medicine*, 1975, *37*, 333–40.

Ahlborg, B. Leukocytes in blood during prolonged physical exercise. *Forsvarsmedicin*, 1967, *3*, 36.

Ahlborg, B., and Ahlborg, G. Exercise leukocytosis with and without beta-adrenergic blockage. *Acta Med. Scand.*, 1970, *187* 241–46.

Amkraut, A. A., and Solomon, G. F. Stress and murine sarcoma virus- (moloney-) induced tumors. *Cancer Research*, July 1972, *32*, 1428–33.

———. From the symbolic stimulus to the pathophysiological response: Immune mechanisms. *International Journal of Psychiatry in Medicine*, 1975, *5*(4), 541–63.

Amkraut, A. A.; Solomon, G. F.; Kasper P.; and Purdue, A. Stress and hormonal intervention in the graft-versus-host response. In B. P. Jankovic and K. Isakovic (Eds.), *Micro-environmental aspects of immunity*. New York: Plenum Publishing Corporation, 1973, 667–74.

Anand, B. K.; Ohhina, G. S.; and Singh, B. Some aspects of electro-encephalographic studies in Yogi. *Electroencephalography Clinical Neurophysiology*, 1964, *13*, 452–56.

Andervont, H. B. Influence of environment on mammary cancer in mice. *National Cancer Institute*, 1944, *4*, 579–81.

Aring, C. D. Breast cancer revisited. *JAMA*, 1975, *232*(7), 742–44.

Bacon, C. L., Rennecker, R.; and Cutler, M. A. psychosomatic survey of cancer of the breast. *Psychosomatic Medicine*, 1952, *14*, 453–60.

Bahnson, C. B. Basic epistemological considerations regarding psychosomatic processes and their application to current psychophysiological cancer research. Paper presented at the First International Congress of Higher Nervous Activity, Milan, 1968.

──────. Psychophysiological complementarity in malignancies: Past work and future vistas. Paper presented at the Second Conference on Psychophysiological Aspects of Cancer, New York, May 1968.

──────. Second conference on psychophysiological aspects of cancer. *Annals of the New York Academy of Sciences*, 1969, *164*, 307–634.

──────. The psychological aspects of cancer. Paper presented at the American Cancer Society's Thirteenth Science Writer's Seminar, 1971.

Bahnson, C. B., and Bahnson, M. B. Cancer as an alternative to psychosis: A theoretical model of somatic and psychologic regression. In D. M. Kissen and L. L. LeShan (Eds.), *Psychosomatic aspects of neoplastic disease*. Philadelphia: J. B. Lippincott Company, 1964, 184–202.

──────. Denial and repression of primitive impulses and of disturbing emotions in patients with malignant neoplasms. In D. M. Kissen, and L. L. LeShan (Eds.), *Psychosomatic aspects of neoplastic disease*. Philadelphia: J. B. Lippincott Company, 1964, 42–62.

──────. Role of ego defenses: Denial and repression in the etiology of malignant neoplasm. *Annals of the New York Academy of Sciences*, 1966, *125*, 827–45.

Bahnson, M. B., and Bahnson, C. B. Ego defenses in cancer patients. *Annals of the New York Academy of Sciences*, 1969, *164*, 546–99.

Balitsky, K. P.; Kapshuk, A. P.; and Tsapenko, V. F. Some electrophysiological peculiarities of the nervous system in malignant growth. *Annals of the New York Academy of Sciences*, 1969, *164*, 520–25.

Baltrusch, H. J. F. Results of clinical-psychosomatic cancer research. *Psychosomatic Medicine (Solothurn),* 1975, *5,* 175–208.

Bard, M., and Sutherland, A. M. Psychological impact of cancer and its treatment: IV. Adaptation to radical mastectomy. *Cancer,* July–August 1955, *8,* 656–72.

Barrios, A. A. Hypnotherapy: A reappraisal. *Psychotherapy: Theory, Research, and Practice,* 1970, *7*(1), 2–7.

Bathrop, R. W. Depressed lymphocyte function after bereavement. *Lancet,* April 16, 1977, 834–36.

Beary, J. F., and Benson, H. A simple psychophysiologic technique which elicits the hypometabolic changes of the relaxation response. *Psychosomatic Medicine,* March–April 1974, 115.

Beecher, H. K. The powerful placebo. *JAMA,* 1955, *159,* 1602–1606.

Behavioral factors associated with the etiology of physical disease. In C. B. Bahnson (Ed.), *American Journal of Public Health,* 1974, *64,* 1034–55.

Bennette, G. Psychic and cellular aspects of isolation and identity impairment in cancer: A dialectic of alienation. *Annals of the New York Academy of Sciences,* 1969, *164,* 352–64.

Benson, H. Your innate asset for combating stress. *Harvard Business Review,* 1974, *52,* 49–60.

————. *The relaxation response.* New York: William Morrow & Company, 1975.

Benson, H.; Beary, F.; and Carol, M. P. The relaxation response. *Psychiatry,* February 1974, 37.

Benson, H., and Epstein, M. D. The placebo effect: A neglected asset in the care of patients. *JAMA,* 1975, *12,* 1225–26.

Benson, H.; Rosner, B. A.; Marzetts, B. A.; and Klemchuk, H. Decreased blood pressure in pharmacologically treated hypertensive patients who regularly elicited the relaxation response. *The Lancet,* February 23, 1974, 289.

Bernard, C. *Experimental medicine.* 1865.

Bernard, C. [*An introduction to the study of experimental medicine*] (H. C. Green, trans.). New York: Dover, 1957.

Bittner, J. J. Differences observed in tumor incidence of albino strain of mice following change in diet. *American Journal of Cancer,* 1935, *25,* 791–96.

Blumberg, E. M. Results of psychological testing of cancer patients. In J. A. Gengerelli and F. J. Kirkner (Eds.), *Psychological Variables in Human Cancer.* Berkeley and Los Angeles: University of California Press, 1954, 30–61.

Blumberg, E. M.; West, P. M.; and Ellis, F. W. A possible relationship between psychological factors and human cancer. *Psychosomatic Medicine,* 1954, *16*(4), 276–86.

————. MMPI findings in human cancer. *Basic Reading on the MMPI in Psychology and Medicine.* Minneapolis: Minnesota

University Press, 1956, 452–60.

Bolen, J. S. Meditation and psychotherapy in the treatment of cancer. *Psychic*, July–August 1973, 19–22.

Booth, G. General and organic specific object relationships in cancer. *Annals of the New York Academy of Sciences*, 1969, *164*, 568–77.

Brooks, J. Transcendental meditation and its potential role in clinical medicine. *Synapse* (School of Medicine, Wayne State University), December 7, 1973, *1*(3).

Brown, B. *New mind, new body*. New York: Harper & Row, 1975.

Brown, F. The relationship between cancer and personality. *Annals of the New York Academy of Sciences*, 1966, *125*, 865–73.

Brown, J. H.; Varsamis, M. B.; Toews, J.; and Shane, M. Psychiatry and oncology: A review. *Canadian Psychiatric Association Journal*, 1974, *19*(2), 219–22.

Buccola, V. A., and Stone, W. J. Effects of jogging and cycling programs on physiological and personality variables in aged men. *Research Quarterly*, May 1975, *46*(2), 134–39.

Bulkley, L. D. Relation of diet to cancer. *Med. Rec.*, 1914, *86*, 699–702.

Burnet, F. M. The concept of immunological surveillance. *Prog. Exp. Tumor Research*, 1970, *13*, 1027.

Burrows, J. *A practical essay on cancer*. London, 1783.

Butler, B. The use of hypnosis in the case of cancer patients. *Cancer*, 1954, *7*, 1.

Cannon, W. B. *Bodily changes in pain, hunger, fear, and rage* (2nd ed.). New York: Appleton-Century, 1934.

Cardon, P. V., Jr., and Mueller, P. S. A possible mechanism: Psychogenic fat mobilization. *Annals of the New York Academy of Sciences*, 1966, *125*, 924–27.

Cassel, J. An epidemiological perspective of psychosocial factors in disease etiology. *American Journal of Public Health*, 1974, *64*, 1040–43.

Chesser, E. S., and Anderson, J. L. Treatment of breast cancer: Doctor/patient communication and psychosocial implications. *Proceedings of the Royal Society of Medicine*, 1975, *68*(12), 793–95.

Chigbuh, A. E. Role of psychosomatic factors in the genesis of cancer. *Rivista Internazionale di Psicologia e Ipnosi*, 1975, *16*(3), 289–95.

Cobb, B. A social-psychological study of the cancer patient. *Cancer*, 1954, 1–14.

Collingwood, T. R. The effects of physical training upon behavior and self-attitudes. *Journal of Clinical Psychology*, October 1972, *28*(4), 583–85.

Collingwood, T. R., and Willett, L. The effects of physical training upon self-concept and body attitude. *Journal of Clinical Psychology*, July 1971, *27*(3), 411–12.

Coppen, A. J., and Metcalf, M. Cancer and extraversion. In D. M. Kissen and L. L. LeShan (Eds.), *Psychosomatic aspects of neoplastic disease*, Philadelphia and Montreal: J. B. Lippincott Company, 1964, 30–34.

Crile, G., Jr. *What every woman should know about the breast cancer controversy.* New York: Macmillan, 1973.

Cullen, J. W., Fox, B. H., and Isom, R. N. (Eds.). *Cancer: The behavioral dimensions.* New York: Raven Press, 1976.

Cutler, E. Diet on cancer. *Albany Medical Annals*, 1887.

Cutler, M. The nature of the cancer process in relation to a possible psychosomatic influence. In J. A. Gengerelli and F. J. Kirkner (Eds.), *Psychological variables in human cancer.* Berkeley and Los Angeles: University of California Press, 1954, 1–16.

Doloman, G. F. Emotions, stress, the central nervous system, and immunity. *Ann. N. Y. Acad. Sci.*, 1969, *164*(2), 335–43.

Dorn, H. F. Cancer and the marital status. *Human Biology*, 1943, *15*, 73–79.

Dunbar, F. *Emotions and bodily changes: A survey of literature-psychosomatic interrelationships 1910–1953* (4th ed.). New York: Columbia University Press, 1954.

Ellerbroek, W. C. Hypotheses toward a unified field theory of human behavior with clinical application to acne vulgaris. *Perspectives in Biology and Medicine*, Winter 1973, 240–62.

Evans, E. *A psychological study of cancer.* New York: Dodd, Mead & Company, 1926.

Everson, T. C., and Cole, W. H. *Spontaneous regression of cancer.* Philadelphia, 1966, 7.

Ewing, J. Animal experimentations and cancer. Defense of Research Pamphlet 4, American Medical Association, Chicago, 1911.

Feder, S. L. Psychological considerations in the care of patients with cancer. *Annals of the New York Academy of Sciences*, 1966, *125*, 1020–27.

Fisher, S., and Cleveland, S. E. Relationship of body image to site of cancer. *Psychosomatic Medicine*, 1956, *18*(4), 304–309.

Folkins, C. H. Effects of physical training on mood. *Journal of Clinical Psychology*, 1976, *32*(2), 385–88.

Fox, B. H. Psychosocial epidemiology of cancer. In J. W. Cullen, B. H. Fox, and R. N. Isom (Eds.), *Cancer: The behavior of dimensions.* New York: Raven Press, 1976.

Fox, B. H., and Howell, M. A. Cancer risk among psychiatric patients. *International Journal of Epidemiology,* 1974, *3,* 207–208.

Fox, E. *Sermon on the mount.* New York: Harper & Row, 1938.

Frankel, A., and Murphy, J. Physical fitness and personality in alcoholism: Canonical analysis of measures before and after treatment. *Quarterly Journal Stud. Alc.,* 1974, *35,* 1272–78.

Friedman, M., and Rosenman R. *Type A behavior and your heart.* New York: Alfred A. Knopf, 1974.

Friedman, S. B.; Glasgow, L. A.; and Ader, R. Psychosocial factors modifying host resistance to experimental infections. *Annals of the New York Academy of Sciences,* 1969, *164,* 381–93.

Galen, *De tumoribus* [About tumors].

Gary, V., and Guthrie, D. The effect of jogging on physical fitness and self-concept in hospitalized alcoholics. *Quarterly Journal Stu. Alc.,* 1972, *33,* 1073–78.

Gendron, D. *Enquiries into nature, knowledge, and cure of cancers.* London, 1701.

Gengerelli, J. A., and Kirkner, F. J. (Eds.). *Psychological variables in human cancer.* Berkeley and Los Angeles: University of California Press, 1954.

Glade, P. R.; Zalvidar, N. M.; Mayer, L.; and Cahill, L. J. The role of cellular immunity in neoplasia. *Pediatric Research,* 1976, *10,* 517–22.

Glasser, R. *The body is the hero.* New York: Random House, 1976.

Gottschalk, L. A.; Kunkel, R.; Wohl, T. H.; Saenger, E. L.; and Winger, C. N. Total and half body irradiation: Effect on cognitive and emotional processes. *Archives of General Psychiatry,* November 1969, *21,* 574–80.

Gottschalk, L. A.; Stone, W. M.; Gleser, G. C.; and Iacono, J. M. Anxiety and plasma free acids (FAA). *Life Sciences,* 1969, *8*(2), 61–69.

Green, E., and Green, A. *Beyond Biofeedback.* New York: Delacorte, 1977.

Green, E. E.; Green, A. M.; and Walters, E. D. Voluntary control of internal states: Psychological and physiological. *Journal of Transpersonal Psychology,* 1970, *2*(1), 1–26.

———. Biofeedback for mind-body self-regulation: Healing and creativity. Paper presented at The Varieties of Healing Experience, Cupertino, California, October 1971.

Greene, W. A., Jr. Psychological factors and reticuloendothelial disease: I. Preliminary observations on a group of males with lymphomas and leukemia. *Psychosomatic Medicine,* 1954, *16,* 220–30.

————. The psychosocial setting of the development of leukemia and lymphoma. *Annals of the New York Academy of Sciences*, 1966, *125*, 794–801.

Greene, W. A., Jr., and Miller, G. Psychological factors and reticuloendothelial disease: IV. Observation on a group of children and adolescents with leukemia: An interpretation of disease development in terms of the mother-child unit. *Psychosomatic Medicine*, 1958, *20*, 124–44.

Greene, W. A., Jr.; Young, L.; and Swisher, S. N. Psychological factors and reticuloendothelial disease: II. Observations on a group of women with lymphomas and leukemia. *Psychosomatic Medicine*, 1956, *18*, 284–303.

————. Psychological and somatic variables associated with the development and course of monozygotic twins discordant for leukemia. *Annals of the New York Academy of Sciences*, 1969, *164*, 394–408.

Greer, S., and Morris, T. Psychological attributes of women who develop breast cancer. A controlled study. *Journal of Psychosomatic Research*, 1975, *19*, 147–53.

Grinker, R. R. Psychosomatic aspects of the cancer problems. *Annals of the New York Academy of Sciences*, 1966, *125*, 876–82.

Grissom, J. J.; Weiner, B. J.; and Weiner, E. A. Psychological substrate of cancer. *Psychologie Medicale*, 1976, *8*(6), 879–90.

Grossarth-Maticek, R. Cancer and family structure. *Familiendynamik*, 1976, *21*(4), 294–318.

Hagnell, O. The premorbid personality of persons who develop cancer in a total population investigated in 1947 and 1957. *Annals of the New York Academy of Sciences*, 1966, *125*, 846–855.

Handley, W. S. A lecture on the natural cause of cancer. *British Medical Journal*, 1909, *1*, 582.

Harrower, M.; Thomas, C. B.; and Altman, A. Human figure drawings in a prospective study of six disorders: Hypertension, coronary heart disease, malignant tumor, suicide, mental illness, and emotional disturbance. *Journal of Nervous Mental Disorders*, 1975, *161*, 191–99.

Hedge, A. R. Hypnosis in cancer. *British Journal of Hypnotism*, 1960, *12*, 2–5.

Hellison, D. R. Physical education and the self-attitude. *Quest Monograph*, January 1970, No. 13, 41–45.

Henderson, J. G. Denial and repression as factors in the delay of patients with cancer presenting themselves to the physician. *Annals of the New York Academy of Sciences*, 1966, *125*, 856–64.

Hoffman, S.; Pschkis, K. E.; and Cantarow, A. Exercise, fatigue, and tumor growth. *Fed. Proc.*, March 1960, *19*(abs.), 396.

Hoffman, S. A.; Paschkis, K. E.; DeBiar, D. A.; Cantarow, A.; and Williams, T. L. The influence of exercise on the growth of transplanted rat tumors. *Cancer Research*, June 1962, *22*, 597–99.

Holland, J. C. Psychological aspects of cancer. In J. F. Holland and E. Frei III (Eds.), *Cancer medicine*. Philadelphia: Lea & Febiger, 1973.

Holmes, T. H., and Rahe, R. H. The social readjustment rating scale. *Journal of Psychosomatic Research*, 1967, *11*, 213–18.

Holmes, T. H., and Masuda, M. *Life change and illness suscepti-bility*. Paper presented as part of Symposium on Separation and Depression: Clinical and Research Aspects, Chicago, December 1970.

Hueper, W. C. Environmental and occupational cancer. U.S. Public Health Report No. 1948, Suppl. 209, pp. 35–47, U.S. Government Printing Office, Washington, D. C.

Hughes, C. H. The relations of nervous depression toward the development of cancer. *St. Louis Medicine and Surgery Journal*, 1885.

Humphrey, J. H. Cited in review of L. L. LeShan's book by P. B. Medawar, *New York Review of Books*, June 9, 1977, *24*(10).

Hurlburt, K. Personal communication, March 1975.

Hutschnecker, A. A. *The will to live.* New York: Thomas Y. Crowell Company, 1953.

Ismail, A. H., and Trachtman, L. E. Jogging the imagination. *Psychology Today*, March 1973, *6*(10), 78–82.

Jaffer, Frances. *Any time now.* Effie's Press, 1977.

Jones, A. D. Theoretical considerations concerning the influence of the central nervous system on cancerous growth. *Annals of the New York Academy of Sciences*, 1966, *125*, 946–51.

Josephy, H. Analysis of mortality and causes of death in a mental hospital. *American Journal of Psychiatry*, 1949, *106*, 185–89.

Katz, J.; Gallagher, T.; Hellman, L.; Sachar, E.; and Weiner, H. Psychoendocrine considerations in cancer of the breast. *Annals of the New York Academy of Sciences*, 1969, *164*, 509–16.

Kavetsky, R. E. (Ed.). *The neoplastic process and the nervous system.* Kiev: The State Medical Publishing House, 1958.

Kavetsky, R. E.; Turkevich, N. M.; and Balitsky, K. P. On the psychophysiological mechanism of the organism's resistance to tumor growth. *Annals of the New York Academy of Sciences*, 1966, *125*, 933–45.

Kavetsky, R. E.; Turkevich, N. M.; Akimova, R. H.; Khayetsky, I. K.; and Matveichuf, Y. D. Induced carcinogenesis under various influences on the hypothalamus. *Annals of the New York Academy of Sciences*, 1969, *164*, 517–19.

Kidd, J. G. Does the host react against his own cancer cells? *Cancer Research*, 1961, *21*, 1170.

Kissen, D. M. Lung cancer, inhalation and personality. In D. M. Kissen and L. LeShan (Eds.), *Psychosomatic aspects of neoplastic disease*, Philadelphia: J. B. Lippincott, 1963, 3–11.

———. Personality characteristics in males conducive to lung cancer. *British Journal of Medical Psychology*, 1963, *36*, 27.

———. Relationship between lung cancer, cigarette smoking, inhalation and personality and psychological factors in lung cancers. *British Journal of Medical Psychology*, 1964, *37*, 203–16.

———. The significance of personality in lung cancer in men. *Annals of the New York Academy of Sciences*, 1966, *125*, 933–45.

———. Psychosocial factors, personality, and lung cancer in men aged 55–64. *British Journal of Medical Psychology*, 1967, *40*, 29.

Kissen, D. M.; Brown, R. I. F.; and Kissen, M. A. A further report on personality and psychological factors in lung cancer. *Annals of the New York Academy of Sciences*, 1969, *164*, 535–45.

Kissen, D. M., and Eysenck, H. G. Personality in male lung cancer patients. *Journal of Psychosomatic Research*, 1962, *6*, 123.

Kissen, D. M., and Rao, L. G. S. Steroid excretion patterns and personality in lung cancer. *Annals of the New York Academy of Sciences*, 1969, *164*, 476–82.

Klein, E. Tumor-specific transplantation antigens. *Annals of the New York Academy of Sciences*, 1969, *164*, 344–51.

Klein, G. Immunological surveillance against neoplasia. *The Harvey Lectures*, 1973–74, Series 69.

Klopfer, B. Psychological variables in human cancer. *Journal of Projective Techniques*, 1957, *21*, 331–40.

Kostrubala, T. Prescription for stress: Running. *Practical Psychology for Physicians*, 1975, 2(10), 50–53.

Kowal, S. J. Emotions as a cause of cancer: Eighteenth and nineteenth century contributions. *Psychoanalytic Review*, 1955, *42*, 217–27.

Krc, I.; Kovarova, M.; Janicek, M.; and Hyzak, A. The effects of physical exercise on the absolute blood basophil leukocyte count. *Acta Univ. Palacki Olomuc Fac Med.*, 1973, *66*, 253–58.

LaBarba, R. C. Experimental and environmental factors in cancer. *Psychosomatic Medicine,* 1970, *32,* 259.

LaBaw, A. L.; Holton, C.; Tewell, K.; and Eccles, D. The use of self-hypnosis by children with cancer. *The American Journal of Clinical Hypnosis,* 1975, *17*(4), 233–38.

Lappe, M. A., and Prehn, R. T. Immunologic surveillance at the mascroscopic level—nonselective elimination of premalignant skin papillomas. *Cancer Research,* 1969, *29,* 2374–80.

LeShan, L. L. A psychosomatic hypothesis concerning the etiology of Hodgkin's disease. *Psychologic Report,* 1957, *3,* 365–75.

———. Psychological states as factors in the development of malignant disease: A critical review. *Journal of the National Cancer Institute,* 1959, *22,* 1–18.

———. A basic psychological orientation apparently associated with malignant disease. *The Psychiatric Quarterly,* 1961, *35,* 314.

———. An emotional life history pattern associated with neoplastic disease. *Annals of the New York Academy of Sciences,* 1966, *125,* 780–93.

———. *You can fight for your life.* New York: M. Evans & Company, 1977.

LeShan, L. L., and Bassman, M. Some observations on psychotherapy with patients with neoplastic disease. *American Journal of Psychotherapy,* 1958, *12,* 723–34.

LeShan, L. L., and Worthington, R. E. Some psychologic correlatives of neoplastic disease: Preliminary report. *Journal of Clinical and Experimental Psychopathology,* 1955, *16,* 281–88.

———. Loss of cathexes as a common psychodynamic characteristic of cancer patients: An attempt at statistical validation of a clinical hypothesis. *Psychologic Report,* 1956, *2,* 183–93.

———. Personality as a factor in the pathogenesis of cancer: A review of the literature. *British Journal of Medical Psychology,* 1956, *29,* 49–56.

———. Some recurrent life history patterns observed in patients with malignant disease. *Journal of Nervous Mental Disorders,* 1956, *124,* 460–65.

Lewis, N. D. C. *Research in dementia praecox.* New York Committee for Mental Hygiene, 1936.

Lombard, H. L, and Potter, E. A. Epidemiological aspects of cancer of the cervix: Hereditary and environmental factors. *Cancer,* 1950, *3,* 960–68.

Luk-yandnko, V. L. The conditioned reflex regulation of immunological responses. Department of Physiology of the Higher Nervous Activity, Moscow State University and Sukhumi

Medical Biological Station, U.S.S.R. Academy of Medical Sciences, June 1958.

MacMillan, M. B. A note on LeShan and Worthington's "Personality as a factor in the pathogenesis of cancer." *British Journal of Medical Psychology*, 1957, *30*, 41.

Marcial, V. A. Socioeconomic aspects of the incidence of cancer in Puerto Rico. *Annals of the New York Academy of Sciences*, 1960, *84*, 981.

Marmorston, J. Urinary hormone metabolite levels in patients with cancer of the breast, prostate, and lung. *Annals of the New York Academy of Sciences*, 1966, *125*, 959–73.

Marmorston, J.; Geller, P. J.; and Weiner, J. M. Pretreatment urinary hormone patterns and survival in patients with breast cancer, prostate cancer, or lung cancer. *Annals of the New York Academy of Sciences*, 1969, *164*, 483–93.

Mason, J. W. Psychological stress and endocrine function. In E. J. Sachar (Ed.), *Topics in psychoendocrinology*, New York: Grune & Stratton, 1975.

Mastrovito, R. C. Acute psychiatric problems and the use of psychotropic medications in the treatment of the cancer patient. *Annals of the New York Academy of Sciences*, 1966, *125*, 1006–10.

Meerloo, J. The initial neurologic and psychiatric picture syndrome of pulmonary growth. *JAMA*, 1951, *146*, 558–59.

————. Psychological implications of malignant growth: Survey of hypotheses. *British Journal of Medical Psychology*, 1954, *27*, 210–15.

Miller, F. R., and Jones, H. W. The possibility of precipitating the leukemic state by emotional factors. *Blood*, 1948, *8*, 880–84.

Miller, H. Emotions and malignancy. Paper presented at the American Society of Clinical Hypnosis Convention, San Francisco, November 1969.

Mitchell, J. S. Psychosomatic cancer research from the viewpoint of the general cancer field. In D. M. Kissen and L. L. LeShan (Eds.), *Psychosomatic aspects of neoplastic disease*. Philadelphia: J. B. Lippincott Company, 1964, 211–16.

Moore, C., and Tittle, P. W. Muscle activity, body fat, and induced rat mammary tumor. *Surgery*, March 1973, *73*(3), 329–32.

Moses, R., and Cividali, N. Differential levels of awareness of illness: Their relation to some salient features in cancer patients. *Annals of the New York Academy of Sciences*, 1966, *125*, 984–94.

Muslin, H. L.; Gyarfas, K.; and Pieper, W. J. Separation experience and cancer of the breast. *Annals of the New York Academy of Sciences*, 1966, *125*, 802–06.

Nakagawa, S., and Ikemi, Y. A psychosomatic study of spontaneous regression of cancer. *Medicina Psicosomatica*, 1975, *20*(4), 378.

Newton, G. Early experience and resistance to tumor growth. In D. M. Kissen and L. L. LeShan (Eds.), *Psychosomatic aspects of neoplastic disease*. Philadelphia: J. B. Lippincott, 1963, 71–79.

————. Tumor susceptibility in rats: Role of infantile manipulation and later exercise. *Psychological Reports*, 1965, *16*, 127–32.

Nunn, T. H. *Cancer of the breast*. London: J. & A. Churchill, 1822.

Old, L. J., and Boyse, E. A. Immunology of experimental tumors. *Annual Review of Medicine*, 1964, *15*, 167.

Orbach, C. E.; Sutherland, A. M.; and Bozeman, M. F. Psychological impact of cancer and its treatment. *Cancer*, 1955, *8*, 20.

Paget, J. *Surgical pathology* (2nd ed.). London: Longman's Green, 1870.

Paloucek, F. P., and Graham, J. B. The influence of psycho-social factors on the prognosis in cancer of the cervix. *Annals of the New York Academy of Sciences*, 1966, *125*, 814–16.

Parkes, C. M.; Benjamin, B.; and Fitzgerald, R. G. Broken heart: A statistical study of increased mortality among widowers. *British Medical Journal*, 1969, *1*, 740–43.

Patterson, W. B. The quality of survival in response to treatment. *JAMA*, July 21, 1975, *233*(3), 280–81.

Pelletier, K. R. *Mind as healer, mind as slayer*. New York: Delta, 1977.

Pendergrass, E. Host resistance and other intangibles in the treatment of cancer. *American Journal of Roentgenology*, 1961, *85*, 891–96.

Peper, E., and Pelletier, K. R. Spontaneous remission of cancer: A bibliography. Mimeograph, 1969.

Prehn, R. T. The relationship of immunology to carcinogenesis. *Annals of the New York Academy of Sciences*, 1969, *164*, 449–57.

Psychophysiological aspects of cancer. In E. M. Weyer (Ed.), *Annals of the New York Academy of Sciences*, 1966, *125*(3), 773–1055.

Rapaport, F. T., and Lawrence, H. S. A possible role for cross-reacting antigens in conditioning immunological surveillance mechanisms in cancer and transplantation: II. Prospective studies of altered cellular immune reactivity in cancer patients. *Transplantation Proceedings*, June 1975, *7*(2), 281–85.

Rashkis, H. A. Systematic stress as an inhibitor of experimental tumors in Swiss mice. *Science*, 1952, *116*, 169–71.

Rasmussen, A. F., Jr. Emotions and immunity. *Annals of the New York Academy of Sciences*, 1969, *164*, 458–62.

Resier, M. Retrospects and prospects. *Annals of the New York Academy of Sciences*, 1966, *125*, 1028–55.

Reznikoff, M. Psychological factors in breast cancer: A preliminary study of some personality trends in patients with cancer of the breast. *Psychosomatic Medicine*, 1955, *18*, 2.

Reznikoff, M, and Martin, P. E. The influence of stress on mammary cancer in mice. *Journal of Psychosomatic Research*, 1957, *2*, 56–60.

Reznikoff, M., and Tomblin, D. The use of human figure drawings in the diagnosis of organic pathology. *Journal of Consulting Psychology*, 1956, *20*, 467–70.

Richter, C. P. On the phenomenon of sudden death in animals and man. *Psychosomatic Medicine*, 1957, *19*, 191–98.

Rigan, D. Exercise and cancer: A review. *Journal A.O.A.*, March 1963, *62*, 596–99.

Riley, V. Mouse mammary tumors: Alteration of incidence as apparent function of stress. *Science*, August 1975, *189*, 465–67.

Rosenbaum, E., and Rosenbaum, I. R. *Mind and body: A rehabilitation guide for patients and their families.* San Francisco: Published by the authors c/o Mt. Zion Hospital.

Rosenthal, R. The volunteer subject. *Human Relations*, 1965, *18*, 389–406.

Rosenthal, R. *Experimenter effects in behavioral research.* New York: Appleton-Century-Crofts, 1966.

Rosenthal, R., and Rosnow, R. L. (Eds.), The volunteer subject. *Artifact in Behavioral Research*, New York: Academic Press, 1969.

Rusch, H. P., and Kline, B. E. The effect of exercise on the growth of a mouse tumor. *Cancer Research*, 116–18.

Sacerdote, P. The uses of hypnosis in cancer patients. *Annals of the New York Academy of Sciences*, 1966, *125*, 1011–19.

Sakurai, N., S. Yamaoka, and M. Maurakami. Relationship between exercises and changes in blood characteristics in horses. *Exp. Rep. Equine Health Lab.*, 1967, *4*, 15–19.

Salk, J. Immunological paradoxes: Theoretical considerations in the rejection or retention of grafts, tumors, and normal tissue. *Annals of the New York Academy of Sciences*, 1969, *164*, 365–80.

Samudzhan, E. M. Effect of functionally weakened cerebral cortex on growth of inoculated tumors in mice. *Med Zhurn.*, AN Ukranian SSSR, 1954, *24*(3), 10–14.

Samuels, M., and Samuels, N. *Seeing With the Mind's Eye.* New York and Berkeley: Random House and the Bookworks, 1975.

Scheflen, A. E. Malignant tumors in the institutionalized psychotic population. *Archives of Neurology and Psychiatry,* 1951, *64,* 145–55.

Schmale, A. H., and Iker, H. The psychological setting of uterine cervical cancer. *Annals of the New York Academy of Sciences,* 1966, *125,* 807–13.

————. Hopelessness as a predictor of cervical cancer. *Social Science and Medicine,* 1971, *5,* 95–100.

Schonfield, J. Psychological factors related to delayed return to an earlier life-style in successfully treated cancer patients. *Journal of Psychosomatic Research,* 1972, *16,* 41–46.

————. Psychological and life-experience differences between Israeli women with benign and cancerous breast lesions. *Journal of Psychosomatic Research,* 1975, *19,* 229–34.

Second conference on psychophysiological aspects of cancer. In M. Krauss (Ed.), *Annals of the New York Academy of Sciences,* 1969, *164*(2), 307–634.

Seligman, M. E. P. *Helplessness: On depression, development, and death.* San Francisco: W. H. Freeman and Company, 1975.

Selye, H. *The stress of life.* New York: McGraw-Hill, 1956.

Shands, H. C. The informational impact of cancer on the structure of the human personality. *Annals of the New York Academy of Sciences,* 1966, *125,* 883–89.

Sheehy, G. *Passages.* New York: E. P. Dutton and Company, 1976.

Silvertsen, I., and Dahlstrom, A. W. Relation of muscular activity to carcinoma: Preliminary report. *Journal of Cancer Research,* 1921, *6,* 365–78.

Sivertsen, I., and Hastings, W. H. Preliminary report on influence of food and function on incidence of mammary gland tumor in "A" stock albino mice. *Minnesota Med.,* December 1938, *21,* 873–75.

Simonton, O. C., and Simonton, S. Belief systems and management of the emotional aspects of malignancy. *Journal of Transpersonal Psychology,* 1975, *7*(1), 29–47.

Smart, A. Conscious control of physical and mental states. *Menninger Perspective,* April–May 1970.

Smith, W. R., and Sebastian, H. Emotional history and pathogenesis of cancer. *Journal of Clinical Psychology,* 1976, *32*(4), 863–66.

Snow, H. *The reappearance* [recurrence] *of cancer after apparent extirpation.* London: J. & A. Churchill, 1870.

————. *Clinical notes on cancer.* London: J. & A. Churchill, 1883.

———. *Cancer and the cancer process.* London: J. & A. Churchill, 1893.

Solomon, G. F. Emotions, stress, the central nervous system, and immunity. *Annals of the New York Academy of Sciences,* 1969, *164,* 335–43.

Solomon, G. F., and Amkraut, A. A. Emotions, stress, and immunity. *Frontiers of Radiation Therapy and Oncology,* 1972, *7,* 84–96.

Solomon, G. F., and Moos, R. H. Emotions, immunity and disease. *Archives of General Psychiatry,* 1964, *11,* 657.

Solomon, G. F.; Amkraut, A. A.; and Kasper, P. Immunity, emotions and stress. *Annals of Clinical Research,* 1974, *6,* 313–22.

Sommers, S. C., and Friedell, G. H. Studies of carcinogenesis in parabiotic rats. *Annals of the New York Academy of Sciences,* 1966, *125,* 928–32.

Sonstroem, R. J., and Walker, M. I. Relationship of attitudes and locus of control to exercise and physical fitness. *Perceptual and Motor Skills,* 1973, *36,* 1031–34.

Southam, C. M. Relationships of immunology to cancer: A review. *Cancer Research,* 1960, *20,* 271.

———. Discussion: Emotions, immunology, and cancer: How might the psyche influence neoplasia? *Annals of the New York Academy of Sciences,* 1969, *164,* 473–75.

Stamford, B. K.; Hambacher, W.; and Fallica. A. Effects of daily physical exercise on the psychiatric state of institutionalized geriatric mental patients. *Research Quarterly,* 1974, *45*(1), 34–41.

Stavraky, K. M. Psychological factors in the outcome of human cancer. *Journal of Psychosomatic Research,* 1968, *12,* 251.

Stein, M.; Schiavi, R. C., and Luparello, T. J. The hypothalamus and immune process. *Annals of the New York Academy of Sciences,* 1969, *164,* 464–72.

Stein, M.; Schiavi, R. C.; and Camerino, M. Influence of brain and behavior on the immune system. *Science,* February 6, 1976, *191,* 435–39.

Steiner, C. *Scripts people live.* New York: Bantam, 1974.

Stephenson, I. H., and Grace, W. Life stress and cancer of the cervix. *Psychosomatic Medicine,* 1954, *16,* 287.

Stern, E., Mickey, M. R., and Gorski, R. A. Neuroendocrine factors in experimental carcinogenesis. *Annals of the New York Academy of Sciences,* 1969, *164,* 494–508.

Stern, K. The reticuloendothelial system and neoplasia. In J. H. Heller (Ed.), *Reticuloendothelial structure and function.* New York: The Ronald Press Company, 1960, 233–58.

Sundstroem, E. S., and Michaels, G. *The adrenal cortex in adapta-*

tion to altitude, climate, and cancer. Berkeley: University of California Press, 1942.

Surawicz, F. G.; Brightwell, D. R.; Weitzel, W. D.; and Othmer, E. Cancer, emotions, and mental illness: The present state of understanding. *American Journal of Psychiatry,* 1976, *133*(11), 1306–1309.

Takahashi, H. Effects of physical exercise on blood: 2. Changes in the hematological picture with physical loads. *Journal Nara Med. Assoc.,* 1975, *26*(6), 431–37.

Tannenbaum, A. Role of nutrition in origin and growth of tumors. In *Approaches to tumor chemotherapy,* 1947, 96–127.

Tarlau, M., and Smalheiser, I. Personality patterns in patients with malignant tumors of the breast and cervix: Exploratory study. *Psychosomatic Medicine,* 1951, *13*, 117–21.

Thomas, C. B., and Duszynski, D. R. Closeness to parents and the family constellation in a prospective study of five disease states: Suicide, mental illness, malignant tumor, hypertension, and coronary heart disease. *The Johns Hopkins Medical Journal,* 1973, *134*, 251–70.

Thomas, L. Reactions to homologous tissue antigens in relation to hypersensitivity. *Cellular and Humoral Aspects of the Hypersensitive States,* 1959, 529–32.

Tillman, K. Relationship between physical fitness and selected personality traits. *The Research Quarterly,* *36*(4), 483–89.

Turkevich, N. M. Significance of typological peculiarities of the nervous system in the origin and development of cancer of the mammaries in mice. *Vopr. Oncol.,* 1955, *1*(6), 64–70.

Ulene, A. *Feeling fine.* Los Angeles: J. P. Tarcher, 1977.

Visscher, M.B.; Ball, Z. B.; Barnes, R. H.; and Silvertsen, I. Influence of caloric restriction upon incidence of spontaneous mammary carcinoma in mice. *Surgery,* January 1942, *11*, 48–55.

Wallace, R. K., and Benson, H. The physiology of meditation. *Science,* March 1970, *167*, 1751–54.

Wallace, R. K., and Benson, H. The physiology of meditation. *Scientific American,* February 1972, 84.

Wallace, R. K.; Benson, H.; and Wilson, A. F. A wakeful hypometabolic physiologic state. *American Journal of Physiology,* September 1971, 795.

Walse, W. A. *Nature and treatment of cancer.* London: Taylor and Walton, 1846.

Waxenberg, S. E. The importance of the communications of feelings about cancer. *Annals of the New York Academy of Sciences*, 1966, *125*, 1000–1005.

Weiner, J. M.; Marmorston, J.; Stern, E.; and Hopkins, C. E. Urinary hormone metabolites in cancer and benign hyperplasia of the prostate: A multivariate statistical analysis. *Annals of the New York Academy of Sciences*, 1966, *125*, 974–83.

Weinstock, C. Psychodynamics of cancer regression. *Journal of the American Academy of Psychoanalysis*, 1977, *5*(2), 285–86.

Weiss, D. W. Immunological parameters of the host-parasite relationship in neoplasia. *Annals of the New York Academy of Sciences*, 1969, *164*, 431–48.

Weiss, D. W.; Faulkin, L. J., Jr.; and DeOme, K. B. Acquisition of heightened resistance and susceptibility to spontaneous mouse mammary carcinomas in the original host. *Cancer Research*, 1964, *24*, 732.

Weitzenhoffer, A. M. *Hypnotism: An objective study in suggestibility*. New York: John Wiley & Sons, 1953.

West, P. M. Origin and development of the psychological approach to the cancer problem. In J. A. Gengerelli and F. J. Kirkner (Eds.), *The psychological variables in human cancer*. Berkeley and Los Angeles: University of California Press, 1954, 17–26.

West, P. M., Blumberg, E. M., and Ellis, F. W. An observed correlation between psychological factors and growth rate of cancer in man. *Cancer Research*, 1952, *12*, 306–307.

Wheeler, J. I., Jr., and Caldwell, B. M. Psychological evaluation of women with cancer of the breast and of the cervix. *Psychosomatic Medicine*, 1955, *17*(4), 256–68.

Wintrok, R. M. Hexes, roots, snake eggs? M.D. vs occult. *Medical Opinion*, 1972, *1*(7), 54–57.

Wolf, S. Effects of suggestion and conditioning on the action of chemical agents in human subjects: The pharmacology of placebos. *Journal of Clinical Investigation*, 1950, *29*, 100–109.

Index

ABOUT THE AUTHORS

O. CARL SIMONTON, M.D., D.A.B.R., is a radiation oncologist, Associate of Oncology Associates, Fort Worth, Texas, and the medical director of the Cancer Counseling and Research Center in Fort Worth. He is a frequent lecturer at hospitals and medical schools, a consultant for cancer counseling programs, and has written numerous articles for professional publications. He co-authored the book, *Stress, Psychological Factors, and Cancer.*

STEPHANIE MATTHEWS-SIMONTON, the director of counseling at the Cancer Counseling and Research Center, is a psychotherapist. She developed the center's intensive psychotherapy program, which has become a model for other programs across the country, and designed a three-phase training program for cancer counselors. Ms. Simonton co-authored *Stress, Psychological Factors, and Cancer.*

JAMES L. CREIGHTON has worked closely with the Simontons as well as independently in cancer patient counseling and care.